CQN ANNUAL 2014 CONTENTS

PUBLISHER
David Faulds
david@241media.co.uk

EDITOR
Paul Brennan
celticquicknews@gmail.com

FEATURES
Jim McGinley

DESIGN
Suzanne Waters

PRODUCTION
Tony Warrington

PHOTOGRAPHY
Vagalis Georgariou and Angus Johnston
Kerrydale Street

**CONTRIBUTORS TO CQN MAGAZINE
IN 2013**
Auldheid, Blinkered Views, Brogan Rogan
Trevino & Hogan, Mark Cameron, Tony
McCann, Chris Collins, Henry Clarson, Bryce
Curdy, Kieran Kaw, Celtic Graves, Celtic Wiki,
Celtic Journal, Patrick Devlin, Denis Doherty,
Michael Diamond, The Doc, Ritchie Feenie,
Vagalis Georgariou, Green Brigade, Hruatski,
Angus Johnston, Leftybhoy, Nik Mirkovic,
Joel McAnallen, Mike Maher, Greg Martin,
Paul McQuade, Steve Mac, Shannon McGurin,
Blaise Plelan, Tony Paterson, Joseph Ruddy,
Stephen Reid, St Martin's Bhoy, Semper Fidelis,
Gareth Savage, St Roch's Football Club,
Setting Free the Bears, Darren Wilson, Suzanne
Waters, Winning Captains and Graham Ward.
Plus all the posters on CQN and the CQN
Magazine Facebook page whose comments we
have relied on.

Thanks to Press Association and everyone else
who has assisted us with photography in 2013.

CQN ANNUAL 2014 – ISBN 978-0-9576171-1-7

CQN Magazine is available to view at www.
celticquicknews.co.uk Print copies are also
available to purchase at www.magcloud.com

If you would like to contribute to
CQN Magazine in 2014 please email
celticquicknews@gmail.com

CQN ANNUAL 2014 is dedicated to the memory
of Miki67, St John Doyle and Lurgan53 who
we lost in 2013 - sadly missed by everyone on
www.celticquicknews.co.uk

MIKI67 LURGAN53 ST JOHN DOYLE PABLOPHANQUE CELTICLOVER

CQN ANNUAL

EDITOR'

1-14

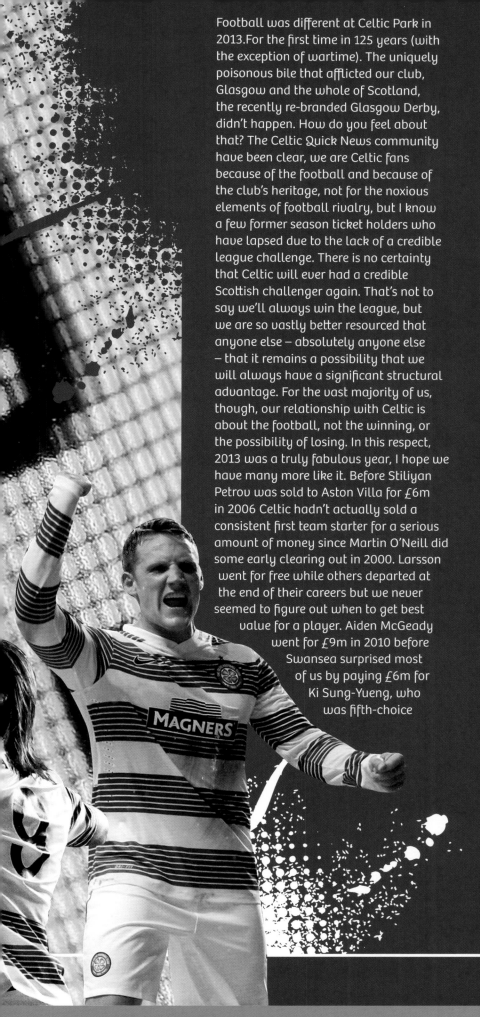

Football was different at Celtic Park in 2013. For the first time in 125 years (with the exception of wartime). The uniquely poisonous bile that afflicted our club, Glasgow and the whole of Scotland, the recently re-branded Glasgow Derby, didn't happen. How do you feel about that? The Celtic Quick News community have been clear, we are Celtic fans because of the football and because of the club's heritage, not for the noxious elements of football rivalry, but I know a few former season ticket holders who have lapsed due to the lack of a credible league challenge. There is no certainty that Celtic will ever had a credible Scottish challenger again. That's not to say we'll always win the league, but we are so vastly better resourced that anyone else – absolutely anyone else – that it remains a possibility that we will always have a significant structural advantage. For the vast majority of us, though, our relationship with Celtic is about the football, not the winning, or the possibility of losing. In this respect, 2013 was a truly fabulous year, I hope we have many more like it. Before Stiliyan Petrov was sold to Aston Villa for £6m in 2006 Celtic hadn't actually sold a consistent first team starter for a serious amount of money since Martin O'Neill did some early clearing out in 2000. Larsson went for free while others departed at the end of their careers but we never seemed to figure out when to get best value for a player. Aiden McGeady went for £9m in 2010 before Swansea surprised most of us by paying £6m for Ki Sung-Yueng, who was fifth-choice central midfield player at Celtic. Ki is an acknowledged talent but he was unable to force the issue at Celtic and was jettisoned by Swansea after a year to take his place at the Sunderland circus. The fruits of what happened during the summer 2013 transfer window will be evident in the years to come. Celtic sold Victor Wanyama for an eye-watering £12m. Gary Hooper left to take up a position on the Norwich City bench before Kelvin Wilson successfully campaigned successfully for a move 'home' to Nottingham Forest. This policy is less radical than it might seem. Hooper and Wanyama had sat on contract offers for 10 months and made it clear they were not going to sign new contracts. Wilson didn't have a contract offer to consider but his desire to return to the Midlands was two years old and getting stronger. For Celtic, it was sell for a gross total of around £20m or sell for less in a year or two. The more important question was how were Celtic going to use their apparent windfall. We went back to Israel for the third time in recent years but most of our spend this year went to mature the markets of Germany and the Netherlands. More significant than the geographical spread of recruits was the age and career profile. Van Dijk, Pukki, Biton and Balde are all young with potential to develop into both stronger, and more valuable, players. Only Derk Boerrigter was signed in his peak years, with no old hands signed. One of the unfortunate consequences of what is almost certainly an inspired long-term strategy was that the crucial Champions League qualifiers had to be navigated almost exclusively with players from last season, minus one or two star players from last season. We successfully navigated the qualifiers but it will be towards the end of the season before we get a good handle whether the recruitment strategy went as well as the sale strategy.

Paul Brennan,
Celtic Quick News

OBBY MURDOCH'S CURLED-UP WINKLEPICKERS • LENNON'S PASSION

TO EVERYONE ON CELTIC QU NEWS – THIS ABOUT WHAT HAVE ALL DO

BROGAN ROGAN TREVINO AND HOGAN ON YOUR BIGGEST ACHIEVEMENT IN A DECADE ON CELTIC QUICK NEWS...

**"This is.....
MISS VANESSA
RIDDLE!"**

Try and cast your mind back, if you will, to those dark and distant days when there was no CQN?

Yes those days, when you didn't reach for your laptop, phone, tablet or whatever to see what you had missed in terms of things Celtic. Those days when, unless you were from East Kilbride, you had no idea what the weather was like there – and to be honest you had absolutely no interest in finding out!

Back to the days when you had never heard of Kojo and his way of speaking or writing, when no one had ever Brattbakkedinanger, would recognise a cash strapped scrofulous hillbilliy outside Beverley Hills , and the only battered

bunnet that you knew of belonged to your Grandad.

I could go on and on with this and it would be fun!

However, the point of the examples above is to point out change. The change that has taken place over the last ten years or so in terms of social media, in terms of the free flow of information, in terms of communication with and from the club we all support, and most importantly the communication flow between---- us---- The CQN'ers.

If you stop and think about it, CQN has brought about a whole host of change in that ten years.

CK
YOU
NE!

The site has changed our daily habits, what we do with our spare time, how we read the news, make comment and much more.

It is a source of information about books, horses, holidays, music, films, theatre, poetry, and politics local, national and international.

It is a place where people who lost touch long ago meet up again, or where they discover news about people that they knew in their childhood from people they have never met, and most importantly it is a place where friendships have been forged, cemented and made strong and binding.

And, of course we have recently had our first engagement, and in due course we will have our first CQN related marriage.

It is also a site where there is often an outpouring of sympathy and goodwill to those who have lost loved ones, where people can find solace, words of comfort and a kind word.

However, principally the site is a place where you can talk all things Celtic, share opinions on things Celtic, disagree about things Celtic and of course is a mine of information about things Celtic past, Celtic present and Celtic future.

It is also a place that serves up a constant reminder that those who support Celtic Football Club do so only partly because of the notion that eleven men—and now women---can achieve something on a football field.

From the very outset, Glasgow Celtic and its support wanted to bring about change—change in the circumstances of the poor, the needy and the disadvantaged, or in the lives of those who were suffering some disadvantage or setback which they themselves, acting on their own, could do nothing about.

It is very easy to bracket everything that has followed from the "Penny Dinners" as simply "Charity" – but that definition and approach is, in my opinion, cold and impersonal.

The Celtic support from its earliest days wanted to support and invest in people not some idealistic concept or notion, but everyday ordinary people who needed a hand and deserved better.

Since the inception of CQN, the site has become a conduit for that notion of helping your fellow man and woman. In my opinion, it is the single greatest achievement of the site—and by far the single greatest achievement of the men and woman who populate the site with their views, chat, jokes and opinions.

Whatever each individual's contribution to the site may be, whether they be regular contributor or occasional or addicted lurker, what cannot be denied is that when the blog acts on masse and takes up a cause that it wants to support then to be frank it can move mountains.

Of course, the Celtic Support is to be found in places other than CQN and I am not for a moment saying that CQN and the CQN'ers are the Be All and End All of the Celtic charity movement—far from it!

However, you only have to look at the vast amount that CQN'ers did in the campaigns for Oscar Knox and MacKenzie Furniss this year to see that no matter what may happen anywhere else, or what is done by anyone

else, when the blog acts as one when stirred to come to the aid of others it represents a mighty force.

It would take one of Winning Captain's by now famous lists to name everyone who has contributed hugely to this year's campaigns, and you have all seen such lists ad nauseam.

So, instead let me introduce the girl in the picture.

This............ is Miss Vanessa Riddle.

Yes, that's right— The girl whose campaign for funds was the first campaign for funds needed to fight Neuroblastoma that was featured on CQN.

Of course, I personally have good cause to highlight the Vanessa campaign as it was I who mentioned it first on the blog. At the time the fund stood at just £10,000 with the target being £500,000.

However, this article is not about me—it is about each and every one of you who reads it—and about Vanessa herself—as I think it is absolutely vital that everyone involved with CQN and beyond sees and knows about the results of that campaign as we approach Christmas 2013.

To recap, the first time I ever met a whole lot of CQN'ers in the one place was in Jury's Hotel in Glasgow where Taggsybhoy (who it turns out I went to Primary School with- but I didn't know that at the time) had organised a music quiz to raise funds for Vanessa.

In my usual fashion, I arrived at the last minute (if not actually late) and within minutes I was faced with the unexpected task of saying a few short words to a room of people I didn't know and who I had not expected to be speaking to—though to be honest I should have anticipated being asked to say something —but I didn't.

So, there I was, standing there with all these people looking at me and essentially I was going to ask them for money to help a little girl that I and they did not know and had never met.

"back at CQN it was as if an army had been unleashed – and once unleashed and harnessed that army would march for Vanessa"

I had no idea what I was going to say.

It was only sometime later—in fact over a year later---- That Paul Brennan admitted to me that initially he thought that there was absolutely no chance whatsoever that you could raise half a million pounds for one child in the short time required.

To be honest, I wasn't too sure myself, but I honestly mean this when I say that I did believe that if the target was at all achievable then it was only achievable with the assistance of the fans of Celtic Football Club.

Anyway, as I stood before approximately 100 or so non music experts (with the odd notable exception) all I could think of to say was what I felt to be the honest and perhaps uncomfortable truth—as I did not want to in any way mislead those who were there and

who would be parting with their hard earned cash.

" Good Evening—My Name is Brogan Rogan Trevino and Boring! But you can call me Jim......."

From there I thanked everyone for coming, Taggsy for his organising the event blah blah blah and then advised everyone that I had no idea if the target money could be raised to get the treatment that this wee girl needed. All we could do is try—and, I stressed, even if we raised all the money in the world, the odds are stacked against her—very heavily against her---- and in all honesty the likely outcome here is not a good one. But here we are—This is what we do—so thanks for coming, have a good night, give what you can, and enjoy the night.

End of speech--- much to the relief of

everyone who perhaps wondered if I talked the same way I wrote?

Vanessa had been visited by Celtic Players at Yorkhill Sick Kids Hospital sometime before when she was first being treated there. For whatever reason, a bond was formed and there was a link between her and the club.

Other people on other sites started to collect for her as well, and in due course other football clubs and even the football authorities rallied to her cause. She played a key role in that year's League Cup Final and was a guest at Hampden.

Loads of other publicity rolled in, thanks to the efforts of family and friends, and the Neuroblastoma Alliance.

But back at CQN it was as if an army had been unleashed – and once unleashed and

and offered to underwrite the balance needed by way of a bank guarantee to get her over the line.

The target was achieved and exceeded in weeks—thanks to people from all walks of life, from throughout Scotland and way beyond and from all sorts of activities. As a money raising exercise it was scarcely believable.

However, you guys need to know what that meant in real terms. What it meant to Vanessa and her family, and to see the results of what all that fund raising actually achieved.

You need to know because it is likely that next year there will be another Vanessa, another Oscar and another MacKenzie somewhere out there who will need our help.

Maybe the Government will take away the need to raise money for Neuroblastoma treatment—fantastic if they do--- but there will always be another cause and someone else facing hardship who could do with a hand up and our help.

MacKenzie Furniss is currently starting a course of treatment that will take years to bring about the desired results--- we can only hope that treatment goes well. Her Just Giving page will be updated but the estimate is that she will need fully FIVE YEARS of treatment.

We all know that Oscar has had a tough battle and is still fighting with the help of medical treatment and care that you helped to facilitate. We can only hope and pray for him and his family that the treatment concerned brings about a full recovery.

But to close, let me give you the direct words of Chris Riddle, Vanessa's dad, who sent me an e-mail when I asked for an update on Vanessa to report back to you. These few short paragraphs spell out what your effort and your money helped achieve far better than anything I could ever write:

Hi Jim,

Got your DM on twitter asking about Vanessa and her current state of health for your article on CQN, thanks for asking.

Vanessa is doing great Jim, she's now back in remission and has no trace of the disease left in her body. She had her last round of scans in Germany in July and those scans showed that she was clear. Since then, she's been back to school, first of all for a few hours each day and now back full time. Her hair is growing back, with curls this time, it used to be poker straight! This has probably come about due to her getting my

wife Connie's stem cells, as she has curly hair and the docs expect Vanessa to take on some of Connie's traits. Hopefully not so much that Vanessa starts giving me into bother though!

She'll be due another round of scans, probably around November time, this time round we should be able to get Yorkhill in Glasgow to do the scans and send the results to Germany. Always a nervous time when she goes for scans, however we fully expect a positive outcome!

So Jim, so far so good, we are not so daft as to think that it can never return, however we don't give it much thought and give Vanessa the best possible life and do lots of things with her as we never know what's round the corner.

Thanks for all your help with Vanessa's appeal when it was going and I know that you've been a REAL help for others such as Mackenzie and Oscar, I'm sure I can speak for us all when I say that we are all indebted to you and your army of Celtic supporters and friends ..... Many thanks!

Best Regards

Chris Riddle

To be clear, it is not MY army of Celtic fans, and were there those on these campaigns, especially the Oscar campaign who did more than I ever could.

YOU are the army of Celtic fans--- YOU and many others like you.

CQN is many things – different things to different people—and it has changed many of our social habits in the last ten years.

However, it will never achieve anything greater, or anything that could or should make the contributors, readers, lurkers or whatever more proud than its amazing collective and individual response in helping these and other children in the name of Celtic Football Club and its supporters.

That achievement is truly fantastic and should be at the forefront of our minds at all times.

Finally, on behalf of CQN'ers everywhere, I would like to wish the families of Vanessa Riddle, Oscar Knox and MacKenzie Furniss a very Happy Christmas and every good wish for 2014 and for many years thereafter.

Celtic Football Club and its supporters--- caring since 1887.

harnessed that army would march for Vanessa, for Oscar, and more lately for Mackenzie as can be seen by the very names of the posters on the blog.

All sorts of people contacted me with offers—to auction wine collections, to do bucket collections in pubs and all sorts of other things that were just fantastic.

Angel Gabriel literally lived up to his name in Ayrshire (and by the way he has some very good book recommendations) and throughout the land all sorts of CQN'ers did amazing things to help Vanessa's target.

Towards the end of the campaign, as it edged ever closer to the magic figure but with tens of thousands of pounds still to go, I was contacted by one CQN'er who demanded complete anonymity but who there and then donated a five figure sum

CELTIC
THEIR PLACE AMONG THE GREATS

Rogan Rogan Trevino and Hogan was annoyed when he picked up a recent edition of a football magazine and discovered that they had unwittingly done Celtic a disservice. Here he replies exclusively for the 2014 CQN Annual...

In October of this year no less a publication than the Internationally respected Four Four Two Magazine ran a feature entitled "FFT's Greatest Club Sides Ever" in which they assessed the merits of the great footballing club sides of the past and attempted the virtually impossible task of comparing them to one another.

In making the fun assessment the magazine declared that in reaching a decision about teams from different eras they decided that "any club could only appear once in the top 20." Thus ruling out different teams from the same club during different eras, and that "the list had to be about more than mere trophies, it had to be about intangibles: how cool a team is, their legacy, their aura."

Having consulted what they describe as the footballing world's "Glitterati" the magazine were left with 38 teams which they had to whittle down to their top 20.

Now, there is no doubt that all of the above would be considered as absolutely fantastic teams, and that to be included in the list has

Revie's Leeds United are nowhere to be seen. The Tottenham Hotspur of Greaves, White and Mackay don't get a look in and there is no side in there managed by the special one.

However, as soon as I saw the list, whilst I was proud that Celtic were in the top twenty and just one off the top ten, my brain started telling me that it disagreed with this assessment on purely logical grounds.

For example some of the "Great Teams" mentioned here were only great for a few seasons, whilst others were apparently great for virtually a decade with only Santos in 7th place being triumphant for more than a ten year span.

Surely a team that is deemed great for virtually a decade has an argument to say that they should rank above a similar team who were only great for say three or four years?

However, it was when I actually started to study the teams above Celtic in 11th place that I determined for myself that with all due respect to the guys at Four Four Two their thinking has to be challenged.

something.

However, cast your mind back to the criteria set out by the Four Four Two guys, who say it is about more than the number of trophies won and should be about the legacy left behind and the impact made at the time.

On that basis alone Celtic should move up the league however when you look at head to head results the argument becomes unassailable.

For example, Celtic only met the mighty Benfica once in a competitive match during the period that both teams are cited for inclusion. Albeit, that the match was won by the toss of a coin, Celtic were the victors. Now whilst Benfica can cite Two European Cups to Celtic's one, and point out that they reached 5 finals in 8 years, the fact remains that they only once faced Celtic when both clubs were at their zenith and they lost!

Not only that, when they reached the last final of their great period in 1968, they were beaten by a Manchester United side which featured many of the same players who had been soundly beaten by Celtic at Celtic park in August 1966 when the score could have been far more than the final tally of 4-1.

In addition, the Grande Inter team of Helenio Herrera had been put together and fashioned in a style which was designed specifically to defeat the attacking football and style of Madrid and Benfica of the early 60's.

This Tactic was successful with Inter putting both Madrid and Benfica to the sword between 1963 and 1965.

It is interesting to note that Four Four Two give La Grande Inter legendary status for the five year period between 1962 and 1967 – precisely half the period of time the same status is granted to Benfica.

Obviously, something happened to Inter in 1967 that caused them to slip from their pedestal.

IN THE END THEY CAME UP WITH THE FOLLOWING LIST:

20 Nottingham Forest 1977-1980	11 Celtic 1965-1974
19 Budapest Honved 1950-1955	10 Torino 1945-49
18 Borussia Monchengladbach 1970-1979	9 Bayern Munich 1967-76
17 Preston North End 1888-89	8 Benfica 1960-70
16 Boca Juniors 1998-2003	7 Santos 1955-1968
15 FC Dynamo Kiev 1985-87	6 Inter Milan 1962-1967
14 Juventus 1980-86	5 Liverpool 1962-1967
13 Independiente 1971-75	4 Barcelona 2008-2011
12 Manchester United 1995-2001	3 Real Madrid 1955-1960
	2 A.C. Milan 1987-1991
	1 Ajax 1965-1973

to be seen as an absolute accolade. This is especially so when you consider the teams which don't make the list.

There is no Arsenal at all for example. Don

Now I know that Celtic have only won the European Cup once whilst others are multiple winners – and I guess that the more often you win the cup with the big ears has to count for

Like Benfica, they played Celtic on one occasion during the period when both clubs were deemed "Great" and like Benfica they lost!

Yet both of these clubs are ranked above Celtic on the list.

There are lots of examples of great teams on that list who were from different times and so could obviously not have met one another. However, these three teams—Celtic, Benfica and Inter --- did meet head to head at the relevant time and only Celtic come out with a 100% record against the other two!

Yet, despite this they rank below their Latin counterparts in 11th place while Benfica sit 8th and Inter Milan 6th.

That just does not seen right to me.

However, even more puzzling is the placing of Bill Shankly's Liverpool in 5th place for their efforts between 1962 and 1967.

Now, I recognise that using my own head to head method above, the records show that the only match between Celtic and Liverpool within the relevant time shows a victory for Liverpool.

Yet, I think it is now even accepted on Merseyside that when the two sides met in the semi final of the European Cup Winners Cup in April 1966 Celtic only lost as a result of a perfectly good Lennox goal being chopped off for no good reason.

However, beyond that, Shankly's Liverpool were not playing at the very top level in Europe in the main, and so were not facing the same level of competition as Celtic during the relevant period. They were nowhere near European Cup Finals at the time unlike Celtic during their cited period of glory.

In fact the nearest they came was the semi final of 1964-65 where they ultimately lost to La Grande Inter whose heyday was to be terminated by Celtic two years later. After the Inter match, Liverpool would not progress past the third round of any European competition for the next 4 years.

Not only that, the only time during the period when both clubs were competing for the big cup at the same time was 1967 when of course Celtic won the trophy outright. Further, in that competition, Liverpool's journey ended when they were thrashed by a Johan Cruyff inspired Ajax by seven goals to three on aggregate. This result persuaded Shankly that he had to change the style of football Liverpool played if they were to ever succeed in Europe.

In that same year, Ajax themselves were eliminated from Europe at the quarter final stage when they lost to the Masopust lead Dukla Prague who were in turn defeated by .... well you know who?

So Basically, I would argue that there is every good reason to suggest that at least three of the teams ranked above Celtic during these zenith years do not deserve their higher billing.

I recognise of course that there are counter arguments and other factors which may well be given more weight by others when looking at a series of head to head results.

However, I am not finished there, because as has been made clear by Four Four Two, of the factors to be taken into account in this purely for fun assessment you are to include how cool a team is, their legacy, and their aura.

Well I suppose it could be argued that a team which wins the European Cup fielding a substantial number of players who all have their false teeth secreted in the goalie's bunnet is not very cool at all!

However, that is not what the Four Four Two guys mean.

No they mean the lasting impression made on football, and when it comes to that category I would argue that Stein's Celtic shoot straight up the league.

There are very few club sides that can actually boast that they changed the shape of the game, but the Celtic of the era cited certainly come into that category in two ways if not three.

First, as we have seen Inter's Cattenaccio had become a dominant and all conquering style which the likes of Benfica, Real Madrid, Liverpool and many more could not handle or overcome.

It was Celtic, and Celtic alone, who consigned that entire system of football to the bin over a 90 minute period. Whatsmore,

"Only Celtic, out of all the teams listed, succeeded in dismantling the Inter myth."

the team's manager made it plain prior to the game that winning by any style was simply not an option.

Stein said in advance that he wanted his team to win with style, with an aura and panache, and in a fashion that made the neutral cheer, thus condemning the anti football of Herrera to the scrap heap.

That is why Four Four Two make it plain that La Grande Inter died in 1967. Prior to that date in Lisbon, many other teams mentioned in the top twenty tried and failed to beat that style of football only to repeatedly fall victim to what was the world's most expensive football team at the time.

Only Celtic, out of all the teams listed, succeeded in dismantling the Inter myth.

However, not only that, the attacking display by the team in Green and White after Mazzola's penalty was to have a profound effect on all others.

Celtic's style of attacking play became the new mantra and this had a subtle effect on all the other contenders of the time. When Ajax played Liverpool in 1966/67 their style was described as a deliberate and patient passing style --- a style far removed from the real glory years of the Dutch masters.

That was to come with the total football Ajax practised between 1969 and 1973 with some saying that the real death of Catenaccio came in the 1972 European Cup Final when Ajax put Inter to the sword by 2-0 in the De Kuip in Rotterdam.

Yet that ignores the fact that after 1967 Ajax changed their playing style and an examination of Celtic's fluid 4-2-4 of the time showed that there were times when attackers were expected to come back and defend and conversely there were goal threats from Celtic from every position bar sweeper and goal keeper. It might be said that total football – including fullbacks

popping up in all sorts of strange attacking places—did not show itself on a major stage until one afternoon in Lisbon and then went on from there, with Cruyff's Ajax being the ultimate exponents of the style.

However, perhaps the biggest impact that this Celtic team had in terms of aura and coolness was the fact that they were all from the one place and were not an expensive team.

One of the Inter Milan players received a signing on fee which was greater than the cost of the whole Celtic team put together, and his wages for the year would have paid the salaries of half the Celtic line up in Lisbon.

Barry Davis viewed the Celtic of 1967-1971 as the finest team in Europe at the time and it was not until the full emergence of Cruyff's total footballing Ajax that you had a clear successor to the title of Kings of Europe...... as Manchester United and others were not consistent in Europe over a period of time.

I have no quibble at all with that Ajax side being rated as number 1 on the list as they were a devastating side to watch and I can testify to that first hand when I watched them beat Celtic 3-0 in Amsterdam before going on to win the big cup in 1971—although to be fair two late goals exaggerated the difference between the teams.

So to conclude, it is flattering to see that great Celtic side being included among those top sides, but there is room for argument to suggest that they should be ranked higher than 11th given the criteria to be applied.

I know I am biased, but I would rely on the opinion of someone who was playing the game at the highest level during the period when Celtic are cited as being of the best. So, I simply remind everyone of the words of Bertie Auld as he went to walk off the turf of the Estadio National on that afternoon

25th May 1967.

" Hey Ronnie Simpson, son! Who are we? Who are we Ronnie?---- We are the greatest son, that is who we are—we are the greatest!"

Although I am pretty sure you all knew that Two thousand, two hundred and forty words ago!

BJMAC · GERRY MCNEE'S SACRED MEDAL · THE GREEN MAN

THE JOURNEY OF GIORGOS SAMARAS

EY
OS

Brogan Rogan Hogan and Trevino pays tribute to the quiet dignity of Celtic's star performer...

In the aftermath of Celtic's champion's league exit there is much speculation in the press about which players will stay and which will leave. I suppose that such speculation in the world of football is only natural.

However, in the case of Celtic Football Club that speculation is heightened by the universally accepted fact that in salary terms Celtic truly is the poor man of Europe. The Club cannot afford the salaries on offer at any of the other clubs in the last sixteen and so Neil Lennon has a unique battle on his hands in attempting to keep players who would hopefully be able to go on and impress again in the same competition next year.

I wonder how many of you have been following the amazing and unique Guardian column that is written by the "Secret Footballer"?

This is a series of newspaper articles supposedly written by a current/former English Premier Player who reveals the life—often the totally shocking life—of an EPL player—earning tens of thousands of pounds per week and living a life style full of huge houses, fast cars, exotic holidays and plenty of willing women—wives and otherwise!

The identity of the player is not revealed, although there is no end of speculation as to who it might be throughout the internet.

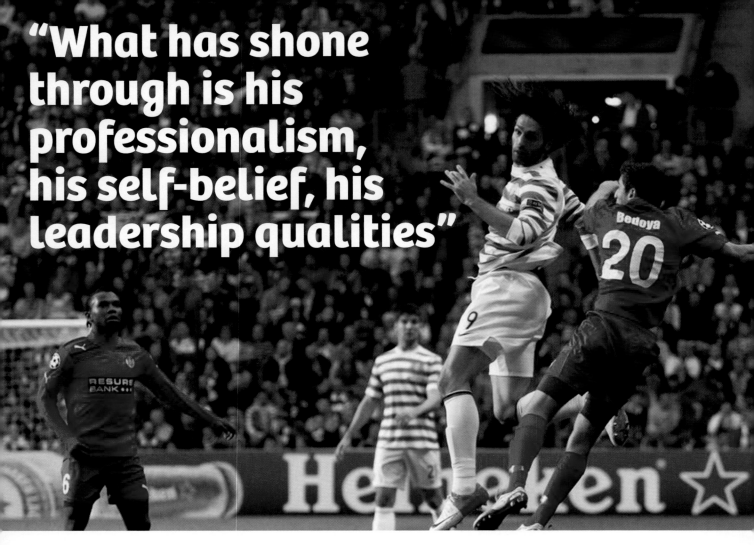

"What has shone through is his professionalism, his self-belief, his leadership qualities"

Of great concern in that Column is the statement by the player that the driving factor in his footballing career has always been money. Now this may be no great surprise to some, but when it is explained that the idea of winning any kind of trophy or medal – anything at all---was looked upon as an absolute bonus, then you can quite clearly see where this young man's priorities lie.

The winning of medals and titles is a complete afterthought—it has at no time been a priority.

He has apparently been sold a few times—including one transfer which represented a record fee for the buying club—and he has played with and against many of the really big names in the Premiership.

Yet winning was a bonus—an add on--- an after thought--- money was everything.

Contrast that to the quiet dignity and the strange and often turbulent career path of Giorgios Samaras.

Samaras was born in Crete and at the age of

ten he joined the local side where his father was a player and would later move on to be coach. Under his father's influence he trained each and every day after school and perhaps most importantly, through his father he got to see the behind the scenes workings of a football club.

By the age of 16 he was transferred to Heerenveen in the Dutch league, making his debut at the age of 18 playing alongside the likes of Klaas-Jan Huntelaar. In three seasons with the Dutch club he scored 25 goals in 88 appearances, and this lead to his £6Million move to Manchester City.

As everyone knows, his time with Manchester City did not go well. Having been signed by Stuart Pearce, it is interesting to note what Samaras himself said of the move, which was that he saw it as "the next stage in my development".

Now, note that phrase. No mention of money, no mention of the league or the prestige etc but an expression about his development as a player.

In his first 6 games for City he scored no less

than 4 times!

However, Manchester City under Pearce were on a downward spiral and as an expensive player Samaras came in for some considerable stick from his manager, his fellow players and the fans. To say that he was not loved would be an understatement.

It is here that I find the words of the young Greek player interesting. In response to the criticism he stated clearly that his self-belief would see him through, that he had overcome more difficult periods in his life than this, and most importantly from our point of view—that it was his foremost desire to become a Champions League player!!

It should be noted that having moved for £6M and given the wage he was on at Manchester City, Giorgios would be financially comfortable no matter what he did on the field of play. However, from the comments above it can be seen that, unlike our Secret Footballer, Giorgios Samaras had a clear goal and that was Champions League Football.

By this time of course he had already opted

He has scored plenty of goals in Europe—important goals at that—this season and more importantly he is seen as someone who causes a severe headache to many opposing teams and managers as they are clearly not too sure what to do about the mercurial Greek in the Celtic ranks. In all, he has made 145 appearances in a Celtic shirt and scored 42 goals.

After the defeat to Juventus he talked of the great learning experience the Champions League campaign had been for younger members of the squad—how they could learn from it and how they could improve as a result of the experience.

On another occasion, when talking about the mysteries of football, about ridiculous wages and transfer fees he is reported to have talked about the pride of playing and being successful rather than the riches that are on offer.

" You can't buy Pride" he is reported to have said.

Further, he has not been slow to release statements and hints through his agent that he is happy in Glasgow and that he rates and recognises the ethos of the Club—another attribute that cannot be bought or sold. In this way he has quickly moved to quell transfer gossip or approaches making it clear that he is a Celtic Player and seems to want to remain so.

I was told by someone who attended the late Sean Fallon's Funeral that Samaras conducted himself with a dignity and in a manner which suggested that the people who have played a part in the football club and who follow the football club are of major significance to him in his thinking and outlook.

Going by what he has said in the past, and what little I know of the man (as outlined above) Samaras is a vital asset in the Celtic dressing room at this time.

Here is someone who, long before he was even considered as a Celtic player, openly stated that he wanted to be a Champions League player. Such a position is not going to be achieved by many of the clubs and players in the top flight in England—and only a few clubs in England will guarantee Champions league football on a regular basis.

The player who is behind the secret footballer column in the Guardian has revealed that for all the almost untold wealth he has accumulated over the years he has received regular treatment for depression. Whoever it is, is also a reasonably bright and caring individual as he says he bears a cross

thinking about the time when one team he played for was consigned to relegation.

He knew that he would not be playing in the lower league the following season no matter what happened to the club. He knew that another premiership side would come and offer money for him so earning himself yet more money—although he did reveal a worry which was that he had by this time built himself a lifestyle that was absolutely dependent on EPL wages—and any relegation which resulted in a cut in wages meant losing a house and a change in lifestyle for him and his family.

However, the player concerned said that he still thought about the club and those people in the backroom staff who lost their job as a result of the team being relegated—possibly only to find that it would be some time before they could get any kind of alternative job to feed their family. He questions whether or not he could have done more to keep that team up and save those jobs. Then he takes comfort in where he is – even though he may be playing at a club where he hates the club itself and the manager he plays for—as long as there is money at the end of the week!

The title of the piece was called " I'm alright Jack".

Contrast that situation to the man who has become Georgios Samaras and his outlook as a footballer in terms of his ambitions and goals.

Samaras' influence, his quiet way, his off field persona may well be his greatest footballing asset and an asset that Celtic would be wise to utilise when dealing with their younger talent such as Watt, Forrest, McGeoch and so on.

As we head on into the madness of the Summer transfer window there will speculation aplenty about who is leaving the club and who is not. No matter what stage they may be at in their "development" as a player or a person, there are those in the dressing room who may be contemplating a move elsewhere for whatever reason. However before finalising things with their agents or whoever they would be well advised to take some Counsel from Giorgios Samaras.

You are always taught the phrase beware of Greek's bearing gifts (such as the Trojan Horse), yet it is equally foolish to ignore Greeks who appear to have Wisdom by the bucket in assessing what they want out of life as a footballer and a person—especially when they are sitting along the bench in the same changing room.

to become a Greek International Player. I stress "opted" because he could have chosen to play for Australia with all the fringe benefits that such a choice would bring—there would be far more competition for a place with Greece--- yet he deliberately chose the harder option for playing for the country of his birth, making his debut a week after his 21st Birthday. He has now gained over 60 caps and played in both Euro and World Cup finals with distinction.

Like the Manchester City fans, Celtic fans quickly became frustrated with Giorgios as his skills and form were very intermittent whether that be under Gordon Strachan or Tony Mowbray, and few could understand Neil Lennon's desire to keep him at Celtic Park.

Yet today, he ranks among the fans' favourites despite his continuing to frustrate at times. What has shone through is his professionalism, his self-belief, his leadership qualities and most of all a dignity and understanding of things Celtic and the Celtic way.

OH AH SAMARAS

Brogan Rogan Trevino and Hogan updates his assessment of the Greek God for the 2014 CQN Annual...

Several months on and we find that the Celtic team has changed significantly with the departures of Gary Hooper, Victor Wanyama and Kelvin Wilson.

Over the summer, new faces have arrived at Celtic Park, and others who have been there only a relatively short time have decided to extend their stay and take the Celtic/Georgios Samaras development course.

Whilst Kelvin Wilson chose to make a return to Nottingham Forrest, a new Herenveen bhoy appeared in the East End of Glasgow in the shape of Virgil Van Dyke. Unlike Samaras he has come straight from Holland to Celtic without going through the quagmire of the English Premier League and as a result finds himself a Champions League

Player.......... Just as Samaras had said he had wanted to be.

Timu Pukki is yet to find his feet at Celtic Park, but he can look to Giorgios and recognise that it took Samaras fully 3 years at least to win over the Celtic support, AND that during those years the management at the club stuck by the player, showed faith in the player, and literally put their faith in not only the player but their initial scouting reaction to what they saw as talent that could be developed.

Efe Ambrose, who many lambasted after his faux pas in the first leg against Juventus at Celtic Park last season, has been sensational this year. More importantly, he has struck a very quick and strong partnership with Van Dyk, and has put pen to paper in signing

Football Club and the attitude of the player himself.

That attitude—as well as his skill, determination and mentality --- has flourished and been nurtured at Celtic park with spectacular results. Players at other clubs can see the change in Samaras and the adulation and respect he receives from the terracing and from the opposition. That respect is not only local, it stretches across Europe --- though at one time had you suggested such a thing many would have laughed at you.

Could it be that someone like Nir Biton could have been swayed to come to Celtic partly because of the Samaras experience? He too was at Manchester City and was predicted to achieve great things amidst the multi millions and the megastars only to find himself back in Israel. Perhaps the sight of another ex City player (perhaps an ex city reject) being discussed across Europe played a part in him deciding that Celtic was the place for him to take " The next stage in (his) development".

And what of the bearded one himself? What have the intervening months brought to Georgios since last season came to an end?

Apart from more winner's medals, it would appear that Samaras continues his development like a thoroughbred race horse who appears at the big race meetings to claim the prize.

After a lacklustre pre season, Celtic had to take a tough and arduous route into the Champions' League group stages.

The question was would they be ready and where were the star men given the departures in the summer?

Enter the bearded, by now experienced, and confident Samaras into the champions arena.

His goals against Cliftonville and Elfsborg were vital in reminding everyone—including the opposition and those at Celtic park--- that Celtic were an accomplished and hardened Champions league team who would be tough to beat unless you were of the right class.

That lesson was hammered home with his performance against Shakther Karagandy at Celtic park.

Needing the win in a tense game, It was the Samaras and Commons double act that secured the vital breakthrough just before half time, with Georgios taking the ball for a walk along the penalty box, dragging opposition players out of their defensive formation, before allowing Kris to take over, walk into the space and unleash a vital

opener for Celtic.

Not long after half time, a mishit Lustig shot was quickly controlled by Samaras and dispatched into the net.

It is often said that Georgios is not " an instinctive goalscorer" however any view of that goal shows sheer instinctive ability and reaction inside the box. Control the ball at pace, shoots, scores--- end of!

What's more, the importance of that goal and his subsequent reaction with the crowd – waving those giant arms and whipping up the Parkhead atmosphere—meant that everyone knew that Celtic were no longer "out" in terms of this tie. They were not through—but they were no longer "out" --- and Samaras wanted everyone in the ground to know it increasing the mental pressure on the opposition who had seen their two goal lead disappear and their defensive wall breached for a second time.

Since then, he has gone on to score a remarkable hatrick against Kilmarnock, and produced a performance against Barcelona where he was a one man battering ram cum ballet dancer against the Catalans -showing a mixture of sheer determination, strength and skill to cause a real problem for a team said to contain some of the most skilful footballers in the world.

Such was his performance against Barcelona—a performance seen throughout the televised world --- that of all the footballers on the planet, Barcelona fans have voted Georgios as the player they would most like their club to sign!

Gary Hooper, Kelvin Wilson and Victor Wanyama did not figure.

Samaras is now 28 years old and heads towards the end of his current contract but unlike last time around there will be no one turning to Neil Lennon at the forthcoming AGM and asking " Why on earth are you giving him a new contract?"

Instead the mood is more likely to be reflected in a comment I recently heard at Celtic park when big Sammy turned, beat a player and sent a shot flying by the far post, inches away from being a spectacular goal.

" Jesus Christ!" came a shout from behind me only to be quickly followed by an instant sharp witted observation from someone else:

" Nah--- he is not quite Jesus Christ... but he is not far off!"

I only hope that the continued Journey of Georgios Samaras...is made on the Celtic bus.

a long term deal, extending his original contract with Celtic.

When explaining his decision to sign the new contract, Ambrose spills words that could be taken directly from the Samaras script book. He talks of being settled here, enjoying the club, the fans, the overall environment and being content within himself. Being at Celtic means something to him and his lifestyle --- it is a script that is far removed from the life of the Secret Footballer and the drive for as much money as possible and a life without winning anything in football.

Whilst these developments in the playing squad (as well as others) can be attributed to Neil Lennon and his backroom staff, his scouting staff and the executives at the club, there is no doubt in my mind that the journey of Giorgios Samaras—with all its ups and downs--- serves as a great advert for Celtic

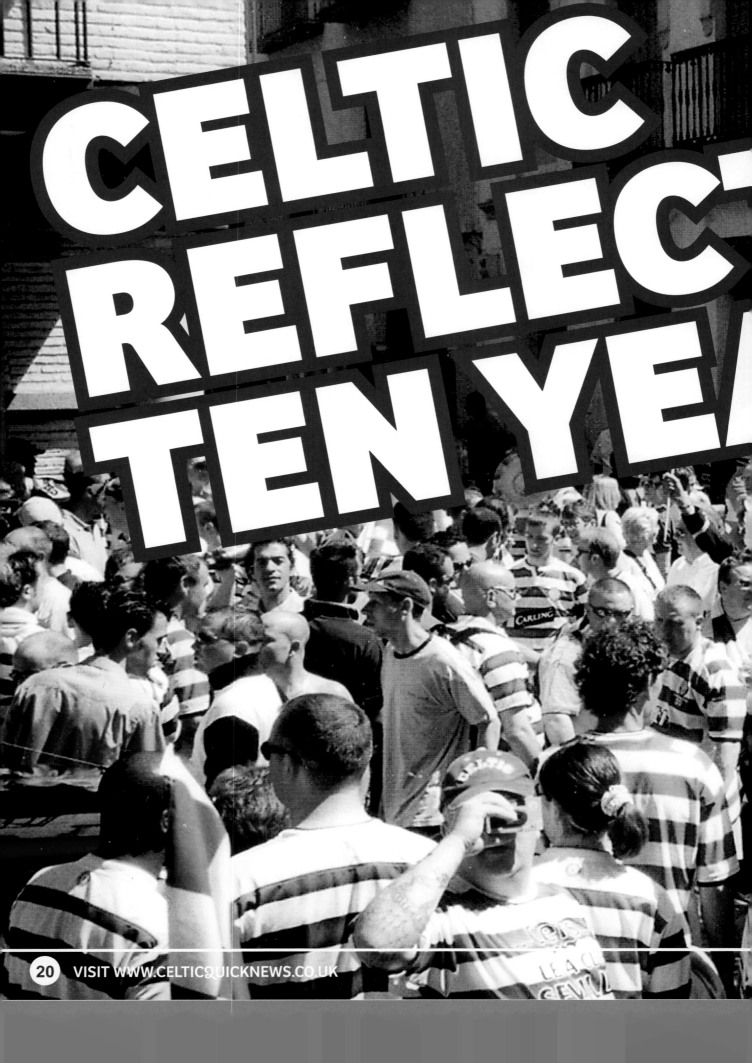

CELTIC
REFLEC
TEN YEA

IONS
RS ON...

Joe Ruddy looks back at Celtic's semi final in the 2003 UEFA Cup against Boavista and on to the Final itself in Seville where Celtic supporters experienced extreme highs and lows as a huge army of Celtic fans descended on Seville for a huge party and the team Losing narrowly, causing such heartbreak...

CLIFTONVILLE CELT FROM BELFAST · MARTI SANDINO · DENIABHOY

Ten years ago to date, Celtic were preparing for two of their biggest games in the clubs history. On the 10th of April 2003 (first leg) and the 24th of April (second leg), Celtic were to play in the UEFA Cup semi-final tie against Boavista. Celtic had already played a fantastic competition, by knocking out Liverpool, Stuttgart, Celta Vigo, Blackburn and Suduva.

Celtic had been playing brilliantly throughout the competition, and had put their fans under some seriously nerve-racking ties, most notably against Stuttgart and Celta Vigo. Their opponents, Boavista, were one of the surprise teams of the competition, and had rode their luck in a fair share of their games in the run up to Celtic, taking nothing away from them, it's the results that count at the end of the day.

After seeing Celtic knocking out much 'better' teams already, there was a sudden expectancy circling among the fans. Before the draw, the teams that Celtic could have came up against were Porto, Lazio and of course Boavista. You could say here that Celtic had the luck of the draw. Lazio were another one of the teams who had been riding their luck a bit, but were still a very deadly team nonetheless. Porto on the other hand, were mauling teams throughout the whole competition, and definitely the team to avoid. The draw was made, and it was very much in our favour.

In what seemed like years leading up to the game, 10th April had finally arrived. Fans were doing what they could to pass the time up until 7.45pm. The fans were again cheering the team onto the pitch, as they always do with such passion and delirium. Everyone was up for this. Before this tie Boavista had collected 26 yellow cards and two red, incurring seven suspensions. Again, it was much the same in the game at Celtic Park, with some atrocious tackles flying in. The first half had passed by, with both sides missing chances, most notably Duda of Boavista.

The teams came out for the second half, much to the support of the fans again, but things went all wrong in the 49th minute, when Boavista went 1-0 ahead. It was a cross into the box from Luiz Claudio, which resulted in Joos Valgaeren scoring into his own net. Panic, for a minute anyway, as Celtic had equalised instantly. Boavista up until now had looked much organised and didn't look like giving much away, but had the goal set their minds on the final instead of the current time? It certainly appeared that way. Stilian Petrov it was with the assist to set up who other than Henrik Larsson, who stroked the ball home, 1-1, game on.

Having turned down numerous penalties already, Frank De Bleeckere (the referee) had decided enough was enough. Penalty awarded to Celtic in the 75th minute. Larsson stepped up to take the spot kick, and missed. To be fair, Larsson didn't do much wrong; it was just a fantastic save by Ricardo. The final whistle sounded, and the first leg score finished 1-1. Boavista had the crucial away goal. Celtic had it all to do in Portugal.

Two weeks went by slowly for Celtic fans, but 24th April had finally arrived. For now, this was Celtic's most important match in years. If they got to the final, then that would be bigger. As expected, this game was played with immense tension and unease. Few chances were being made between either side in the first half. Celtic's best chance fell to Larsson, who shot wide. Elpidio Silva had Boavista's best effort just before half time, but Douglas was on hand to parry away the header. On the hour mark, Douglas had all fans hearts in their mouths, as he was in no man's land. He misjudged a cross, and it went straight to Elpidio Silva, but Johan Mjallby saved the team, by knocking the ball out for a corner.

Time was ticking away, and it was looking as if Boavista were going through on the away goal rule. Henrik Larsson had other ideas though, when he put Celtic 1-0 ahead on the 78th minute. 12 minutes to hold on. Celtic fans were going wild. Time was ticking down, then Didier Agathe made a tackle in the box, in which he appeared to make contact with Jocivalter, but the referee seen nothing wrong with the challenge. Celtic held on for a 1-0 victory in Portugal. They had done it! Celtic were to play in the UEFA Cup Final against Porto in Seville, on 21st May 2003.

Fans were preparing for the final, arranging travel arrangements to Seville. Unfortunately I was unable to attend the game, as at the time I was only 14. I had to settle for the settee! This was now their biggest game, emulating that of the 2nd leg semi-final. The fans had been singing, partying, drinking in Seville in the build up to the game. We weren't stupid though, we knew Porto were clear favourites to win it. Porto got into the final with relative ease, beating Lazio 4-1 on aggregate. They had been doing it throughout the competition, destroying teams.

The game got underway, Celtic again being cheered on by the fans. The noise was unbelievable. Porto got off to a bad start, when

Francisco Costinha was taken off on a stretcher, with a thigh injury. Celtic's chances were few and far between in the first half, Deco proving to be a real problem for the Celtic defence. In first half injury time, Porto had finally undone the Celtic back line, going 1-0 ahead. It was Deco who assisted, setting up Alenitchev, whose volley was saved but only parried out to Derlei to put it in the net. Half time, 1-0 to Porto.

Martin O'Neill had to deliver one hell of a speech. Whatever he said though, it seemed to pay off, as Celtic had equalised on the 47th minute through Henrik Larsson. Didier Agathe put a cross into the box, and Larsson rose magnificently to make it 1-1. That was Larsson's 200th goal in the green and white Hoops. Game on.

It wasn't long before Porto found themselves ahead again. In fact it was only 7 minutes Celtic were equal. It was the magician Deco who assisted again, setting up Alenitchev, who supplied a neat finish. 2-1 Porto, Celtic with it all to do again. Two minutes later, Celtic were level again. Alan Thompson swung in the corner, which again met the head of Larsson, his bullet header making it 2-2. Game on, again. What a match. It seemed whatever Porto were doing, Celtic were matching it. It stayed 2-2, and in the final moments of injury time, Aleitchev had a great chance to win the Cup, but he couldn't keep his composure, and put it way over the bar.

Extra time was to be played to find the winner. Four minutes into extra-time and Celtic found themselves a man down. Bobo Balde was sent off for his second bookable offence following a woeful challenge on Derlei. The complete opposite of what Celtic needed. Celtic held on for the first half of extra-time. It looked to be heading to a penalty shootout, but it wasn't to be. Five minutes from time, Porto had struck again. Derlei had scored. Celtic hearts just sunk, fans and players. Porto's Nuno Valente was also sent off for a second bookable offence in the dying seconds, but it was too little, too late, there wasn't enough time for Celtic to level. Porto had broken hearts, beating Celtic 3-2.

I don't know how to best describe the thoughts and feelings of the fans once the full time whistle went. It was sheer devastation. Many tears were shed that night, mine included. It was a very, very emotional night. There was certainly no shame in this loss. Nobody had expected Celtic to get anywhere near the final, and Porto were one of the best teams around at that time. In fact, to date, Porto are still one of Europe's deadliest teams.

Even though from my own viewing from the sofa, it is a night that will stay in my memory for the rest of my life. It will be a night for many Celtic fans to saviour in years to come. A story for the kids, the grandchildren. I was there. I witnessed it. I have seen my team, Celtic Football Club, getting into a major European final.

Hopefully, I can witness it again. It's one of the best memories I'll ever have.

DELANEYS DUNKY · GREENSIREUR · MOUNTRLOW TIM

1771 MILES IN MAY

Tony McCann travels not quite a million miles, but would do so if required...

"The Woodstock of fitba? Whit you slabberin aboot?!"

He was right, I was drunk, it was roasting hot and the beer had be going down easier than a Rivaldo in the penalty box. Swept away with the euphoria of seeing a coursing, live sea of green and white almost 100,000 strong I was letting the drink pick the vocabulary and it was a sentimental composer.

Even though we had no tickets we were there, carried 1771 miles to Seville by the biggest football buzz to hit my mates and yet; the 2002-2003 UEFA Cup final. Well the buzz and my trusty Ford Focus, which looking back was a suspect greeny, bluey, why would someone-buy-a-car-that-colour hew. I was 22, on a budget and totally in love with my vehicle, even if the colour was repugnant.

We had started our journey at roughly 2030hrs on a sunny Sunday May evening in 2003. The sun was bright as it optimistically set blessing the car with its last light and warmth as I cruised down the M8. Before me, if the carefully printed out AA map was to be believed, lay 1771 miles of tarmac until Seville and not one inch of the tarmac between me and Seville daunted me in the slightest. This was destiny unfolding.

The logistics pre-journey had been assembled with military precision. I had fetched

2 x 24 can crates of Red Bull from Costco and my compadres, Ped & the legend in the making, the Bead had arranged food, sleeping bags and camping gear. The energy first conjured up whilst disgustingly drunk after watching Celtic dump Boavista out of the UEFA cup hadn't died down. This was on. We were going.

The first leg of our journey involved making the 0630hrs Euro Tunnel train, leaving us a 10 hours to make Felixstowe. The journey flew in, and in no time at all it seemed like I was driving my Focus tentatively onto a train. We were second in the queue to enter the train behind a crisp blue Mondeo ST 220. As we drove I realised we had to go right to the front of the train, it was like driving to the end of the tunnel. Everything this trip seems destined to be an adventure.

Turns out I hadn't counted on driving through Paris. And also that the navigator, in this instance The Bead hadn't been studying the map and was winging it in a country he had never even considered visiting. Hindsight is a wonderful thing but even the Bead's utter navigational ineptitude (for want of an expression less expletives) is just another facet to this life-affirming event.

And standing here on this ornate Spanish bridge, gibbering semi-coherent superlatives to my beery buddies, comparing the scene to Woodstock, a great number of ideas carried me momentarily out of the scene.

"The Woodstock of fitba? Whit you slabberin aboot?!"

AESTRO-NUMBER8 • THEBHOYDAVEJAPAN • MASTY • DONTPATMADUG

Seeing so many bodies mobilised, all marching under the same banner so to speak was mesmerising. Mass camaraderie, that appears so abundant in the past but so scarce in the present was a mighty force. And we seemed to be a force for good, elated zealots here to spread peace through bonhomie, football and song.

That morning I had woke up face down on the pavement in the city centre. Grit was welded to my cheeks and the Cadbury's Dairy Milk bar shaped pavement had collected some of my salvia, no doubt excreted during a delightfully deep sleep. Who knew pavements were so comfy? The quick inventory check revealed that during the night I had lost a Celtic top and gained a Betis top. In the taxi back to the camp site I started to piece together the night. Ped, Bead and I had gone to see Charlie and the Bhoys. The gig was incredible. Then when the bar was drunk dry we all dispersed. Scene missing. Then we were getting shooed from a tapas bar where I seem to recall swapping my Celtic top with what I think was a bemused local.

The taxi swept into the campsite. The place was electric, music, song and laugher were everywhere and the place reverberated with positive vibes and tales punctuated frequently with a random "Hail Hail!" It me in mind of some Roman front line infantry camp like in Gladiator, all corners of the far-flung Celtic Empire here to pay tribute, Ozzies, Yanks, hardcore German bikers sporting St. Pauli gear and even the soul member of the Wigan CSC. So he said anyway. And his missus.

Its one thing to be told you have global reach, it is quite another to witness it. There was no doubting any of the hyperbole of old, this was real and it was happening. The best natured army ever assembled had descended upon Andalusia and I was part of it.

The city rocked and on the way to watch the game Seville was green and white. Every artery of the city pulsed and pounded to the rhythm we took and the vibe we made. Nothing before or after would match that march towards the stadium.

The result hurt, like Icarus flying too close to the sun and suffering for it. If we had been royally stuffed then I suppose it wouldn't have been so much of a tough one to take, but as Henrik Larsson said "to score two goals in a final and not win is tough, very tough".

"If it hud been the Woodstock ah fitba we wouldnae huv goat beat ya nugget", the Bead declared from under a ferociously furrowed brow. Before he could compound his point, in a moment of rare clarity I countered with "if ye knew the result beforehand would ye have still came?"

In the periphery of my vision a guy wearing a full Celtic kit, tricolour worn as a cape and holding aloft a framed painting of Da Vinci's The Last supper with Jesus and the Apostles replaced by Martin O'Neill and the squad. The Bead and I both caught each others eye and smiled, "too right" he roared with a 'whit you talking aboot' look plastered all over his Chevy Chase.

The 1771 miles back home were easy, largely silent and reflective, not burdened by the result and spurred on by what we had seen. Events like this are as frequent as Halley's comet and as magical as a 5-year's Christmas and we had been there. The pride in our club we were often so derided for by many sections of society disappeared. We had made Scotland, our club and most of all ourselves proud and it had been effortless. Even almost 10 years after the event my pride hasn't subsided. This affirmed all things Celtic to us and to I'm eternally grateful I got to drive those 1771 miles in May.

We don't care if we win lose or draw, what the hell do we care? For we only know that there's going to be a show and the Glasgow Celtic will be there!

ALL MY PEOPLE RIGHT H RIGHT NOW – KNOW WH

 **v**

Estadio Olímpico
21 Mayo 20:45
Sevilla 2003

E I MEAN?

SEVILLE TORY

UEFA CUP FINAL
PRESENTED BY
Carlsberg

Part One – Bless this House

L Monaghan

WEEBOBBYCOLLINS · MAYNOOTHBHOY · GERRYBHOY · EXCATHEDRA44

L Monag[...]

Fans of The Beatles will remember when their 'Anthology' was shown on TV in the mid 90s. One instalment dealt with the legendary Shea Stadium gig. I remember being quite impressed with the editing of one trailer, in which all surviving members of the group name checked the venue in quick succession with faces still betraying a sense of awe at the gravity of an event held thirty or so years prior.

I think that's the way it's going to be with Seville.

My Seville story really started while I watched the Boavista away leg with my wife at home. This had become a superstitious arrangement through progressive away ties in the competition. I'd come to feel that we wouldn't win if the dynamic consisted of anything more than her and I. Irrational yes, but hardly unusual for someone who dribbles a mini football around the house during live radio commentaries somehow believing that I'm contributing to the match in progess.

Of course we'd loved Blackburn, Stuttgart, Anfield etc, but with twenty minutes to go in Oporto, I sat with my stomach recreating a range of football related sinking feelings from the past. You know, being told I was 'shite' by the high school team prima donna as another of his cannonball passes

rocketed out for a shy under my foot, or the time I ran home from primary school to watch Celtic lose to.... someone...on a black and white television during the seventies. I've never wanted to find out who we lost to or what year it was. The memory's more intriguing left blurry like footage of the moon landings.

I can recall having one of those whiney fits that kids have who've been dragged around the shops for too long. The ones when their bones have disappeared and mum's carrying their entire body weight by the wrist. At the end, I threw cushions at the telly and my dad suggested I toughen up and stop greetin'.

Back in 2003, I'm out of the seat, whole body wound in tension. I've only breathed in. I'm gonna have to breathe out eventually. The ball, the ball...it's hit off Hartson, no he passed it...wha'?.... HENRIK, PLEASE, PLEASE.

I never stopped to think about dad's instructions. Toughen up? Stop greetin'? When you love Celtic you've got no chance. BANG, my head went off like a beetroot grenade. I got those wee stars and psychedelic patterns in my eyes as I let out a throaty skrike again and again. Still, hold it, calm it, easy baw etc. We're no' out the woods yet. The spell at the end was sheer

L[...]

CELTIC QUICK NEWS ROLL OF HONOUR 2013-14

...ell. I celebrated Bobo's clearances louder than ...do goals at most SPL home games.

...he final whistle blew. I'd look at a tape ...f events later I thought. I always love ...crutinising the scenes and interviews at the ...nd of cup finals but now is just for us to ...njoy I kept repeating to a still seated other ...alf 'We've done it, We've done it'. Now, most ...f the time I speak (a lot) without thinking ...bout it but I really felt the 'we'. Not just in ...ur living room but in Oporto, crofts on Barra, ...owntown Boston and all the Celtic bars I'd ...ver drank in.

...threatened the mood a wee bit by getting ...erself in an affectionate headlock. Obviously, ...gallon of adrenaline wasn't jetting through ...er system as a stupid, tearful ape flew at her ...om the other side of the room. She forgave ...e though after much apologising. I mean, I ...ad to keep on her good side – Seville wasn't ...oing to come cheap.

Part Two – The Office

...s I lay horizontal on the living room floor, ...ecking the last can of celebration Stella from ...e fridge, I beamed as yet another bevvied ...c fan challenged J.Traynor to deny we were ...rilliant on the post-match phone ins.

...wo hours after the final whistle and I was still ...enching my fist and spitting 'Yessss' every ...ow and then like it was a twitch. How was I ...oing to get there and how might I get a ticket? ...eople all over the world were thinking the ...me thing. It was to be a big exciting, nervy, ...nd periodically depressing game of musical ...ckets (and flights). During my quest to reach ...eville I would see the best and worst of ...uman traits (in context you understand) and ...so rediscover what I already knew – Celtic is ...ot just a football club but an ideal concerned ...ith fair play for everyone.

...ights were fairly easy. I queued outside a ...avel agent on Cathcart Road in Glasgow ...n a drizzly Monday morning before work ...ong with a dozen or so other hyper hoopites. ...was to end up on a French jumbo more ...sed to taking Serge and Monique long haul ...ps to Tahiti than carting 500+ Celtic fans to ...ndalusia. It's quite a sight to see that many ...eople on a plane wearing the same top. Still, ...on't imagine anyone thought 'damn, I must ...ange'.

...o far so good. I'd resigned myself to simply ...aking a pilgrimage to Seville, ticket or no ...cket. Over the next few weeks at work I tried ...make connections via email to every long ...ot I could think of. Two lines of enquiry ...main with me for different reasons.

...esar is a Basque doctor who lodges with a ...ate of mine in Edinburgh. When I explained ...y dire need he asked his father to suss out

the ticket scene across there. The old boy called his business contacts in Seville only to draw a blank. Even though he looks like an able Bilboa centre back, Cesar's not really a football fan. The fact that he tried to help was much appreciated though.

Maybe I should have known better but keeping tabs on the various CFC messageboards really brought me down. I realise there would be a proportion of wind up merchants and full time touts on the sites but I also caught a whiff of some selfish, profiteering fans. The popular line of argument seemed to be 'what would you do in my place'? That's easy – sell at face value.

The weeks drifted past and all my options dissolved one by one. It would be the big screens for me. In the days leading up to the final, TV reports were coming live from Seville. I was just desperate to get out there. Everyone in the office was talking about it all the time.

I got the impression that fans of all other teams (except the obvious) and none were as excited as us, and that the whole event had become one for Scotland. I think it's worth remembering that we don't, and have never felt the need to sing 'no-one likes us we don't care'. Many do like us and we do care.

Monday the 19th of May 2003 was like any other day at work except I was chain guzzling coffee and pacing the floor like an expectant father. The phone went. Call from a colleague:

Caller - 'What are you doing on Wednesday?' (Yeah, nice one smart arse)

Me – 'Erm, I'm on annual leave'

Caller – 'I'm your fairy godmother' (Whit?)

Me- 'Sorry, in what way?'

THE LONG WAIT IS OVER • BARCABHOY • SOUTHCOASTJHIM • MINX1888

Caller – 'Och, I'm kiddin' you on – just phone Tommy on his mobile'

Tommy's speaking to me from Spain when he answers. After denying all knowledge of me for a minute he casually tells me I've got a ticket - from Jesus.

ALLLLLLLLLLEEEEEEELLLLLLLLLUUIIIAAA, ALLLELLLUUUIII

Now that might sound cornier than a cornfield in Cornwall but it's literally true. Tommy's brother works for a multinational company. He had asked his Spanish colleague Jesus to secure some extra briefs if possible. After copious thanks, I retired to the male lavvie to punch the air in delight many, many times and croak out 'yes, ya beauty' over and over.

So this was it. I was going to be there. After a trip to the Celtic shop to get freshly togged out the next day, it was just a matter of counting down the hours.

Part Three – Eldorado

Yes, I know it was the city of gold but we all hoped Seville was going to be the city of silver for Celtic. I'd ordered a 5 a.m. taxi to Glasgow Airport. Naturally, my cabbie was a kind of tattooed, bluenose caricature who wouldn't talk to me all the way there. I was desperate for some banter. Imagine if I'd puked in the cab with excitement. Tempting.

Soon met up with mates and got the breakfast pints in. Brilliant match atmosphere in the airport. The teeming departure lounge was chaos with ad hoc green hair-dos being administered to half cut punters and fans of all ages chatting nervously and laughing at any patter at all.

I just couldn't get my head around the sheer mass of Celtic fans...

The journey on the plane was just something to get through. I 'm not a great flyer. I do remember using the toilet about 23,000 times and discussing the merits or otherwise of violent horror films with a mates' 11 year old son.

As the aircraft door swung open it felt like standing in front of a hairdryer firing squad set to hot. We were escorted to our buses and conveyed through the scorched outskirts of Seville. The stadium looked small and compact to me as we were dropped off. Little did I know that I would later walk into the coliseum scene from Gladiator, complete with CGI-like animated hordes of Celtic fans.

A group of us walked up to the centre of town through the EXPO site complete with Arianne rocket. For some reason the whole area seemed like a ridiculous theme park from an episode of the Simpson's. What do I know? – it's better than the shows across from the Victoria Infirmary in Glasgow.

I took my first picture on the bridge over the river. We'd heard that a Porto fan had died after falling from this bridge. It's too easy to dismiss these things in among mass human

traffic but I remember feeling (not for the first time) how profoundly sad it would be to leave home for a football match and never come back.

We found a neighbourhood bar and settled down for a while. I still had to meet the bhoys with my ticket, so made a series of shouty mobile calls as the reception was so poor. The plan was set. Cathedral at three. After a couple more cervezas we began to wind our way through the narrow streets. I was lagging behind the others and I took my favourite picture of the trip. It shows many of my friends filling a sunny street lined by distressed orange trees. Everyone is walking tall in the hoops. All my people right here right now. D'ye know what I mean?

The night before I'd made myself a t-shirt tribute to my Grandfather. He died in 1990 but I wanted him with me today. Younger fans feed off stories from the past and I love that he lost his false teeth in 1957 and had to be brought home pallbearer style by three or four neighbours. I also remember when he was older and much frailer after a couple of strokes that the old fire was still there as Charlie scored his second penalty at Ibrox in that 4-2 game from the early eighties.

In any case, as we moved through the town and the crowds got bigger, I felt great in my home-made t-shirt with hoops tied round my waist.

I met Tommy and the bhoys who had just hoovered up armloads of left wing freebies at the local offices of the Spanish Socialist Party. After being offered a fraternal fan to cool myself down, I received my ticket in the entrance of a pub that Billy Connelly had apparently cleared for a private party. The owner shooed us out of the place but I didn't care, I was Charlie Bucket with a golden ticket. The other day, someone gave me a framed photo of a celebratory me after being passed the brief. The face is in its thirties but the body language is in its early teens.

After more beer in a bustling wee bar, we began the walk back to the stadium. The nerves started then. I hadn't thought about the football much all day. Now the cold fingers of fear and doubt gripped my guts.

L Monagha

CELTIC QUICK NEWS ROLL OF HONOUR 2013-14

had a great seat between the main stand and the Celtic end. Next to me were three empty seats that stayed that way all night. Unbelievable. The hour before kick off went past like a three minute pop song. I just couldn't get my head around the sheer mass of Celtic fans. This was where it was at in world sport that night.

We all know what happened on the field.

At both goals I was showered by crash test dummy Celts firing all over the seats as if out of cannons. If I'm being honest, once Bobo went, I was just waiting for them to score. We came close but I think we just came up short on the night. That allied to a weak referee meant we didn't win the UEFA cup. The cup though is all we never won. We gained new respect for our team, club and ourselves. We proved we are big time. On the way out I was sad but proud. A teenager walked past me crying and unconsciously I clapped the back of his head and said 'never mind son – we done well'. I never told him to toughen up and stop greetin'.

With wet eyes, I would have had no credibility.

L Monaghan

The jokes were getting less frequent and the smiles nearer grimaces. Some of our party were suffering from kilt rash and walking decidedly bow legged. I spotted Jim McInally and his kids all decked out in the hoops as we neared the stadium.

With time on our hands we stopped by a fence and quaffed a few beers bought from a vendor with a bin full of bottles. The crowds were massive by this time. We had to move on. I remember thinking the security seemed fairly lax until I realised that the bar code on the ticket really did have a use.

Then I was in.

L Monaghan

KEVTIC • FALKIRKBHOY • CALTONTONGUES • SPARKX • DRAMBOWIECELT

THE SEV TIC

Where to begin? I always said I'd keep this story to the select few who knew the details, however with the passing of ten years (so hard to believe), I guess I can finally put the facts as I remember them down on paper (virtual, that is).

Following our magnificent win over Liverpool, three of us ardent supporters were of the unshakable belief that we were going all the way this time. So confident, in fact, that we booked a week's package holiday on the Portuguese Algarve to coincide with the Uefa Final in Seville. We figured, sure if the worst comes to the worst, at least we'll have a "lads" holiday in the sun. So, after the plan was hatched and a gallon of porter drank, we informed our respective wives/partners of our plan. Glad to say that the news was favourably received, although a large amount of Brownie points were used up. Consequently, we watched the first leg of the Semi-Final in complete confidence, in the certain knowledge that Celtic would be once again in a European final.

Sadly, in between the games our greatest supporter, Charlie Murray, passed away. Only those who knew Charlie, a beautiful wee Belfast man, can understand the grief this caused. He was the originator of the idea of a Celtic Supporters Club in the Irish Mid-West. His club, The Charlie Tully CSC drew members from Clare, Limerick, North Tipp and North Kerry. These eventually formed their own clubs, but back then, Charlie was the heart and soul of Celtic. I am delighted to report there is now a CSC named after this humble man. After his funeral we watched the second leg against Boavista, but I have to say, we barely registered the result. Within a few days, however, we were back on track; we now owed it to Charlie to represent him at the game.

3-14

MAGIC ILLE KETS

...or how Celtic fans are all equal in times of need.

SWINDONBHOY · EDWARDBURNS5 · BIG MIKE · GRETNABHOY

It was then the hunt began. We knew that every Celtic fan and their cousins would be scouring the world for the precious tickets. Out own supporters club had 16 season tickets and could therefore hope to get a small amount from Celtic FC, these would have to be raffled amongst the season ticket holders, of which I was one. Our band of three decided to write, phone, email everybody that had the remotest of chances getting tickets. I unashamedly used my father's connections to the GAA to obtain a promise of All Ireland hurling or football tickets for whoever came through for us. I got in touch with several well-known international politicians whom I persuaded owed me big time. The word was out.

I had a friend who was fairly well got in the Vatican and so I had him contact all the bishops and priests he could, both in Rome and on the missions (he was really well got). In fairness and despite him knowing my religious beliefs had long gone from the Catholic faith, he did what he could. In the meantime, May was drawing ever closer. My comrades were having no luck either and it seemed like the club draw would be our only chance. It was then I had divine inspiration!

I had heard that our largest shareholder, at a personal level, was a sound guy, not remotely like the media image that had been built around him. But how to approach him? Well, first I obtained his home address

through a very old story in a national newspaper. That done I now had to compose the correct type of letter. Begging? No way, demeaning to both him and I. Boisterous? nah, to crass. Humble? Mightn't get the correct result. I know, sez I, humour mixed with business. And so it was that I composed the following .

A Chara,

As a fellow Shareholder and indeed, supporter, I wish to address you with regards to our upcoming Uefa cup final. I could write for hours on how much Celtic means to me and tell you hair raising stories of our numerous trips to Glasgow over the years but that would only be taking up your valuable time, so I will cut to the chase. Having

booked a package holiday on the strength of our win over Liverpool, myself and my friend find ourselves in Praia da Rocha, with a night booked in the San Pablo hotel, but with no feckin match ticket. I have called in favours from mates going back over the years, but all to no avail and since it appears that selling ones wife and children into slavery is now illegal, we are up the Swanee. After some soul searching and meditation I decided on offering you a deal. Having read various articles about you over the years (although I take newspapers with a large dollop of salt) I came to the conclusion that offering money would not get me the two desired tickets. So here is the deal. I have two possessions that may be of interest to you. I must admit I do not know the monetary value

Sadly, in between the games our greatest supporter, Charlie Murray, passed away. Only those who knew Charlie, a beautiful wee Belfast man, can understand the grief this caused.

of either, but I do know the value to myself and my friend of attending this upcoming magnificent occasion in Seville. The first item is a pristine condition programme from the Ireland v England rugby international in Lansdowne road in Feb 8th 1947. The second item is of huge sentimental value to me and indeed should show just how important this occasion means to fans like me. It is a postcard sized photograph of the Celtic team that won the double in 1954. What makes this photo invaluable is the fact that all the players autographed the back of it! Including Bobby Evans, Sean Fallon and Charlie Tully. It breaks my heart to offer this photo, but to see Celtic run out on the pitch in a European cup final would be amazing. If you are interested perhaps you could contact me at the above address or even phone or Email me. If not, so be it. I genuinely hope you have as much craic in Seville as we intend having, win, lose or draw. Hail Hail.

Well, letter sent, calls made to the Vatican and GAA carrot dangling, there was nothing else to do but wait. Two days before our flight, my boss tells me there was a guy looking for me on the phone during my lunch break. Fifteen minutes later they called back.

"Is this Blaise Phelan." Says this strong voice, (indistinguishable accent).

"Tis" said I. "Who am I talking to "

"This Dermot Desmond, I received a letter from you a couple of weeks ago. Sorry about the delay in getting back to you."

"Tom, is that you. This isn't f*e'king funny, I have work to do".

Laughter. "No it's Dermot Desmond,

honestly".

"Billy, you bo**%x, don't joke about this".

More laughter. "Seriously, it's Dermot Desmond".

The penny began to drop, jayzus, this might be genuine! And so it was. I sat at my desk and had a conversation about team tactics, Martin O'Neil and Celtics future with my new friend, Dermot Desmond. After a bit,

ROBERT TRESSELL · MAESTRO · GLENDALYSTONSILS · ROY CROPPIE

he excused himself, he had a meeting to go to and then informed me that indeed he did have two tickets for myself and my buddy, Tom. I asked to what address would I send my offerings, but was told that this was not necessary, the tickets were a gift. He offered to have them mailed that day, but with two days to the flight, I told him I would be in Dublin before close of business. And so it was that Tom and I drove the straight to Dublin, hitting the road in the odd spot, we arrived in time to receive our precious tickets in the plushest office of the Irish Financial Centre.

Ironically, I won a ticket in the Club draw, but was able to have it re-raffled so another member could benefit. There is more to the story, about the offers I received for the ticket, offers I had from two Scottish newspapers for the story with a copy of the letter. Then there were the adventures in Seville and the Algarve, but they are for another time. On a

L Monaghan

very sad note my great comrade, Tom, passed away last year leaving a void that has yet to be filled. But I do have the great memories of him. The one thing I'll say is that on entering the stadium, I took out a photo of the late Charlie Murray and let him look around at the awe inspiring green and white, knowing that his spirit was somewhere with us.

A strange thing happened to the 1954 photograph. I donated it the original Kano fund, to be raffled. However, it never reached the organizers. On contacting the Post Office I discovered there was an industrial action taking place and mail could be delayed up to several months. There has been no word since.

There are various views on Dermot Desmond's stewardship of our club. I for one am extremely happy that he didn't allow us to take the route of others and leave our club in dire financial straits. On a personal note, I

have always thought that his gesture, not so much giving me the tickets, but to take time out and phone for a chat, shows him to be a man of character and decency. The kind of person I would wish to be in charge of our beloved Celtic.

Written by Blaise Plelan.

OUR CELTIC TEAM OF THE '70S

Setting Free the Bears selects
his Celtic team of the 1970's
for CQN Magazine...

One careless evening on C2N and the challenge was laid down...

Name your Celtic team for the decades!: a team for the 60s, the 70s and the 80s. I don't know if the 90s was thought to be too recent or too traumatic to be a subject for nostalgia, but recollections were not sought! As I identified myself as a child of the 70s, even though I first remember seeing Celtic as a 7 year old in 1963 and fully enjoyed our success in that decade, my teenage years were in the 70s and I turned 21 there, so that is where the Celtic shackles and chains have fixed my memories. Being a thrawn individual, I did not want to pick the routine Legends list, though there are some who cannot be left out if you do not want your judgements to receive instant condemnation. Anyways, I give this selection about 5 seconds before the brickbats come flying.

Oh! One last caveat, I have omitted some Celtic Legends who played in the 70s but their best was behind them or they left too early in the decade. But like all rules, they can be broken by or for exceptional men.

Goalie: Ally Hunter

No Ronnie Simpson, who left in 1970. No John Fallon, a more athletic keeper who left in 71. No Peter Latchford, who played 187 games for us, or the revered Packie Bonner who appeared near the end of the decade. No my choice was Ally Hunter, who played between 73 and 76. He had already been capped by Scotland as a Killie player and, early in his Celtic career, he seemed to promise a reliability and consistency which had been absent in many previous keepers. His presence saw Evan Williams, one of our few successes in our Feyenoord final defeat in Milan, depart for Clyde.

Hunter competed with Dennis Connaghan and seemed to have the upper hand but Big Jock was already detecting a psychological weakness in the keeper's constant worrying over lost goals and, though his error in Scotland's successful World Cup qualifier with the Czechs in 74 was supposed to signal the downturn in his performance, he was still a regular pick until 1975 when, like many

a Celtic goalie before or since, a nightmare performance at Ibrox signalled the end.

Ally had 31 shut outs in 61 appearances for a winning Celtic team. He gav us a brief glimpse of a standard of keeping that we were not to see surpassed until the days of Boruc and Forster.

RB: Danny McGrain

Not much room for argument here. Danny was recognised as a World class full back for Celtic and Scotland. Along with Kenny Dalglish, he carried the team during a period where we were struggling to replace the Lions. I have vivid memories of the two of them inter-passing from our box to the opponents goalmouth with no opposition player getting near to a dispossession and few of their team mates trusted to become involved (Ronnie Glavin occasionally got one touch). He recovered from a fractured jaw in 72, a diabetes diagnosis in 74 and a 16 month absence in 77/78 for injury. He stayed with us till 1987 and would be in our team of the 80s too. 441 league appearances, 62 caps and umpteen medals. Nobody leaves Danny McGrain out.

CB: Pat McCluskey

Affectionately known as "Fat Pat" because he possessed what CQN's The Token Tim, reckons is the prerequisite for defending the ball, an ample bahooky. Pat was a converted midfielder and, for me, he managed the transition far more effectively than Roy Aitken did, and I would cite in evidence the stats of penalties conceded by both players which I feel would favour Pat. He played from 71 to 77. He could take penalties and contributed goals. He was a formidable figure in many ways. He was one of the Copenhagen 5 who went out on the lash and were caught. To the SFA's credit, his ban was lifted and he did get one more cap afterwards. It was a different era in many ways.

CB: Pat Stanton

We were used to seeing Pat as a cultured Hibbee trying desperately to stem a rampant Celtic side that always seemed to beat his team. We did not know if he would manage the transition to our version of the big time at the age of 32, which was old for a player arriving at Celtic then. He was bought to help settle some youthful defenders in 76 and only played for little over a year before a long term injury ended his playing days. In that short period as a Sweeper for Celtic, he showed an intelligence and game-reading ability which was a bit of a novelty for us. Only 37 appearances for Celtic and yet he makes my team. We really did not emphasise defence enough in those days. If Pat was an Italian, he would have been more appreciated.

LB : Davie Hay

Davie was my favourite player then and now. Of course I knew that Kenny was more of a genius but Davie was a bridge for me between the toughness of the players of the 50s and 60s and the athleticism which became dominant in the late 70s and 80s leaving Scottish football a bit behind the times. Davie made no fuss about sorting out opponents who were harming our flair players.

He did not indulge in posturing and squaring up to people to intimidate. He just sorted them. Then he went back to playing a marauding ball carrying style of football. Davie was a class act but, there is no way I am going to repeat the Scotland Boss error and move Danny to left back to accommodate a lesser talent, so Davie has to play left back.

RM: Jimmy Johnstone

The greatest ever Celt. There are no words of mine that can do this talent justice. Just watch the videos. He left Celtic in 1975 and, yes, he was a reduced shadow of the player he had been. His shadow could still outplay all who came before and have been here since.

CM: Bobby Murdoch

Along with Jinky, Buzzbomb, and Tam Gemmell (who left Celtic in 71), we had 4 world class players in the Lions alongside several very good craftsmen and a few forces of nature. Bobby obviously makes the team of the 60s but, despite playing only 3 years into the decade before leaving for Middlesboro, he still makes my team of the 70s because nobody else could touch that level of ability. Boro fans of that era will let you know that we were mad to let him go.

CM: George Connelly

The enigma. The Scottish Beckenbauer- yes, he WAS that good. He arrived in the team at the end of the 60s and developed to be Player of the Year in Scotland in 1973 and, yet, a year later playing football was all too much for him and, in 1975, he walked out, for the second time, having lost his love for football. He was as good a long passer as Bobby Murdoch but lacked his dig and scoring drive. For a big man, with a fair heft about him, he moved as if he was gliding and the word "graceful" was appropriate for his football demeanour.

Rather than focus on his tragedy of promise not sustained, I will remember George as a star who burned short and bright. Short as it was, he played 136 times for Celtic. I do not recall a bad performance on the field of play.

LM: Steve Murray

Not his natural position but Stevie was, to my young mind, adaptable wherever he found himself on a pitch. He was one of those players who rarely seemed troubled in possession and knew when to pass and when to retain. Though he was never guaranteed a starting spot, he seemed to excel in Europe and scored an extra time winner in a European Cup quarter final in 74 to earn us that infamous tie with Atletico Madrid. He played between 73 and 76, managing a round 100 appearances for the Celts. Did I tell you he knew about timing?

FW: Kenny Dalglish

Like Henrik, Kenny did not fulfill his ambitions with us but he still fulfilled them. A young man with no great pace, it is hard to discern why Kenny was so good, except he could pass, shoot, retain possession, and tackle. He scored goals of elegance rather than power but he managed this feat regularly. Anyone watching the grumpy, acerbic Kenny, of his managerial days, would find it hard to picture what joy he showed on a football field. Rod Stewart fell in love with Celtic because of Big Jock and Kenny. I wish we had a team worthy of him in the mid 70s but we did not and he moved on.

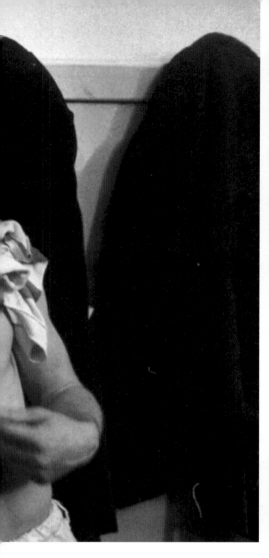

FW : Bobby Lennox

Standard Psychological Personality Tests include items for the purposes of detecting liars and delusionals. An item such as "I never tell lies" or "I always give of my best" should not be ticked as only the amnesiac or sociopaths believe they are that good (deities excepted). Excluding Buzzbomb Lennox from your Celtic team of the 60s and 70s would lead to equal derision. 335 appearances, 167 goals and 25 winners medals in two separate periods with our team are impressive stats. At least with Bobby, we realized we let him go too soon and rectified our mistake. As good a judge of footballers as Bobby Charlton rated Bobby as a team mate. He is undroppable.

Well that's my final pick. I give brief honourable mentions to Shuggie Edvaldsson, Dixie Deans, Andy Lynch and the young Brian McLaughlin. On another day, George Connely would drop into defence to replace Fat Pat and one of the above would get the chance to play in this team. What a great privilege it has been to have seen them all."

GREENYINFURRAFENIAN · TRUTH BEAUTY AND FREEDOM

CHAMPIONS 2012 ~ 2013

CELTIC QUICK NEWS ROLL OF HONOUR 2013-14

HOW WE WON THE LEAGUE

Patrick Devlin charts how Celtic retained the SPL Championship...

FREDDIEBHOY • ACGR • RWE • MIHAL • MNCELT • GG • MICHAEL

August

Celtic started season 2012/13 as Champions of Scotland with a home tie versus Aberdeen, where the league flag was unfurled by the late Sean Fallon. A 1-0 win ensured the domestic season started positively, as the Hoops looked to make it 2-in-a-row. With vitally important Champions League qualifiers at the forefront of Neil Lennon's mind, slightly weakened Celtic teams made two successive trips to the Highlands, where Celtic drew 1-1 with new boys Ross County and thrashed Inverness CT 4-2, youngster Tony Watt bagging a fine double in the latter. By the end of August, Celtic had a place in the Champions League group stages for the first time in four years, and had started the league campaign brightly.

September

Celtic opened the month with a home fixture against Hibernian, with an entertaining match finishing 2-2, the start of a good run for Hibs that would see them in the top three for most of the first half of the season. Unfortunately, defeat was tasted in only the fifth game of the SPL away to St. Johnstone, the Perth side claiming all three points despite Kris Commons opening the scoring after only three minutes. Celtic bounced back and comfortably beat Dundee (Club 12) 2-0 at Paradise. Celtic won 2-0 again in their next league match, away to Motherwell in a very impressive display. Outside league duty, Celtic claimed a crucial Champions League point against Benfica, and progressed in the league cup with victory over Raith Rovers.

October

Only three league games were played in October as Celtic tried to balance domestic issues and performing on the big European stage. After their first away win the Champions League group stages in Russia only days earlier, the Celtic supports joyous mood continued as we beat Hearts 1-0 at Celtic Park. The Bhoys made it four consecutive league wins as they thrashed St. Mirren 5-0 in Paisley, a game that will always be remembered for Efe Ambrose's acrobatic celebration after scoring his first ever Celtic goal. However, Celtic were suffering from European hangover when Kilmarnock visited Glasgow, as they lost 2-0 to the Rugby Park outfit, though it was understandable after the Hoops suffered a devastating last minute defeat to Barcelona in the Camp Nou only days earlier.

November

November proved to be a memorable and historic month for Celtic, as they celebrated 125 years of tradition, success and charity since their formation in 1887. Despite this, it started with disappointment in Dundee as Celtic threw away two points by losing a two goal lead at Tannadice, drawing 2-2 to United when they were two goals to the good with, funnily enough, two minutes to go. This mattered little though as three days later Celtic beat Catalan giants Barca 2-1 at Paradise in the Champions League in one of the greatest recent European nights. Naturally, no game could match the atmosphere of that night, so a subdued Parkhead witnessed a tired Hoops team draw 1-1 with St. Johnstone. A tough visit to Pittodre followed but Celtic performed professionally to beat Aberdeen 2-0, but dropped more SPL points as Inverness CT stunned the Champions, winning 1-0 in Glasgow. Again, this defeat came after a trip to Lisbon where Celtic fell to a decent Benfica side. Thankfully, all was made up as Celtic ended November by hammering Hearts 4-0 in Edinburgh, always a nice result for Celtic fans.

December

The festive period proved to be as hectic as always as Celtic continued to balance three competitions, with the Scottish Cup coming into play. Eight days of December passed by the time Celtic played their first league game, by which time they

were miraculously through to the last 16 of the UEFA Champions League after a second victory in the season against Aiden McGeady's Spartak Moscow. The Bhoys avenged their earlier defeat by Kilmarnock to sweep them aside 3-1 at Rugby Park, before two comfortable home wins were recorded when St. Mirren and Ross County visited Paradise. A Boxing Day visit to Dens Park was next on the agenda, and another 2-0 win followed, with spectacular goals coming from Georgios Samaras and Gary Hooper. There was slight disappointment as the last SPL game of 2012 finished in defeat for Celtic away to Hibernian, but on the whole 2012 was a fantastic year for everyone involved with Celtic.

January

For the New Year, the SPL brought back the winter break, but before this two week break kicked in, Celtic faced Motherwell at Parkhead, where Fraser Forster saved a penalty and Gary Hooper scored to win the game 1-0. After the break, Hearts were the visitors to Glasgow but left empty handed as Celtic turned on the style to win 4-1, and the Celts scored 4 again three days later when hosting Dundee United, this time with no goals conceded. These fine performances should have set Celtic up nicely for the League Cup Semi Final against St. Mirren, but the Hoops continued their so called Hampden Hoodoo to be defeated 3-2 by the Paisley outfit. As ever, Celtic bounced back and thrashed Kilmarnock 4-1 at Paradise, with Welsh dragons Joe Ledley and Adam Matthews shining.

February

The month of February saw European football return again in the shape of a Last 16 Champions League tie with Italian giants Juventus, as well as the next round of the Scottish Cup, where Celtic eased past Raith Rovers. With the big game on the forefront of Neil Lennon's mind, a weakened side made the trip to Inverness, but still beat Caley Thistle comfortably 3-1, who were second in the SPL at the time. Disappointment in Europe followed as Juve won 3-0 in Glasgow despite an excellent performance from the Bhoys, who were unlucky to lose at all. Celtic responded well and hammered Dundee

MEA CULPA • JUNGLE JIM • PARKHEADCUMSALFORD • FOURGREENFIELDS

3-14

United 6-2 at Celtic Park, in the rearranged game from August before drawing away in Perth to St. Johnstone, meaning the Saints remained unbeaten against the Champions in the season. Bottom club Dundee travelled to Glasgow but left with nothing after getting smashed 5-0 as Celtic's title march stormed on, but this was momentarily halted when Motherwell claimed all three points in a 2-1 win at Fir Park to finish the month.

March

Celtic avenged their League Cup loss by knocking St. Mirren out of the Scottish Cup in the first game of March, and then travelled to Turin for the second leg of the Champions League Last 16 Round, where Juventus saw off a spirited Celtic display to win 2-0 and 5-0 on aggregate. The Bhoys returned to league duty and looked to have claimed all three points in the early stages of the game in Dingwall versus Ross County, but last year's Division One winners fought back from two goals down and stunningly won the game 3-2. But Celtic made a comeback of their own in the next game at home to Aberdeen, who were 3-1 up with half an hour to go but lost out 4-3 after a magnificent fight back, finishing with Georgios Samaras scoring an overhead kick in the dying seconds. A now tiring Celtic team went to Paisley and drew 1-1 with St. Mirren in a controversial game remembered for the shocking performance of referee Bobby Madden rather than any football played.

April

The point at Paisley meant only four points stood in the way of Celtic and title number 44 with six fixtures remaining. The first of these came at home to Hibs, where Kris Commons inspired Celtic to a 3-0 win. The league then split, with Inverness CT the team to face Celtic in the first game where the Hoops could win the league. Before this, Celtic saw off a brilliant Dundee United performance at Hampden to win 4-3 AET and progress to the Scottish Cup Final. After a subdued first period in the ICT game, the party started when Gary Hooper fired Celtic in front, moments before Joe Ledley poked home another. Hooper was at it again with a cheeky flick to make it 3-0, and Georgios Samaras finished off proceedings with a scintillating strike to seal the three points, and the championship. Caley Thistle pulled one back but it mattered little as Paradise entered party mood, knowing it was mission successful once more for the Bhoys in green and white.

FROM THE GOLD COAST TO GLASGOW – TO PLAY FOR CELT

CELTIC QUICK NEWS ROLL OF HONOUR 2013-14

On his last day in Scotland before heading back to Australia, Willie Wallace stood up Brogan Rogan Trevino and Hogan and Winning Captains. The three were supposed to be having lunch but Willie forgot and instead was out at Lennowtown with Bertie Auld and John Clark. Willie was organising a trial at Celtic for a young Australian player called Nik Mirkovic and at the end of June he duly arrived in Glasgow to have a trial with Celtic. Here is his account of what happened, in his own words...

ROW Z – LET CELTIC FLOURISH BY THE CLEANSING OF THE 'DEN!

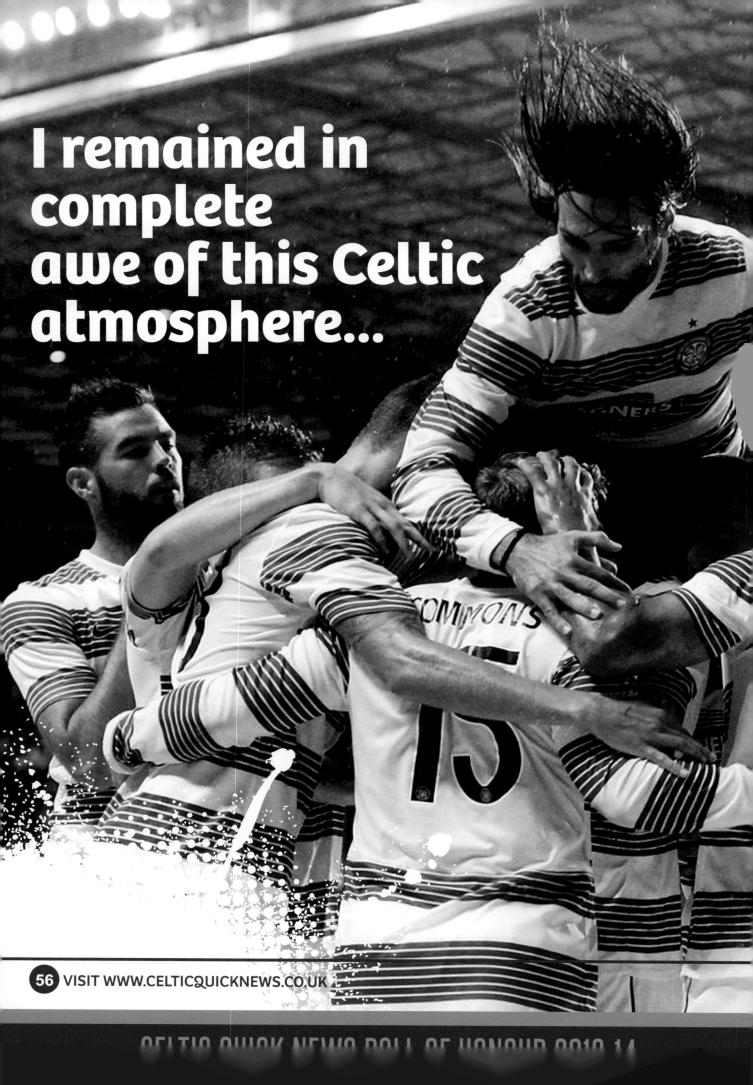

I remained in complete awe of this Celtic atmosphere...

CELTIC QUICK NEWS ROLL OF HONOUR 2013-14

I arrived in Glasgow around midday on Thursday 27th of June. The purpose of my trip was to try and get a contract in Celtic's renowned youth set up. I was recommended to Celtic by club legend Willie Wallace. Willie was my coach on the Gold Coast three years ago when I was 15 and we have kept in touch ever since. Being 18 and having finished school, we both felt that it was the right time for me to try my luck in Europe and Willie said to me that there is no better club than Celtic. He had arranged for me to stay with Winning Captains and he was waiting for me as I arrived in Glasgow where I would discover if I had what it takes to become a professional football player.

As an Australian our main exposure to the game in Britain is via the EPL. Straight away I struggled to comprehend the size and magnitude of the Celtic, from the impressive shop in the airport to the supporters wearing those famous green and white hoops- Celtic looked massive! Winning Captains had bought me a ticket to watch the game against Elfsborg in the Champions League Qualification round and It was not until I entered Celtic Park itself did I truly understood Bill Shankly's famous words- "football isn't a matter of life and death, it's much more important than that." For the entire 90 minutes Celtic Park transformed into a cauldron, making it nearly impossible for the other team to get going. The goosebumps and chants will always remain a great memory for me whenever I hear anyone mention the famous name - CELTIC. Yet Winning Captains told me that this was a quiet night at Paradise and there would be bigger games ahead!

However I remained In complete awe of this Celtic atmosphere so I decided to watch as many games as I could find on You Tube etc. The next day Winning Captains gave me a DVD to watch. I sat down and watched in absolute awe the famous game in 1967, where the Lisbon Lions were formed. This is a day that will forever be remembered by all Celtic fans, lifting the famous European Cup. It was strange watching a young Willie Wallace take to the field on the biggest stage of all. The game was fantastic, to see a club like Celtic destroy a legendary Inter Milan team. This match only made me an even bigger Celtic fan and showed me the roots behind the success of the famous green and white.

During the month of August I was at Celtic FC for a trial. On the first day I was immediately impressed by the world class facilities. From the training facilities to the staff, the entire youth set up was outstanding. I was somewhat in awe at the professionalism of the youth game in Scotland. I feel this is one thing that most of the boys from Celtic take for

granted. I doubt they realise how lucky they are to be involved with such a professional club. Everyone made me feel welcome and for the three weeks that I was there I felt at home and part of the squad.

As you will all know, Celtic have two training facilities which they use to develop both youth and first team players. Lennoxtown is the modern state of the art training facility, which is mainly used by the first team and some youth teams. The other training ground is Barrowfield, situated down the road from the famous Celtic Park. For the majority of my time I was at Barrowfield, which like Lennoxtown, has high quality pitches that are looked after on a daily basis leaving the playing surface like a carpet to pass the ball on. Coming from Australia, I was surprised at the pristine quality of the pitch. Back home the fields at majority of football clubs are not maintained well, which results in an uneven playing surface.

The training sessions were intense and the standard was always high. One thing that I noticed was that all of the drills would revolve around the emphasis of high pressing when you don't have the ball and being efficient with the ball when you attack. The overall standard of players was good, however, like in any team, there are a few that, in my own opinion, are lucky to be there.

Another surprise was the amount of preparation that goes into the youth game. From the amount of coaches to the type of food that has to be consumed; the only thing that the players have to do is play football. After every session we were driven by bus to Celtic Park to have lunch. The meals would change every day, the only thing that remained the same was the nutritious value of each meal. Everything had to be prepared well and it all had to contain the correct amount of protein, carbohydrates and fats to best benefit a growing sportsman.

The professionalism and entire set-up was what I will remember, as the teams in Australia do not have this sort of focus on any team, other than the first team. The way in which Celtic develop and nurture their young players is a credit to them, and is evident in their success and longevity.

The highlight of my time with Celtic was having the opportunity to play against some quality teams such as Manchester City and the Republic of Ireland. These experiences are ones that will be etched in my memory for a lifetime.

Although I was not fortunate enough to secure a place in the squad on this occasion, the overall experience was priceless, and

I will take all that I have learnt back to Australia, and continue to pursue my goals of improving as a player and becoming a professional footballer.

Following on from the disappointing news from Celtic, I was fortunate that Willie then organised for me to have a training session at Clyde. Former Scottish Premier League players, Jim Duffy and Chic Charnley worked together in training and managing Clyde. It was at Clyde where I experienced a real culture shock; the rain, midgies and astro turf surface made for a rather unpleasant experience. The pace of the play was incredibly fast and everyone was like a bull at a gate. Being the first time on an all-weather pitch, I struggled to play and did not enjoy it at all. I was glad to meet both Jim and Chic, and I will take back the positives from that experience.

Prior to leaving Glasgow, I went to the Shakhter Karagandy game. After already witnessing a spectacle at the Elfsborg game, I knew from Winning Captains that I should expect an even better experience and he was 100% confident that Celtic – who had been really poor in the away leg – would overcome this team and qualify. I admired his confidence but thought it would be difficult for Celtic to get through but if they did then it would be something special. Celtic, having to overturn a two goal deficit, would need the crowd to be the 12th man. The entire 90 minutes was unbelievable and kept me on the edge of my seat. When the shot from James Forrest in the 91st minute hit the back of the net, the stadium erupted. I felt as though I was a life long Celtic supporter, the happiness and joy that ran through my veins was electrifying. This was an experience that I had never enjoyed before in football. It was an amazing night in Paradise!

I came to Glasgow only knowing Celtic as the team who wore green and white hoops, and left as a life long follower of the club. The Shakther game has inspired me to follow the progress of Celtic FC right through the Champions League in not only this season but many more to come.

This whole experience would not have been possible without the assistance of Celtic legend Willie Wallace. It is with thanks to Willie that I have had the chance to be around a professional football club. I would also like to take this opportunity to thank Winning Captains and his family. They were amazing. They made me feel completely

welcome and part of their Celtic family.

This journey was not only a life changing experience, but it also gave me a taste of what professional football has to offer. It has equipped me with more drive and hunger to train harder and make it to the top of this great game - Football!

I have decided to come back to Australia to continue to work hard, hone my skills and chase my dream in becoming a professional football player. Due to the gradual rise in football here in Australia my ambition is to secure a contract in the next 2 years with one of the A league sides. Another one of my goals in life has always been to start up and run my own business. Being home in Australia makes it easier for me to reach both of my aspirations in life, with support of my family and friends.

Thank you to all at Celtic for a once in a lifetime opportunity. The football experience and the friendships made, will be treasured for ever.

I hope to return one day, in the not too distant future, an improved, wiser player, and secure a spot in the Celtic squad! Like Celtic I will never say never!

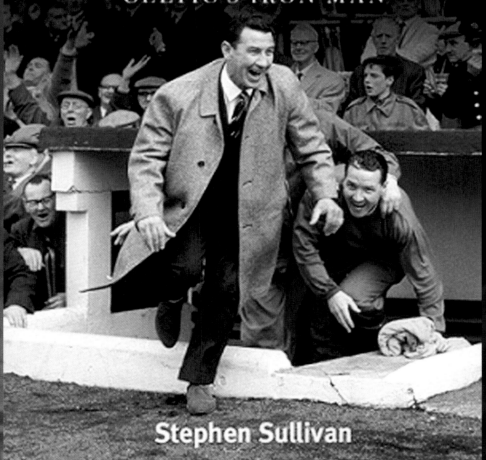

THE AUTHORISED BIOGRAPHY

SEAN FALLON

CELTIC'S IRON MAN

Stephen Sullivan

AVAILABLE TO BUY FROM CELTIC QUICK NEWS – SEE THE BLOG FOR DETAILS!

THE T DAYS

With the Festive Season upon us, St Martin's Bhoy reflects on events in November that proved a timely reminder of what Celtic is all about...

CELTIC QUICK NEWS ROLL OF HONOUR 2013-14

WELVE OF CELTIC

The 6th November saw the rain of Newcastle give way to slightly lighter clouds as I drove north past Gretna en route to a very special occasion. It was Celtic's Birthday and I had donned my best suit! I had a ticket to the Celebration and I knew how fortunate I was. As I arrived at Celtic Park in plenty time on that chilly November afternoon my timing, for once, was perfect. First Bertie Auld and then Billy McNeill walked past, so at ease with the awe and respect that is still rightly shown to them after all these years. Then a number of current heroes emerged to board the team bus, Messrs Forster, Hooper and Wilson among them. This was the eve of the Champions League clash with Barcelona. Celtic's Birthday, then Barcelona at Paradise - all my Christmases at once.

People gathered in small groups, huddled against the cold wind that blew, before we made our way round to where it all began, St Mary's in the Calton. As I arrived at the Church I waited outside and a mini-coach pulled up with some of the dignitaries of Barcelona FC on board. Our Catalan cousins had come to remember the humble beginnings of our beloved Celtic. Another coach arrived and off stepped Neil Lennon, resplendent in grey suit, white shirt and Club tie. At the same moment, Dermot Desmond appeared at the side of the coach and greeted Lenny with warmth that was plain for all to see. They made their way into the Church, followed by many more. You could sense just what a special evening it was to be.

For those that weren't there, I shan't spoil it too much as the Birthday Bhoys DVD may well be released as you read this but a packed St Mary's echoed with laughter and memories and Celtic. From my balcony vantage point in that truly beautiful Church I looked down on a host of stars of Celtic. A short film, beautifully put together by Tony Hamilton and the team featuring heroes past and present, on the park and off, was played before our Club Chairman Ian Bankier, Church of Scotland Minister, XXXXX and Historian and raconteur, XXXXX reminded us of Celtic's origins, Celtic's present and assurance on Celtic's future. A short play intertwining our inception and a modern day scene preceded Mass. A simple meal was to follow in the Kerrydale Suite, Tony joked that due to the length of the service it may well be breakfast! Three hours after entering the Church we returned to Celtic Park.

WINNING CAPTAINS · BIG JOE · JOHANN MURDOCH · CHARLIEBHOY

Once there I had the pleasure of spending time in the company of some of the group who would mark Celtic's Birthday by cycling from Andrew Kerins' birthplace of Ballymote in Co. Sligo to his statue on Kerrydale Street. We watched a short film about the marvellous work of Mary's Meals, the beneficiary of the evening's collection and then it was time for the trip back to Newcastle. The night had been inspirational. For much of the journey home I drove in silence and reflected on what our Club had become: a Club that spans the globe despite the somewhat suffocating environs of Scottish Football. A force for good, just as Walfrid had envisaged. I went to bed delighted that I had had the opportunity to be part of such an evening and delighted that in less than 12 hours I'd be making the same journey up the road to see the best Club in the world take on the best team in the world.

You all know what happened on that incredible night so I'll not dwell on it here. Sufficed to say the team were inspired -perhaps by the calibre of the opposition and undoubtedly by the most unrelenting supporting noise I, and they, have ever encountered. However, I like to think the players took inspiration from the knowledge that they were involved, particularly that night, in something that stretched beyond the ninety minutes and the parameters of the hallowed turf. The passion of Walfrid appeared to coarse through the veins of those in Green and White on the pitch and in the stands and it was magical to behold.

The determination and fierce will to succeed displayed 125 years previously by our founding Fathers was replicated and led to a victory that will remain one of our greatest when our Celtic celebrates its 250th year of unbroken history. Those who were present and those who sat in front of TVs in Ballymote and far beyond will never forget it.

Two special days in Celtic history were over but these were not just "Another 48 Hours".

Over a week had elapsed before the next journey to Glasgow. My better half and I watched in a pub as we won at Pittodrie before we got ready for the main reason for our trip and the final part of this Celtic trilogy. It was time for Wee Oscar's Racenight.

You all know about Oscar, you all know of his courage. You all will be aware of the love and strength of his family and you will know that the CQN Community has been keen to help them. A small team from this Parish organised an army of bucketeers earlier in the season as we stood in the Paradise sunshine and the same team worked like Trojans to provide an evening full of entertainment, fun and emotion. That team ought to be incredibly proud of what they have done and continue to do in the name of Oscar and Celtic and are the living embodiment of Walfrid's dream. In the region of 400 people attended and helped raise around £27,000. TeamOscar, it simply wouldn't have happened without you, take a bow.

For much of the journey home I drove in silence and reflected on what our Club had become: a Club that spans the globe despite the somewhat suffocating environs of Scottish Football...

I like to think the players took inspiration from the knowledge that they were involved, particularly that night, in something that stretched beyond the ninety minutes...

The wonderful Lisa Hague spoke warmly of Celtic and the Celtic Family. She said she was proud to be part of it and would continue to be, not only as long as Kris was at Celtic, but beyond. They were words from the heart and words that summed up entirely the feeling of those gathered. It was yet another great occasion.

From the 6th November in St Mary's to the race night on the 17th, these "Twelve Days of Celtic" had been

the modern day reality of Brother Walfrid's vision. The Celtic Family had remembered our history. Our team and management had delivered in unforgettable manner. Our 1254125 cyclists had arrived safely to be warmly received by our Club's custodians and the Faithful gathered in our modern, vibrant home. And then a fortunate 400 had been assembled by the hard work of a few to do what we do – help. The essence of Celtic.

THE LITTLE GENTLEMAN IN THE BLACK VELVET WAISTCOAT · SCOTTISHLEAF

As I sit with those dear to me this Christmas I'll enjoy the festivities. In a quiet moment I'll think of those close to me who have passed and doubtless dab a watery eye. I shall also remember, remember those days in November and what they mean to me. Most of us will give and receive gifts this Christmas. Some will be expensive, others less so. Few will last for 125 years and still have a bright future ahead of them. None will be a vision that has charity as its lifeblood and football as its heartbeat.

Brother Walfrid gave us a wonderful gift, a gift for life. Enjoy it and cherish it.

Happy Christmas!

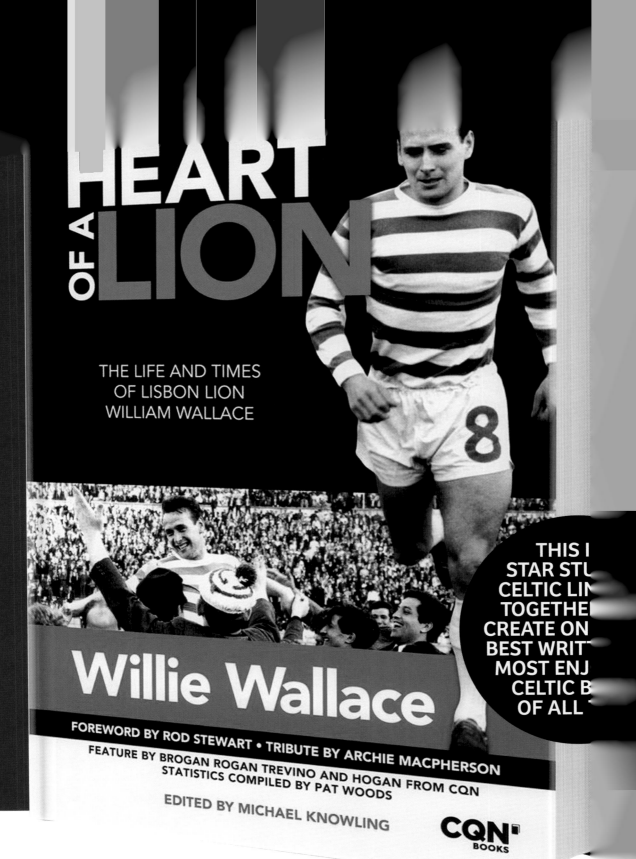

HEART OF A LION

THE LIFE AND TIMES OF LISBON LION WILLIAM WALLACE

Willie Wallace

FOREWORD BY ROD STEWART • TRIBUTE BY ARCHIE MACPHERSON
FEATURE BY BROGAN ROGAN TREVINO AND HOGAN FROM CQN
STATISTICS COMPILED BY PAT WOODS

EDITED BY MICHAEL KNOWLING

CQN BOOKS

THIS I
STAR STU
CELTIC LIN
TOGETHE
CREATE ON
BEST WRIT
MOST ENJ
CELTIC B
OF ALL

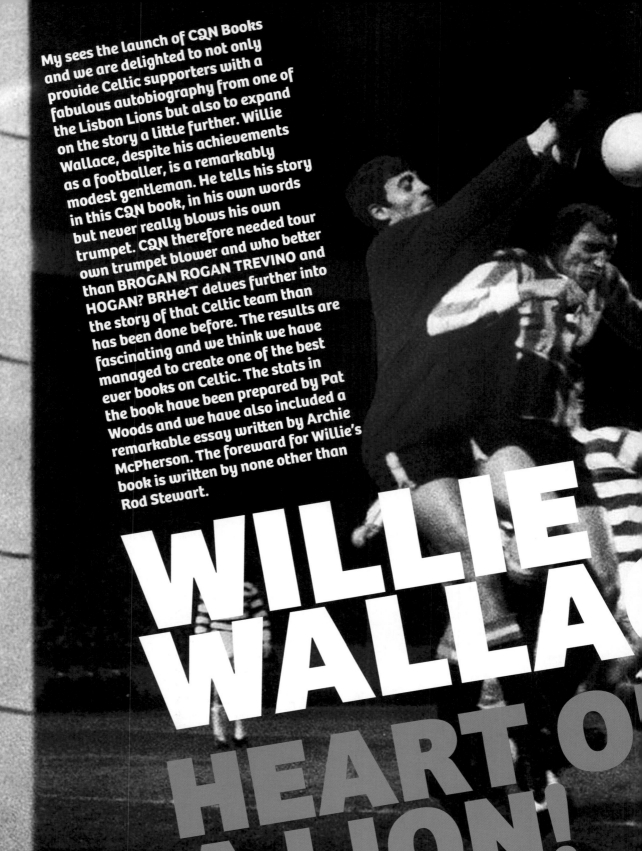

My sees the launch of CQN Books and we are delighted to not only provide Celtic supporters with a fabulous autobiography from one of the Lisbon Lions but also to expand on the story a little further. Willie Wallace, despite his achievements as a footballer, is a remarkably modest gentleman. He tells his story in this CQN book, in his own words but never really blows his own trumpet. CQN therefore needed tour own trumpet blower and who better than BROGAN ROGAN TREVINO and HOGAN? BRH&T delves further into the story of that Celtic team than has been done before. The results are fascinating and we think we have managed to create one of the best ever books on Celtic. The stats in the book have been prepared by Pat Woods and we have also included a remarkable essay written by Archie McPherson. The foreward for Willie's book is written by none other than Rod Stewart.

WILLIE WALLA

HEART O A LION!

Now this has to be an impressive line-up for the first ever CQN Book?

What is remarkable is the way all of these characters – legends in their own way – interacted in the past. A six year old boy, feeling poorly at an airport in Argentina, is comforted by a professional footballer in 1968. The boy – a young Brogan Rogan and the footballer is Willie Wallace, a Lisbon Lion! Here is a little flavour of Willie's book, as BRH&T describes Willie's unconventional role in the European Cup Semi Final return match in 1967...

Willie Wallace, Heart of a Lion is out on 24 May on CQN Books and will be available on CQN and available at the Celtic stores and all good bookstores including Waterstone's. It will also be available on Amazon and there will be a Kindle version.

Wille Wallace is coming over from Australia to help promote the book launch and there will be various book signings – see Paul's posts on CQN for details. Willie is also the guest of honour at the CQN Golf Day at Aberdour in Fife in June.

We hope you will all support CQN Books and are sure you will absolutely love WILLIE WALLACE – Heart of a Lion!

Now over to Brogan Rogan...

I once read that Diego Maradona was in no doubt about the name of the toughest opponent he ever faced on a football field. Without any hesitation he would provide the same answer any time he was asked to name the guy who had given him the most trouble on the park— Lothar Herbert Matthaus.

On two occasions (1981 and 1986) Matthaus would be given the job of sticking to Maradona "like a limpet" with the view to preventing him dictating the game. On the first occasion the German performed such a task, he was no more than 20 years old and received rave reviews for doing such a great job. A great defensive job, despite being an attacking and creative midfielder who would score his fair share of goals.

Almost 15 years earlier, Jock Stein

would turn to another attacker and creator and ask him to do a similar "limpet" job on Josef Masopust in the second leg of a European Cup Semi-final.

Masopust was, as we have heard, nearing the end of his days in top class football, and at the end of season 68/69 he would be allowed to leave his beloved Dukla and play out the last two seasons of his career in Belgium with a degree of success.

However, in April 1967 he was still the central cog in the Dukla Prague wheel and from his position in midfield it was he who made the side tick - and Jock Stein wanted to make sure that he did not tick effectively against Celtic.

Masopust was known for breaking runs forward - described in the press reports of the time as the Masopust slalom - and for his crisp intelligent passing of the ball. It had been one of his runs up the park in the first leg that eventually led to confusion in the Celtic defence allowing Strunc to score in the 44th minute.

Accordingly, Stein decided he had to be man marked and more or less sat on for 90 minutes! Stop Masopust and in many ways you stop Dukla!

In choosing who he wanted to perform this task he opted for Willie Wallace - withdrawing him somewhat from the forward line and putting him in midfield instead to joust with Masopust.

As everyone now knows, the second leg in Prague would not be a footballing spectacle, and at times it would best be described as a gritty, backs to the wall, performance by Celtic whereby they got the job done with none of their, by now, customary flair.

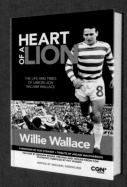

Stein and Celtic also had to keep an eye on the referee Mr Gottfried Dienst from Switzerland. While he was considered to be the best referee in the World at the time, this was the same official who had taken charge of the 1966 World Cup Final at Wembley and had awarded a goal to Geoff Hurst which many thought was not a goal at all.

Dienst had been the man in the middle for the 1961 final that saw Benfica defeat Barcelona to become champions and the 1965 final that saw Inter lift the big cup at the San Siro when they defeated the almost ever present Portuguese. Very few referees have ever taken the final twice - in fact Deinst was one of only 4 officials ever to do this.

He was also only one of two referees who would officiate for both the World Cup final and the European Championship final, and it was those European Championships that would lead to his

greatest controversy.

His officiating in the 1968 European Championship final was marred by real controversy. In that game, a 1–1 draw between Italy and Yugoslavia which was played in Rome, Dienst came to be accused of favouring the home team. The final was replayed later (the Italians winning 2–0) in a game refereed by the Spaniard José Maria Ortiz de Mendibil.

By 1967 Dienst already had a reputation of being a "home" referee.

In deciding to deploy Wallace on Masopust Big Jock will have gone through the options.

Bertie Auld would be an obvious choice to do a job on the Czech midfielder, but if Bertie was over keen or his fiery temper got the better of him, the official

might find an excuse to take Celtic down to ten men, which would undoubtedly spell disaster.

Bertie's partner in the middle, Bobby Murdoch, was most effective playing deeper, and Stein would not want him trailing all over the park after the tricky Masopust and so leave his Celtic team out of shape.

Bobby Lennox and Jimmy Johnstone were extra cover on the wings. If they could get forward - great - but they also had a defensive job to do in front of Jim Craig and Tommy Gemmell.

Accordingly Stein opted for the man who he had described as the equivalent of a whole forward line when he signed him. Remember Bobby Lennox saying that Willie was good enough to drop into midfield and do a top

class job, and both McNeill and Auld pointing out that Wallace could take care of himself physically and was no soft touch?

Well these qualities plus Willie's pace, stamina and ability to follow instruction convinced Stein to play Wallace on the Czech playmaker.

Willie has said that Stein told him to let Masopust know he was there early - to give him a wee dunt to let him know that Willie was there and would be there throughout the game.

There was no way in the world that Josef Masopust had not received such treatment before and in his own book Bertie Auld would stress that his Celtic team-mate played Masopust fairly all day whilst effectively negating his influence on the game.

PETEC · BAWSMAN · GORDON J BACKING NEIL LENNON · RRC:

Accordingly this second performance of Willie's was just as valuable in getting Celtic to the final as his two goals in the first leg.

If ever Jock Stein was to get a great return for his money, then he got it out of Willie Wallace in the two semi-finals with Dukla. It is at least arguable that cometh the hour cometh the man and that Celtic would never have been in Lisbon if it were not for Willie Wallace!

The man himself will, in all likelihood, not thank me for saying that, and will highlight the fact that it was the whole team that took them to Lisbon rather than one performance. Equally, without Gallagher's corner and McNeill's header in the previous round, Willie may not have even got the chance to play in the European Cup of 1967!

However, there is no doubt that the semi-finals of the European Cup belonged to Willie Wallace and no Celtic fan should ever forget that because without him Lisbon was by no means certain.

Before leaving the story of this tie there are two things I have to highlight.

I have never read any account of the second leg in Prague by any of the Lions without them mentioning the disappointment shown by Josef Masopust in not progressing to the final. Everyone to a man has commented on his refusal to shake hands at the final whistle and his attitude towards Willie in particular.

Equally, everyone again acknowledges that this great player put that disappointment

behind him very quickly and made a point of going out of his way to apologise for his surliness and then going on to congratulate Celtic wishing them all the best for the final.

This story has been repeated so regularly by the members of the Celtic team that it is quite clear the incident and the player made a lasting impression on them. It is to the credit of the Celtic team that no one has ever even thought of criticising Masopust for apparent churlishness. On the contrary, the Celtic players who have written and talked about the incident have said that they would not have blamed Masopust for his behaviour and would have thought no less of him had he not taken the decision to apologise very quickly, shake Willie's hand, and wish them all the best for the final.

However, I have to end this section with a Masopust story, which may explain his actions at full time, and which more likely, explains his complete volte face and the decision to apologise immediately and wish his conquerors well.

As we have seen, Josef Masopust was the European Footballer of the year in 1962.

Masopust was the star man of an unfancied Czech team captained by fellow Dukla Player Novak, and his skill was instrumental in dragging his team all the way to the final against Brazil. However progress to that stage was thought most unlikely especially as the Czechs were drawn in the same group as the holders at the start of the tournament along with Spain and Mexico.

Having won their opening match, Czechoslovakia would play the holders Brazil in the knowledge that another surprising victory would put them in a great position to progress from a very difficult group.

It is in this game, that the man from the Eastern Bloc with all the skill would do something that made both footballers on the park and the footballing public in general stare in astonishment.

Before half time, Pele would be badly injured leaving him virtually hobbling on the sidelines as a spectator and of no use to his team at all - he would take no further part in the competition at the final whistle.

However, from time to time the ball would be played out to him out of sheer instinct and he was virtually unable to control the ball and play it back to a team-mate.

In the middle of the Park, Brazil fielded the magnificent Didi and it was Masopust's job to go head to head with him.

The Czech player kept the irresistible Didi quiet as Czechoslovakia held Brazil to a shock 0-0 draw, however it was a match in which his class showed both professionally and personally.

This was the pre substitution era and with Pele severely injured and forced to hobble helplessly around the field there were numerous chances for Josef Masopust to win the ball without fear of challenge. However, when the ball went towards the Brazil No10 the elegant Czech No.6 refused to challenge his opponent at any time despite the importance of the game and the opportunity for a fantastic result.

In a show of true sporting integrity Masopust simply allowed another Brazil player to collect the ball from Pele rather than make a challenge.

"It was a gesture I will never forget," said Pele afterwards.

Pele's team mate, the legendary Djalma Santos who would play in four World Cup finals remarked at the time: "It was moving to see the respect with which Masopust treated the situation. It was not just respect for Pele but for the entire Brazil team and the tournament. He was a great player and, moreover, a gentleman."

Whilst I appreciate that this is a book about Willie Wallace it has to be said that at times sport throws up a true great and Josef Masopust was truly great in every single way.

So that is one of the two things I have to highlight.

The second is that this game was played in the afternoon of 25th April and there was no television coverage and so back home everyone was tuned into the radio commentary provided by a certain Archie McPherson.

When the final whistle went and Archie proclaimed, " That's it! They've done it. Celtic are in the final of the European Cup!"--- Well with my old man in London potentially chasing planes for the final, my Mammy just burst into tears!

WILLIE WALLACE Heart of a Lion launched on 24 May 2013 on CQN Books.

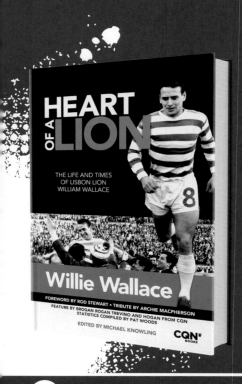

HEART OF A LION

THE LIFE AND TIMES OF LISBON LION WILLIAM WALLACE

Willie Wallace

FOREWORD BY ROD STEWART • TRIBUTE BY ARCHIE MACPHERSON
FEATURE BY BROGAN ROGAN TREVINO AND HOGAN FROM CQN
STATISTICS COMPILED BY PAT WOODS

EDITED BY MICHAEL KNOWLING   CQN BOOKS

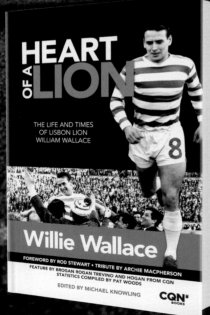

A WEEK WITH WALLAC!

Brogan Rogan Trevino and Hogan on a very special week for CQN shared with Lisbon Lions Willie Wallace and Bertie Auld, as we promoted Willie's new book, A Heart of a Lion...

When I was first asked to write anything at all about Willie Wallace, the last thing that I thought I would ever write is that Willie Wallace is a funny wee bowlie legged man!

However, the fact of the matter is that--- Willie Wallace is a funny wee bowlie legged man!!

Yes he is a former Celtic player, a Lisbon Lion, a former Scottish Internationalist and a member of that select group of people who have scored over 100 goals for Celtic—but he is far far more than that—and first and foremost he is chatty and very funny with a great sense of humour.

I have just spent the better part of a week touring about with 72 year old Willie and have seen him hold court in book shops, in BBC studios, with Journalists with the public at large and in private.

His persona just never changes—he talks, laughs, and is so obviously genuine and

natural that is it a joy to spend time in his company.

" Do you know that Olive loved Celtic too?" he asks.

Olive is his wife of 50 years plus, and he goes on to explain that she didn't go to too many games throughout his career with Hearts or Raith Rovers or even at Crystal Palace in London. She went to some of course, but she was not that enthusiastic.

However, Celtic was different.

" She loved the atmosphere at the club" says Willie. " She loved the crowd and the banter, the camaraderie between the players and the excitement of the European nights. All these years later she still loves that support and all the stuff that is special about this club."

Earlier in the week I witnessed Willie team up with the non-stop tour de force that is called

Bertie Auld.

I asked Willie when he had last seen Bertie?

" Oh—he came out to Australia about 18 months ago with Charlie and the boys and he came to see me." Says Willie. " I tried to pretend I was out but I never got away with it—he found me in the end!"

In the BBC studios where they were recording a special radio show on the Lisbon Lions, those present were very quickly presented with an impromptu session of the Bertie and Willie double act--- a twosome that is so automatic and natural that anyone can see that these two were not just team mates from 40 years ago— but are great friends, happy in one another's company irrespective of the passing of years and the thousands of miles that separate their respective homes.

" Is this wind up radio?" asks Willie

" Don't you start" sayd Bertie " You are the best wind up merchant in the business – and the one that never gets the blame! Mr " It wasn'y me boss!'".

" Well most of the time it wasn'y me"

" Yer arse—it was always you!"

Kenny McIntyre and others in the BBC studio can't help laughing—tears of laughter roll down cheeks as the two continue.

" Do you remember the bottle of Whisky that we used to have in the showers? Bert"

Bertie mocks indignation " Whisky has never passed these lips in my entire life!"

" Aye I know it didn'y pass your lips—it went between them and straight down your throat!" replies Willie as quick as a flash.

Apparently there was always a wee nip of Whisky in the showers—BEFORE THE GAME--- and each of the players would take a nip!

" Oul Bob Rooney used to finish the bottle right enough when he thought we weren't looking!" Willie adds.

The conversation goes on to Neilly Mochan, and both former players agree that "smiler" used to be great fun in the dressing room.

" He used to say some brilliant things that had us in stitches" Says Willie.

" My favourite was when there had been some high jinks somewhere and Neilly had been involved and we started taking the mickey out of him. I remember him shouting back " People in Glass Houses shouldn't throw Tomoatoes!".

Wallace and Auld—both in their seventies--- burst into fits of laughter like two schoolboys at this—and to be honest everyone else in the studio does likewise.

" How did big Jock handle wee Jimmy" asks Kenny McIntyre trying to get a serious answer to something.

" Handle him?" asks Willie " He spent most of his time just looking for him?"

Again there were peels of laughter as Willie describes Jimmy Johnstone escaping from a ground floor flat through a window.

" He still needed a ladder right enough"--- more laughter.

And on it goes.

The humour gets even worse off air with stories that can't be repeated on air nor repeated here in print.

Later in the week I have the bizarre experience of sitting down for a cup of tea and a roll and sausage with Willie—in Auld's the bakers.

" Right—one thing son--- when you next see Bertie don't tell him we were in here—tell him we went to Greggs rather than Auld's—wind the Ba****d up at every opportunity!"

Later, a photo opportunity arises with Willie being photographed with two glamorous models. These are gorgeous girls in their late teens or early twenties.

" Phone Bertie—Phone Bertie—make sure he knows about this!" cries Willie.

Soon all I can hear is Bertie Auld throwing good humoured abuse at his former team mate down the phone and asking if Willie has reversed the charges?

Yes—a week with Willie Wallace came as a bit of a surprise—full of fun, full of laughter, full of stories about football and life in Australia.

He says his life is like the weather in Australia:

" One day its great--- and the next day is just perfect!"

That just about sums it up!

CAN I HAVE RASPBERRY ON THAT CHAMPIONS LEAGUE ICE CREAM

MARYHILL FOODBANK COLLECTI

CELTIC QUICK NEWS ROLL OF HONOUR 2013-14

Celtic supporters rounded off the 125th year with a final charity event – at Firhill on Sunday 27 October where Celtic legends Bertie Auld and Frank McAnennie both lent a hand for the Maryhill Foodbank collection. Both sets of supporters from the Glasgow derby set aside their footballing differences to particulate as these photographs demonstrate. The need for Foodbanks in Glasgow in 2103 – 125 years after Celtic was founded to provide this very social service was not lost on the support. Well done to everyone involved in organising this event and everyone who contributed. Celtic won the match by two goals to one but the real winners on the day are those who will be helped by such generosity.

1254125
CELTIC CHARITY

1254125

LET'S M[A]
OUR LE[G]

Mark Cameron looks back on a memorable year for Celtic Charity...

Over the last twelve months the Celtic Charity Supporters Committee have grabbed fans interest with their "1254125" campaign – encouraging supporters to raise £125 for worthy causes during the clubs 125th anniversary year.

The committee put together an ambitious and varied event list, all of which were extremely well supported. The Lions Roar Again evening in the Kerrydale Suite at the start of March sold out in a few days and such was the feedback that another evening was held in the summer.

The much publicised Highest Huddle

which took place on top of Ben Nevis in June proved to be as memorable as it was worthwhile. Over 100 supporters climbing the Ben and then "huddling" in the snow managed to raise over £25k for the charity. The photographic images from the day went global and have become an iconic symbol of the supporters engagement in the 1254125 campaign, those images will inspire even more to participate next year.

In the autumn a large group took part in a cycle from Celtic Park to Cardenden, hometown of legendary Celtic goalkeeper John Thomson. Only a few weeks later similar numbers took part on the Great

1254125
CELTIC CHARITY

KE IT
ACY

Scottish Run in Glasgow. All of this in aid of Celtic Charity.

Of course many fans came up with their own novel way of fund raising during the year – from climbing all the steps inside Celtic Park, bike rides to Celtic matches as well as to mainland Europe, fun runs, head shavings & body waxing's to motorcycling in a Onesey, our supporters soon realised that it's not what you do that's important, it's all about what you are doing it for.

The need to support the poor and vulnerable at home and abroad is still as relevant now as it was when Brother Walfrid uttered those immortal words in St Mary's Hall. The 1254125 campaign can be the springboard for our generation to make a measurable difference.

Let's make it our legacy.

1254125
THE CELTIC CHARITY FUND

1888 Our First Game	**1967** European Cup Win	**1974** 9 In A Row	**1988** Centenary Double	**2003** UEFA Cup Final	**125 YEARS OF PASSION**

THE BATTERED BUNNET · SOUKOUS · I'M NEIL LENNON (TAMRABAM)

CELTIC QUICK NEWS ROLL OF HONOUR 2013-14

THE WEARING OF THE GREEN

After watching the 2 Scottish Cup semi-finals, Mike Maher couldn't get some thoughts about the meeting of Hibernian and Celtic in the final out of his head. So he decided to put pen to paper and submit another fine article to CQN Magazine ahead for the forthcoming Scottish Cup Final!

CRAIG IN 'I QUIT' SHOCK

By DON MORRISON

THE cheers and applause for record-breaking Celtic were still ringing round Hampden yesterday when manager Jock Stein came out with the shock news that right back Jim Craig is quitting the club, and migrating to South Africa.

It was news that brought the only tinge of sadness to the celebrations after the 6-1 trouncing of Hibs—a result which gives the Celts their 22nd Scottish Cup win, and that by the biggest margin in the tournament in 84 years.

Craig, who is 29 years old and has won one European Cup and four Scottish Cup medals in his seven years with the club, leaves for Cape Town on May 16 to take up his profession of dentistry.

"I just thought it about time I did this," he said. "After all, my career is more important. I would have hated to play for a club other than Celtic. This is a wonderful way to bow out."

Celtic have agreed to cancel Craig's registration and contract so that he can move to South Africa. He has already agreed to join Hellenic as a part-timer.

"We are very sorry to lose him," said manager Jock Stein, "but we realise he must think of his own future.

Craig, who played his 237th first team match yesterday, is the seventh of the "Lisbon Lions" to leave Parkhead. Only McNeill, Johnstone, Murdoch and Lennox remain.

The only Celt injured in yesterday's match was the tireless Bobby Murdoch. He took a knee knock early on and twice took further knocks on the same spot.

With 10 minutes left he wanted to come off but manager Jock Stein insisted he stay on.

And last night there was no big celebration for the Celtic players. So experienced in the trophy winning business, they went home to their families.

However, tonight in Glasgow the club will hold a special dinner-dance.

Hampden's happiest player, Dixie [Deans] ... spectacular hat-trick in his ...

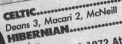

12

CELTIC.............................6
Deans 3, Macari 2, McNeill
HIBERNIAN.........................1
Gordon
Hampden, May 6 1972 Att: 106,102
Celtic: Williams, Craig, Brogan, Murdoch, McNeill, Connelly, Johnstone, Deans, Macari, Dalglish, Callaghan.

Hibernian: Herriot, Brownlie, Schaedler, Stanton, Black, Blackley, Edwards, Hazel, Gordon, O'Rourke, Duncan (Auld).

THE most convincing Scottish Cup Final win of the century as Celtic ran riot. Hibs competed for the first quarter as Gordon cancelled out McNeill's opener. But then Jock Stein's Hoops who had already won the league went into overdrive, Deans grabbing a hat-trick and Macari adding a late double.

DIXIE Deans celebrates after writing himself into cup folklore with a stunning hat-trick against Hibs

... begin ... the greatest day in football for Dixie Deans as he heads Celtic's second goal at H...

is to be an "All Green" Scottish Cup
[...]. Except that it will be more likely Black
[...]low as both Celtic and Hibernian will
[...] change strips. My son and I always
[...] the same argument when these teams
[...]. I don't see the need for a change while
[...] tells me that there is a colour clash. If a
[...]ee cannot distinguish between green and
[...]e hoops and a green shirt he should not
[...] the job! I had no difficulty recognising
[...] Deans scoring that incredible goal in
[...]972 Cup Final and on a dark December
[...]noon that same year as I stood on the
[...]s Park terracing at Hampden I was in no
[...]t that it was Pat Stanton and Jimmy
[...]urke scoring the goals at the Mt Florida
[...]o win the League Cup for Hibs. However
[...]ss I am fighting a losing battle in trying
[...]ep the traditional colours on the field of

[...]ot just colours of course that connect
[...]rnian and Celtic. Every Celtic supporter
[...]us that after Hibs won the Scottish Cup
[...]bruary 1887 at Hampden they went to
[...]ary's Hall in the East End of Glasgow to
[...]orate with their supporters in the west of
[...]land. (It is intriguing to think that in 1887
[...]u had asked Br Walfrid, John Glass, Pat
[...]h etc. who they supported their answer
[...]d presumably have been Hibernian!)
[...]ey were about to leave the Hibernian
[...]tary John McFadden suggested that the
[...]gow Irish should consider organising
[...]own club. The rest, as they say, is
[...]ry.

[...]I was back in Scotland a few years
[...] managed to pick up "The Making

of Hibernian" by Alan Lugton. I would
recommend this book to anyone with an
interest in Celtic's history. It is a bit like
reading a prequel to the Celtic Story. Names
like Dan Doyle and Tom Maley appear. One
of Hib's nicknames was "the Bhoys" and of
course they were the first to wear green and
white hoops. Celtic fans know the story of
Michael Davitt laying a sod of Irish turf at
Celtic Park in 1892, well he had performed a
similar ceremony at Easter Road years earlier
(incidentally that book has an interesting
take on who stole that sod of turf from
Celtic Park a short time later).Hibernian had
initially been refused entry to the SFA as they
were Irish not Scottish. They lobbied until
they were eventually admitted. That was a
hurdle that Celtic would not have to face.

One thing that would be different about the
new Glasgow Irish club would be the name. It
appears that the name "Glasgow Hibernian"
was strongly promoted but apparently Br
Walfrid was strong in his insistence on the
name "Celtic". In recent years this choice
is explained by saying that he wanted the
new club to appeal to more than just the
Irish. I have no doubt he wanted to make the
club wide ranging in its appeal but I am not
sure that is why he chose the name he did.
In those days I feel that to most people the
name Celtic would have had much more Irish
than Scottish connotations. Any Scottishness
would have been more related to the
Highlands than the local Scottish population.
I think his choice of name may have had a
more pragmatic aspect. The name Hibernian
was already well established. Hibs had
helped organise clubs throughout Scotland
and there were teams such as Dundee
Hibernian, Coatbridge Hibernian, Carfin
Hibernian and even Larkhall Hibernian!
Walfrid would have wanted to make it clear
the new club was not just an offshoot of the
more famous Edinburgh club.

He would also have seen the support Hibs
had throughout Scotland and even in
England. Although Hibs were more or less a
"parish team" they had supporters wherever
they played as the Irish people of the area
would turn out to cheer them rather than
the local side. If Celtic could be successful
they could surely expect such support and
also had a bigger Irish population close to
home. (At that time the media did not seem
to have problems accepting that people
might support a team for ethnic rather than
geographical reasons).

The arrival of Celtic did cause problems for
Hibs and for a short period they went into

recess to re-build and restructure before
returning to the main Scottish Football fold.
In 1902 they defeated Celtic in the Scottish
Cup Final – their last success in that trophy. A
newspaper of the time reviewed the game in
this way-

"It is a peculiarity of Scottish Football to find
two Irish clubs contesting the final tie for the
Scottish Cup; but if we remove these teams
from the sport much of the life and attractive
power of the game would disappear"

Over the years I have witnessed many great
games between Celtic and Hibernian (without
changing strips!) so let's hope we have
another one at the end of May.

A final suggestion. As neither team will be
wearing their traditional colours what about
something else that was in the tradition of
both clubs? The first time singing was heard
en masse at a Scottish match was when
Hibs won the Cup in 1887. Their supporters
started singing a popular song of the time
and the players joined in. That night the
same song was sung heartily by everyone
in St Mary's Hall. It was also sung at early
Celtic occasions, in particular the opening of
Celtic Park. Most people know the tune and
the words so how about on Cup Final day we
have 50,000 voices belting it out-All together
now-

"God save Ireland said the heroes, God save
Ireland say we all..."

HOW THE
WAS WO

CELTIC QUICK NEWS ROLL OF HONOUR 2013-14

CUP

William HILL

hill.com · CARLING · William

AULDHEID · AN TEARMANN · JAMESGANG · IKI · SCOTTISHLEAF

DATE	ROUND	VENUE	TEAM	SCORE	SCORERS
1/12/12	4th Round	Celtic Park	Arbroath	1-1 D	OG
12/12/12	4th Round Replay	Gayfield	Arbroath	1-0 W	Matthews
3/2/13	5th Round	Stark's Park	Raith Rovers	3-0 W	Commons (p), Forrest, Mulgrew
2/3/13	Quarter Finals	St. Mirren Park	St. Mirren	2-1 W	Ledley, Stokes
14/4/13	Semi-Finals Park	Hampden	Dundee United	4-3 W (AET)	Commons 2, Wanyama, Stokes
26/5/13	Final	Hampden Park	Hibernian	3-0 W	Hooper 2, Ledley

Report

Having last won the Scottish Cup in 2011, 35 times winners Celtic looked to get their hands on the famous trophy once more in 2013, after controversially missing out on a place in the final last season after defeat to eventual winners Hearts. First up for the Hoops on the road to Hampden was the visit of Second Division outfit Arbroath. However, a weakened Celtic side, with many players rested because of the Champions League tie against Spartak Moscow in Neil Lennon's mind, failed to impress at Celtic Park as Arbroath earned a deserved replay by drawing 1-1. The Bhoys opened the scoring in comical circumstances, as a clearance from

an Arbroath defender cannoned off his team mates back and flew into the back of the net. The lower league side though continued to work hard and equalised late on when a deflected free kick left deputy keeper Lukasz Zaluska with no chance.

Just over a week later, a stronger Celtic side visited Gayfield for the replay on a bitterly cold December evening. The Bhoys opened the scoring when Adam Matthews brilliantly drilled the ball into the top corner after a burst of pace took him away from a couple of defenders in what was the Welshman's first Celtic goal. There were no more goals to come as Celtic booked their place in the fifth round, although Fraser Forster had to pull off a great save on the slippery surface to prevent extra time.

Raith Rovers were next on the Scottish Cup agenda for Celtic in early February,

and after a goalless first period, Celtic found the breakthrough from the penalty spot following a clumsy challenge on Kris Commons in the box. Commons himself stepped up and fired low into the corner. The Scottish Champions continued to dominate and doubled their lead after a fantastic solo effort from James Forrest, which was bettered only by Celtic's third goal, Charlie Mulgrew curling home from 20 yards.

Celtic faced SPL opposition for the first time in their cup run, and were made to work hard for their place in the Semi-Finals against a stodgy St. Mirren side. Joe Ledley opened the scoring early on with a glancing header, but the Paisley side drew level after a defensive horror show from Emilio Izaguirre. It didn't take long though for the Hoops to be back in front when Anthony Stokes nodded in at the back post.

LENNYBHOY · GREENDREAMZ · THE HOOPED CRUSADER · !!RADA RING!!

The score remained the same despite some minor scares as Celtic booked their place at Hampden once more, maintaining Neil Lennon's 100% record of reaching at least the semi-finals of the domestic cups every season he's been in charge.

This Semi-Final arrived after the SPL split, with Celtic three points away from two-in-a-row in the league. Dundee United were the opponents and performed heroically in one of the games of the

Scottish season. It initially looked as if Celtic were on easy street after Kris Commons opened proceedings after only three minutes with a phenomenal hit from 25 yards, and Mikael Lustig hitting the post from all of 6 yards with the net expected to bulge. However, United came back into the match and levelled with a quick counter attack, Mackay-Steven finishing past Fraser Forster following a crisp passing move. The Arabs then stunned Celtic by taking

the lead when Jon Daly nodded home from a free kick. About a minute later, with the United faithful gloating, Victor Wanyama immediately silenced them with a bullet header from an Izaguirre cross, meaning the sides were drawing at half time. After the interval, Celtic put the foot on the gas and went 3-2 up when Kris Commons turned in with an unorthodox finish! Dundee United kept on preserving and incredibly equalised again following a terrific back post header

from 'Soon To Be Division Two Star' Daly. Celtic then almost won the game at the death but couldn't find the net in a last gasp bombardment of the United goal, meaning the game went to extra time.

Extra time signalled a rejuvenated United, who almost went in front, but Daly only managed the woodwork with his latest headed attempt. Fortunately, a few minutes later substitute Anthony Stokes didn't miss with the head, as he got on the end of a brilliant James Forrest cross

to leave United dejected. The side from Dundee couldn't find another route past Forster in the remains of extra time, and Celtic were through to the final, ending their 'Hampden Hoodoo' too.

It was the Battle of the Green's and White's in the showpiece finale at the end of May in the Scottish Cup Final, when Celtic faced Hibs, with the side from the capital looking to win the cup for the first time in 111 years. Celtic, having to play in their black away strip, were under the

cosh for the opening seven minutes, and relied on Fraser Forster to make a good save from Doyle header. Thankfully, the Bhoys controlled the rest of the game after scoring with their first attack. Mikael Lustig's low cross was picked up by Stokes at the other end of the box, and the Irishman duly found his strike partner Gary Hooper with his curling delivery, the English striker cushioning the ball into the back of the net. Celtic, missing Victor Wanyama and Beram

TURKEYBHOY · SUMMA OF SAMMI... · JIMMCI · BLANTYRETIM

Kayal through suspension, continued to dominate and doubled the lead after Stokes and Hooper combined to great effect once more. Commons fed Stokes and he crossed with his left foot, finding Hooper's head with stunning accuracy. Hooper placed his header back towards goal and into the bottom corner in a Larsson-esque moment. Into the second period, with Celtic in second gear and Hibs posing no real attacking threat, the Hoops finished off the Hibees with ten minutes to go. Stokes turned brilliantly in the centre of the park to beat his man before feeding Lustig on the right flank. The Swedish international crossed early for Hooper but the former Scunthorpe man couldn't score his hat-trick as he missed the ball, but Joe Ledley was on hand to thump the loose ball home and seal a delightful domestic double. Scott Brown went up and lifted the cup to cap off a memorable season for Celtic in our 125th anniversary season.

Player of the Tournament

Tough to choose, with Joe Ledley consistently good throughout the rounds, Kris Commons shining against Dundee United and Gary Hooper's fantastic double in the final, but this award goes the Anthony Stokes for scoring the winning goals in the St. Mirren and Dundee United games, plus his Man of the Match performance in the final.

Goal of the Tournament

There were some excellent finishes on our Scottish Cup journey, but I think Kris Commons' stunning strike for the opening goal in the semi-finals takes some beating. Adam Matthews and Gary Hooper (his header in the final was pure class) will count themselves unlucky though!

-14

JOCK STEIN, BILLY McNEILL AND NOW NEIL LENNON. CAPTAINED THE CLUB TO THE DOUBLE AND MANAGED THE CLUB TO THE DOUBLE. THREE CELTIC LEGENDS - NEIL LENNON YOU ARE NOW IN THE COMPANY OF THE GREATEST EVER CELTS. STAY FOR THE TEN. IT IS YOUR DESTINY. ADD TO THE UNBROKEN HISTORY!

THE HONEST MISTAKE LOVES BEING FIRST • TOMTHELEEDSTIM

CQN PLAYER OF THE YEAR

With a little assistance from the regulars on CQN and on CQN Magazine Facebook page, Paul Brennan sets out the first ever CQN Player of the Year Awards…

CELTIC QUICK NEWS ROLL OF HONOUR 2013-14

Lustig

SAMARAS

After dominating the Scottish Player of the Year awards for much of the last 20 years, in sunshine or in shadow, I couldn't believe the upset that no Celtic players were nominated for the PFA awards. Neil Lennon was variously reported as "outraged" and "furious" but I suspect he was indulging in some motivational tactics to maintain players edge in the weeks between winning the SPL title and the Scottish Cup final.

Eventual winner, Michael Higdon, and fellow nominees, Leigh Griffiths, Andrew Shinnie and Niall McGinn, were star performers for their clubs, although none will have had the blood rushing in the veins of Celtic scouts. Celtic's top performers were less clear-cut, as the bulk of the squad contributed at various stages. I'd like to highlight a few players:

Most Improved Player: Mikael Lustig

Mikael joined Celtic in January 2012 and set about competing for the right back slot with Adam Matthews, who was already demonstrating what effective player he is. It was an odd signing. Season 2012-13 proved how much football is now a squad game. Mikael's pace and ability to throw in early crosses was became a dependable feature of Celtic last season.

His adaptability was also an indication of how Neil Lennon plans his squad. Lustig and Matthews were regularly used together on the right, one overlapping the other. Their disciplined performances in the Champions League was one of the main reasons Celtic progressed in the tournament, in particular in that home victory against Barcelona.

The early ball into the box for Gary Hooper in Moscow will be the most persistent memory of Mikael this season. That was Celtic's first attack of the game, and their first goal of the group

stages, and set the scene for their first win away from home in the history of the tournament.

European Player of the Year: Georgios Samaras

Georgios proved to be the commensurate European player this season. Scoring in five consecutive away games, including Barcelona, Benfica and at Spartak Moscow, was genuinely historic, I don't have the time to research this one, but few players, at any club, will have been able to match this achievement.

All those things people complained about Georgios for: holding onto the ball, taking it for a walk instead of releasing it, were evidently what the team needed in Europe. With eight minutes left of their home game against Spartak, Celtic were level and needed a win to qualify for the knock out stages. It was Georgios who opened play up inside the Spartak box, daring a defender to lung in and concede a penalty.

PLAYER OF THE YEAR

COMMONS

With so much transfer speculation around Victor Wanyama and Gary Hooper it is perhaps surprising that Hooper featured well down my list of nominations for the top spot. A good case could be made for Wanyama, who had all the raw material to make it to the very top of the game, but the same could be said for Fraser Forster. All three were edged out by Kris Commons. Kris arrived at Celtic in January 2011 like a Force of Football. He blew away opposition defences with craft and outstanding finishing, I remember writing his arrival maintained our league challenge until the last day.

The following season was a write-off. The goals dried up and he found himself in and out of the side. Whatever happened last summer Kris returned after the break at his very best. He and Samaras between them ensured Celtic's qualification for the Champions League group stage and once there, he didn't disappoint.

Kris is never going to be a player with the best pass completed ratio, most tackles won or most ground covered, but he is an intelligent player. He knows where to go, when to take a player on and when to wait on the challenge. His use of the ball and his off-the-ball running are educational. His game is not primarily played with his feet, it is played in his head.

You also suspect that head is always thinking 'goal'. He can make anywhere within 40 yards of goal a dangerous place for opponents, either with a cross or a shot.

Along with Georgios Samaras you also get the feeling Kris is a player who has made his home at Celtic. He 'gets' the club, as does his incredible partner, Lisa Hague. The good causes which the Celtic support are well known for, for so long survived with little more than the efforts of the ordinary fan. When Lisa heard of the Wee Oscar Campaign she stepped forward and offered to patron the cause.

It is unsettling to think that in the weeks before he signed for Celtic, Kris Commons was subject to a bid from Oldco Rangers. He was neither expensive nor greatly sought-after when available for transfer from Derby County, but he was incredibly grounded.

CELTIC QUICK NEWS ROLL OF HONOUR 2013-14

CELTIC JOURNAL
THE SUPPORTER'S VOICE

The Celtic Journal is one of the latest upcoming platforms in which anyone is welcome to write an article about Celtic. It has gone down very well amongst readers with the site now featured on one of the biggest internet news websites, News Now. Articles are written on a wide variety of subjects, all Celtic related. I've been writing for the Journal more or less since its birth and I've reached 50,000 views on all of my current articles, something I never thought I'd achieve! I fully recommend that, as well as CQN Magazine, you bookmark Celtic Journal, you won't be disappointed. If purely Celtic related articles are your thing then look no further.

The Journal currently has three senior editors, myself, Kieran and Alex. Myself and Kieran write articles regularly at least one each week. Alex does the technical side of things, keeping the website up to date, doing all the designing and logos. The website welcomes all contributions. We have people writing articles as a one off, or even people that write them every month or so. There is plenty of variation on the site and space to leave your thoughts about what you've just read. We like to promote each other's work and ensure that we try our best not to repeat articles found elsewhere.

The website will soon be joining up with Google News as well as News Now, so even more views are guaranteed in the future. It was actually through Celtic Journal that I started writing articles and since then I haven't looked back. I love writing about Celtic now.

Please feel free to follow me on Twitter @joebhoy2412. Kieran (@Kieran_Celtic) and Alex (@alexbaskhanov) are also on Twitter. All articles are available to read at any time and can be found on Twitter @CelticJournal, or on the website, http://celticjournal.org/. A massive thank you to CQN for publishing this article to gain a bigger audience for the Journal.

BRYCE CURDY • CULTSBHOY LOVES BEING 1ST FOREVER & EVER

C2N'S CELTIC EIGHT

Setting Free the Bears selected the Celtic team of the 1970s in the last edition of C2N Magazine. In this edition Winning Captains selects our Celtic team from the 1980s. In terms of formation the 80s team can be either 4-4-2 or 4-3-3 – this was the system that a very good Celtic team employed in the first half of the decade. However a shrewd young Aberdeen manager would often take advantage of Celtic's tactical naivety and maybe we should have been using 4-4-2 sooner?

TEAM OF THE TIES

BHOYL083 · BIG NAN · KOJO · BOBBYRUSSELL · YORKBHOY

A few players haven't been considered for selection – the obvious one is Maurice Johnston. In actual fact he wasn't good enough to be in this team anyway. The other player who subsequently talked himself out of consideration for a place in the team is Charlie Nicholas. He had the potential to be a Celtic great – what a player he was in that very short period when he first wore the Hoops. Ultimately he couldn't wait to get away and the rest of his career in London, Aberdeen and back again at Paradise, was a huge anti-climax, given the talent at his disposal. Nicholas clearly failed to realise his potential. He's not worthy of a place in this team!

GOALKEEPER

In goals who else but PAT BONNER? I remember sitting in the seats behind the dugout at Celtic Park on St Patrick's Day in 1979 watching Celtic beat Motherwell 2-1. We had been really poor for weeks before this and as a 14 year old I was a little bemused at this loss of form. In fact this game was the beginning of a superb turn around that saw Celtic win match after match and this led us to a a title decider on a Monday night in May. More on that game later on. Paddy made his debut that St Patrick's Day replacing Peter Latchford who was a real fans' favourite. To be perfectly honest, I watched Paddy throughout his entire career and was never totally comfortable with him in goals. In particular I always thought he was pretty weak at Ibrox and McCoist would all too often get the better of him. I never felt we had a really top quality goalkeeper until Artur Boruc arrived. It is always easy to blame the keeper I suppose!

Paddy was Jock Stein's last signing for Celtic and he played for our team well into the 90s. He is the goalkeeper in CQN's team of the 80s.

Paddy played across the entire eighties decade but most of the outfield players, in my mind are divided between two distinct Celtic sides. Firstly the Celtic team of the early part of the decade that competed against the so-called New Firm challenge and were actually better than Aberdeen or Dundee United. This team that went to

a return leg in Amsterdam with only a 2-2 to show from the first leg at Celtic Park and dramatically defeated a top quality Ajax side 2-1 with a very late winner! Then there is the Celtic team of the Centenary season – a real band of brothers. A story of dramatic late winners – one up away to Dundee springs to mind. A team that was full of experience and determination and faced the financial onslaught from the Bank of Scotland's open cheque book which they'd given to David Murray and his loathsome manager Souness.

The first Celtic team in the 80s was naïve but superb to watch. They were so good that despite winning championships and cup finals they left me with a feeling that they under achieved. They were also robbed out of a real chance of a European Trophy by one idiot throwing a bottle and the subsequent cheating antics of a Rapid Vienna side – despised to this day that club. The Centenary Celtic side was all about the short-term objective. That season was wonderful but the cracks were there and after another cup win the following season in 1989, we went through a long barren spell, that was just

horrible to endure. Endure it we did.

BACK FOUR

Anyway back to the CQN team selection. The back four sees DANNY MCGRAIN at right back. There is an argument to move Danny to left back to accommodate Chris Morris in the side and Danny is probably our best left back of the decade too! He was a wonderful player and when he had a long period out

the side through injury he was badly missed. Danny was a world-class footballer. Loved it when he played in front of the Jungle.

The two central defenders are MICK McCARTHY and ROY AITKEN. Big Mick played a huge part in getting Celtic across the line in the Centenary season – he was a tough, uncompromising player and certainly made sure we were no pushovers. We can forgive him his dressing room fights with Tommy Burns, but only just!

ROY AITKEN seemed almost super human to me. Getting the ball in defence and going on one of those runs of his with the Jungle singing Feed the Bear, Feed the Bear...I remembered him from 70s often scoring against Rangers and he scored again and was man of the match when Ten Men Won the League on that aforementioned Monday in May 1979. He was a superb Celtic player for 15 years.

With Danny McGrain in the side at right back, it's a straight choice between Anton Rogan and Mark Reid for the left back slot and I am opting for MARK REID. He was Mr Dependable for five seasons before a change of manager saw him lose his place in the team to Brian Whittaker or Graeme Sinclair. Davie Hay didn't fancy Mark as a player and he moved on to join Charlton. He was a very cool customer from the penalty spot and when called upon to take crucial spot kicks he wouldn't miss. He is worthy choice as our left back. Mark Reid is an unsung Celtic hero.

MIDFIELD

Easy – PAUL McSTAY – 100% class. MURDO McLEOD – a hero, I will never forget that last minute goal to make it 4-2 that Monday night! And of course TOMMY BURNS – always was my favourite Celtic player. I had a Higher English exam at school in 1981 and the night before Celtic were away at playing Dundee United and if we won we'd Champions. Thumbing a lift at the traffic lights at Moodiesburn and on my own – I made it to Dundee, studying hard for the exam on the bus there and back. Tommy made it a very special night and years later when we next won the League at Tannadice; I had a tear in my eye thinking about Tommy and the wonderful goal he scored that night. I got an A in that English exam, although you probably won't believe that judging by this article.

I was there too in 1981 up Pittodrie when Paul McStay scored his first ever goal for the club. Again like Danny McGrain, Paul McStay was a world-class footballer. Celtic should have done more for him after he was forced to retire due to an ankle injury.

FORWARDS

Our number 7 is DAVIE PROVAN on the wing. Before joining Celtic he had played second fiddle to Davie Cooper, who denied him his dream move to Rangers. Instead Davie signed for Celtic and with his socks down at his ankles, he was a joy to watch as a Celtic player. His most memorable goal was probably in the 1985 Cup Final – that curling free kick against Dundee United to equalise before FRANK McGARVEY with an amazing header from a great cross from The Bear gave Celtic a dramatic late winner and another Scottish Cup win. How we partied! Davie Hay then got rid of Frank – probably too soon for my liking anyway. Frank had joined Celtic from Liverpool where he never really got a chance. They were winning European Cups at that time – and when he came back to Scotland to join Celtic he was a sensation. He made Charlie Nicholas look good by doing all the hard work. One goal just before half time against St Mirren at Celtic, where he seemed to beat just

about everyone on the park before hitting a screamer into the top corner, is a memorable McGarvey moment. The Rubber Man is my No 9 for the Celtic team of the 80s.

BANKIEBHOY1 · SAINT STIVS · O.G.RAFFERTY · OINEY HOY · LEFTCLICKTIC

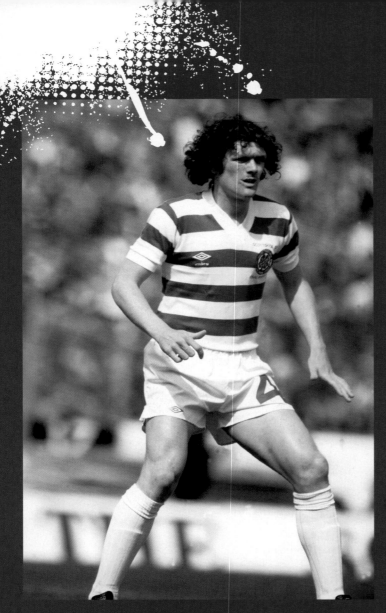

That just leaves a striking partner and I am opting for another player who was liked when the majority of the support was loving the guy he made look good. BRIAN McCLAIR was an excellent footballer, intelligent, skilful, and effective. He left Celtic to sign for Alex Ferguson at Manchester United and Fergie is on record as saying he was one of his best ever signings. That says it all.

Subs – we were allowed only two subs back then so we will go for Mr Super Sub himself GEORGE McCLUSKEY and BILLY STARK for the importance of his winning goal against Rangers in the Centenary season.

Manager – Billy McNeill. Didn't he land a right hook on Gerry McNee? Legend!

In summary my team BONNER, McGRAIN and REID. AITKEN, McCARTHY and McLEOD. PROVAN, McSTAY BURNS, McCLAIR and McGARVEY. McCLUSKEY and STARK are our subs. I think would wipe the floor with Setting Free the Bears Celtic team of the 70s and would probably beat any Celtic team since. It's all a matter of opinions!

We need someone to step forward and write up the Celtic team of the 90s for the next edition. Email Celticquicknews@gmail.com if you would like to do this for the magazine.

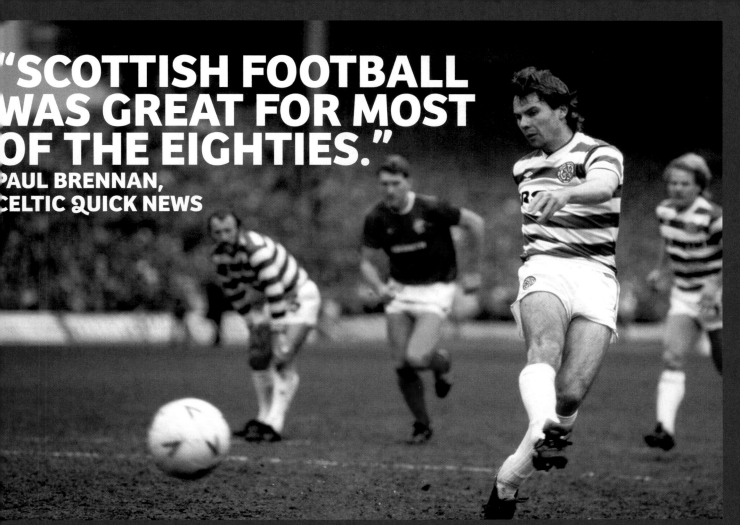

"SCOTTISH FOOTBALL WAS GREAT FOR MOST OF THE EIGHTIES."

PAUL BRENNAN, CELTIC QUICK NEWS

"If you were too young to remember watching Celtic in the 1980s ask someone who was there and you would be forgiven for being a bit cynical about the reaction you get. The 80s didn't have Stein or the Lions (apart from the odd cameo from Bobby Lennox early in the decade). They started with Celtic losing the championship to Aberdeen and ended with us slipping miles behind Rangers, but in between we some fantastic times.

Few things will get Celtic fans reaching for the channel changer these days than Charlie Nicholas or Davie Provan but in the early 80s they were incredibly gifted footballers. Nicholas was special, but like a lot of naturally gifted talents, he was lazy. His goals at Celtic made him an irrepressible hero, in particular, he was a scourge of Rangers. Memories of him drifting past Rangers players at Hampden in the rain during the 1982 League Cup final, before thrashing the ball into the net, or jinking left and right and smacking one home at Ibrox remain vivid. He was an irrepressible image of what we wanted Celtic players to be.

Unfortunately, Charlie wasn't the smartest

jock strap in the hamper. He left but instead of moving to Liverpool he took the highest salary on offer, from a notoriously dull Arsenal. His lack of mobility stood out as soon as he arrived in England.

Provan was a favourite of mine. He was skilful, had pace and his work ethic was the antithesis of Nicholas. He destroyed Rangers during that 1982 League Cup final.

The story of the 80s was really the story of strikers. Frank McGarvey pulled defences this way and that, creating space for Nicholas to tend his fringe. His joy at scoring for Celtic, the 25 yarder against St Mirren, which made him sick with excitement afterwards, and the 1985 Cup Final header, were the embodiment of a Celtic fans joy at playing for his team.

Arguably the best Celtic forward during the 80s was Brian McClair. McClair was quiet. Bought by Billy McNeill as a parting gift before he left, we had to wait each game until the young striker was given his chance by new manager, Davie Hay, while Brian Melrose was given a starting spot.

There was, of course, one man, singed from

Watford, who played to the gallery. The dyed hair and blessing himself against Rangers, it was cringe-worthy stuff. He as a headline maker but he couldn't lace McClair's boots.

Scottish football was great for most of the 80s. It is to Billy McNeill's credit that he won consecutive league titles against Alex Ferguson's Aberdeen, who were one of Scottish football's all-time great teams. We had Dundee United too, who won a marvellous evening game at Celtic Park 2-3 on their way to the 1983 title.

United came within a whisker of being the second Scottish club to reach the European Cup final but let a two goal first-leg lead slip. They would go on to reach the 1987 Uefa Cup final, beating Barcelona home and away in the process, but the glory days were about to end. Rangers had won only three leagues in over 20 years. They flooded the club with money and the century-old tradition of meritocracy was over."

Paul Brennan.

IT MAY BE THE WRONG ROAD...

A CQN TURIN TRIP via CROATIA, VENICE and stopping off to find Craigy Whyte for a beer in MONACO! CQN photographer Geo from Biglens.co.uk explains his logic in getting to the Juventus match by taking the long road…

ULYSSES MCGHEE · JUDE2005 IS NEIL LENNON \0/ · DODDO

"And Celtic will play...... Juventus" – The one draw I didn't want. For very different reasons I`d have preferred Malaga or Dortmund, but after being trackside for the group stage Barcelona match in the Camp Nou, I couldn't not book up for Juventus vs Celtic in Torino.

After listening to so many people who had previously been to Torino, I decided to do a euro trip with a difference. I spent hours poring over Google Maps looking at Central Europe and possible stop offs. I'd already decided that I'd rather only stay in Torino only for two days, on the day Celtic would train in the Juventus Stadium and on match day itself.

Here is the logic. I know that when I am travelling to a Celtic match in the North of Scotland, it would usually would normally take me about 6 hours all in and I am comfortable with that length of drive. So for my European adventure, I looked at places within similar range to Torino and Croatia fell right into that category. With my family coming from Greece, I thought it would be a nice place to visit and that of course the food would be great! So for the first part of the journey, I booked a hotel for a couple of nights in Rovinj.

Next I looked at what I would do after the match, and seeing that Monaco was only about 2 ½ hours away from Torino I thought that I'd head up there. Well it would have been rude not to. I couldn't resist the thought of bumping into Craigy Whyte that's for sure! I'd buy him that beer he's been promised on CQN by Paul67.

I booked my flights booked from Stansted to Torino on the Sunday morning, I set off on Saturday night for the first leg of my journey from Glasgow and the 6 hour, 400 mile drive. There is nothing better than stopping halfway through a huge journey like that and finding the service station you stop at has ice cold bottles of Irn-Bru!

I attempted to catch up on my sleep on the flight over. I collected my hired car and headed straight to the first destination Rovinj in Croatia - just over 600km and over 6 hours of driving away! Driving on Italian roads is an experience in itself, indicators are only to be used if you can be bothered and you can just change lanes whenever you like really! Although for all the last minute lane changing and driving centimetres from the car in front of, there wasn't any road rage, no drivers going mental. They accept the crazy driving, so when in Rome...

Stopping part of the way through for something to eat, you can't help but notice that even petrol station food in Italy is pretty good. From Panini's to Lasagne to Bolognese with plenty of parmesan cheese, and I'm good to go and back on the road for the rest of my drive to Croatia.

I've never visited Croatia before, but the place I stayed, from the pretty Venetian style 'old town' to the fishing harbour, was very picturesque, and definitely

somewhere I would go on holiday. Spending the couple of days there, I found the Croatian people really friendly and spent a few hours in the various shops and harbour restaurants where they served very traditional Croat food. Before leaving, I picked up a few presents from the market in the main square for people, and found out that the Istria area of Croatia is very famous for truffles, I just need to figure out what to cook them with now.

On the way back from Croatia and I passed through Slovenia before heading back into Italy. At one point I checked my map and saw that Venice wasn't too far away so I thought it would be a worthwhile stop off. I was only in Venice for a few hours, purchasing a few tourist trap fridge magnets, taking a few photos on the phone, and paying for the world's most expensive car parking! I was then back on the road to catch up with Celtic who were training in the Juventus stadium.

Arriving at the stadium I started to get butterflies for the match that was coming tomorrow. 3-0 from the first leg was a tough ask, but stranger things have happened in football. From the outside, the stadium is great, but doesn't really impose itself on the Torino skyline. As I walked down and through the inside of the stadium before walking out onto the trackside, I was very impressed by the compactness of the new stadium and as a photographer, how bright it is lit inside at night. Fantastic floodlights for me!

The players went through their paces in preparation for the match with the photographers and journalists standing on the touchline and the one thing that struck me, and everyone there, was the condition of the pitch. One half was an immaculate bowling green, the other wasn't far removed from the condition of Fir Park after a hard winter.

Next day I attempted to arrive at the stadium in plenty of time but drivers in Torino had other ideas! When I eventually got to the stadium, the atmosphere was building outside at the various stalls, whether it was Celtic fans singing our songs, or Juve fans responding with theirs. I was really looking forward to this one. Getting into the stadium I set up my equipment in front of the Curva Sud ultras for the first half and even before kick off the atmosphere generated by the Juve Ultras was starting to build nicely. We all know what happened during the match so I`ll not go into any details there but switching sides and sitting in front of the Celtic fans for the 2nd 45 was an experience and a half.

"Here we go, 10 in a row.." rang out for pretty much the entire 2nd half and the other photographers sat and watched Juve fans applaud the Celtic fans, throw flags over and trade scarves with the Celtic fans. One photographer who travelled from France looked at me, pointed at the Celtic fans, smiled and said "Fantastique!" I think the fans left a lasting impression on a lot of people in the stadium, not just the opposition fans.

So the game ended, my photos were processed, and I went back to the hotel to get ready for my trip to Monaco. A 3 hour journey was all that would separate the skint me and the rich jetset of Craigy Whyte in Monaco, I knew I would fit right in! Monaco is another place I'd definitely go back to, but unless you are minted, it really isn't somewhere to spend a 2 week holiday.

MARGARET MCGILL · SIXTAESEVEN · WEEMAN67 · EDDIEINKIRKMICHAEL

CELTIC QUICK NEWS ROLL OF HONOUR 2013-14

Down to my last few euros and with my reason for visiting only 400m from my hotel, I made the trip to Le Casino in the hope of bumping into Craigy Bhoy or at least winning a few Euros to help fund the trip. A few hands of blackjack and a few hours later I walked out with some winnings to cover the drive back to Torino the next day.

I flew back to Stansted from Torino airport, then started the long journey back to Glasgow, arriving back at 4:30am. 4 hours sleep later and I was back in the car for the trip to Dingwall that would end my weeks worth of driving. 6 days, 7 countries, over 2300 miles, 3 different currencies and 4 different languages. If only the players could have given me 2 victories.

THE LITTLE GENTLEMAN IN THE BLACK VELVET WAISTCOAT

CQN IS ON THE MARCH!

"So who's up for a CQN FAC meet on 6/4?" With that post Moonbeams started the road to the Fans Against Criminalisation Rally for around 80 CQNers. Doc organised a 2m x 3m banner to be printed. CQNers arranged collectively to chip in a fiver each to cover the costs with any balance going, in traditional CQN style, to charity. Doc reports for CQN Magazine…

CELTIC QUICK NEWS ROLL OF HONOUR 2013-14

The Demo started at 12 noon in George Square, Glasgow but the CQNers met in appropriate fashion outside the nearby Gallery of Modern Art (GOMA) around 11:45, for some culture, coffee and of course the option to pop into a Café that sells beer! This is who came along from the CQN blog...

Doc, Miss Doc, Cowiebhoy, MWD, Mini MWD, CelticRollerCoaster, Mrs CRC, CaityRollerCoaster, DeccyRollerCoaster, HamiltonTim, Minx1888, The Boy Jinky, Jobo Baldie plus mini, Roy Croppie, Ten men won the League, Palacio67, Mini Palacio67, KevJungle, EmbraMike, Neganon, OldTim67, FourGreenFields,FourGreenFields

Jnr(16), FourGreenFields Jnr(10), Mouldy67, BJMac, VMhan, Che, VoguePunter, Gordon 64 and Willy O ,the bold Fenian Mhan (lurker), MightyTim, Iki, Praecepta, FanadPatriot, Johann Murdoch, Kilbowie Kelt, LostinBonnybridge, Frantic07, Mrs Frantic07,The Good Ship Celtica, Jungle Jim, Bamboo, Neganon2, Swatson neil lennons 6ft skinny twin, Gourockemeraldbhoy, Thebhoyfromoz and thebhoyfromoz jnr, Houl yer Wheest, BognorBhouyle, Tommysbhoy, The Red Telephone, Youssarian67, Stairheedrammy, Sipsini, Lennybhoy, Vale Bhoy, Troon Tim, Troon Tim Jnr, Leftclick, Mrs Mighty Tim, SeanyBhoy, SarahGhirl, The

MACANBHEATHA OSCAR ABÚ · 16 ROADS · DESSYBHOY

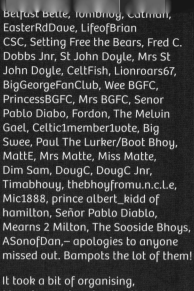

Belfast Belle, TomBhoy, Catman, EasterRdDave, LifeofBrian CSC, Setting Free the Bears, Fred C. Dobbs Jnr, St John Doyle, Mrs St John Doyle, CeltFish, Lionroars67, BigGeorgeFanClub, Wee BGFC, PrincessBGFC, Mrs BGFC, Senor Pablo Diabo, Fordon, The Melvin Gael, Celtic1member1vote, Big Swee, Paul The Lurker/Boot Bhoy, MattE, Mrs Matte, Miss Matte, Dim Sam, DougC, DougC Jnr, Timabhouy, thebhoyfromu.n.c.l.e, Mic1888, prince albert_kidd of hamilton, Señor Pablo Diablo, Mearns 2 Milton, The Sooside Bhoys, ASonofDan,– apologies to anyone missed out. Bampots the lot of them!

It took a bit of organising, Moonbeams keeping the list going individuals, the banner, transport, but that isn't the whole story here.

The CQNers who turned up are. They did it with humour. They did it with solidarity of purpose. They wanted to let it be known by the powers that be that it is not only the young, radical Celtic fans who oppose this "Mince", copyright Sheriff Richard Davidson, legislation.

The Auld Brigade are right behind the Green Brigade and every other Celtic fan who has been affected by this stupid legislation. We got our message across. We listened to the speakers and were impressed. This wasn't rabble rousing, this was considered and to the point. This wasn't just about the platform speakers although we should acknowledge that the speeches of MSP Michael McMahon and Jeanette Findlay of FAC were very well delivered and both made important points.

Again as you would expect from a gathering of CQNers there was plenty of humour. This wee anecdote sums it up.

The rally had a warm up speaker. He outlined some of the things wrong with the legislation. Things like the attempt to "even up the figures" copyright Christine Graham – ie even up the amount of convictions comparing fans of Rangers Football Club (In Liquidation) with those of the fans of Celtic Football Club. As he listed these wrongs, a voice

from behind shouts out, "Down with that sort of thing" a quote from Father Ted, but it was a Pythonesque moment. Michael Palin could not have timed it better!

I turned to those around me laughing, "That has to be a CQNer" someone said. It was Richie, and it was comedy genius.

CelticRollerCoasters daughter CaityRollerCoaster had to hobble her way to the demo after being hacked down playing 5 a sides with her Dad and another CQNer who just couldn't keep up, sorry about that. Still she managed along and showed her support, along with DeccyRollerCoaster and their Mum.

Another when KevJungle came over to me shook my hand and handed over his contribution to the banner fund, as he walk away Jobo Baldie pipped up he's " Off oot" – as regulars on the site this is KevJ's signature when he signs off on a post or from the blog for a bit, another bit of comedy gold.

Moonbeams was going to take some photos, Young Moonbeams was handed the empty camera case, but didn't fancy carrying it - "You can cycle 70 miles but cant carry an empty bag?":-)

Now to the real story, the charity. The essence of our club, the very spirit that founded Celtic. Moonbeams asked for help in organising a banner. I emailed him to volunteer as I had a contact who I have used before and was fairly confident I could get a banner printed in the time frame. I contacted Phil the Printer and asked him what he could do. Next day we met up, simple was his advice, so I thought about the Green Brigades chant, "All Celtic Fans Against the Bill", as in both Legislation and the old types. Emails were exchanged, and Moonbeams added to his post that I had arranged a banner and if those going could contribute a fiver to help cover costs.

I arrived at The Gallery of Modern Art just about on time, CowieBhoy needed a cup of tea from the KFC on the Gallowgate, so it was just, taxi into the city centre. A group of

dodgy looking middle aged men were lurking on the corner, guess who?

It was that lot mentioned above. I've only once seen that amount of CQNers where there was no sign of alcohol and that was the Green Bucket day.

From the moment I got out of the taxi people were coming up to me saying, "You Doc?" hand shake "I'm so and so from the blog", and a fiver thrust into my hand. Too many to try to remember the names, I just kept stuffing money into my pockets. I had no idea how much I'd been given, but I knew cost had been covered a few times over.

So the protesters moved off. They marched to Celtic Park and the police praised them for their behaviour. I hope you see the irony there.

We all went our separate ways – and everyone expressed a desire to meet up again with their fellow CQNers.

I was intent on walking to Celtic Park, wandering along behind the march but...

"Where are you going?" ask CRC.

"On the March" I replied,

"Not the pub then?" he queried!

And so it was de-tour time with CRC, CowieBhoy, Praecepta, Andy, Moonbeams and various other CQNers. Surprisingly many found their way to this watering hole. I had a chance to count the cash, £277 after the cost of the banner. Well done Bhoys and Ghirls. I emailed Paul67 as agreed with those present and asked for a suggested charity. Mary's Meals gratefully received the money, I sent a copy of the receipt to Paul67 and Moonbeams, more for the sake of probity than sobriety of course.

The Doc

SEAN FALLON

TRIBUTE DAY ON C2N

C2N's older generation posted in numbers on Friday 18 January to mark the passing of Celtic legend Sean Fallon. These posts, together with Paul's moving tribute, deserve to be preserved. Accordingly we have reproduced some of them in the magazine and we will also feature these posts in print in the C2N Annual at the end of the year. Rather than just memories, shared for one day on the internet and then lost, they will be permanently available, as part of the rich history of the Celtic family.

Sean Fallon
31 July 1922
-
18 January 2013

:52

Paul 67

Sean Fallon was known as The Iron Man, a hard left back at a time when pretty much all footballers were hard. I met him and his wife Myra at their home a few months ago to prepare an interview in advance of his autobiography, which is due for release soon, the hard-man reputation could not have been further from the character of the person.

He was the most generous spirited man I have been in the company of for years. Myra is a force of nature, unquestionably the wind in his sails. You have never met a happier couple.

The stories he told about how Celtic were transformed from a sporting irrelevance into one of the most powerful and feared clubs in Europe were incredible. His story was one of huge and dramatic achievement. You and I are the beneficiaries.

The players he signed are legendary. Kenny Dalglish, who was in tears in Sean's home the night he agreed to go to Liverpool, Danny McGrain, a person Sean could not speak highly enough about, and countless more. He was a committed Celtic man but took no

pleasure in the death of Rangers; such was his generosity of spirit.

Sean described Jock, himself and Sir Robert Kelly as a three-man team who had the vision to drive Celtic forward. He believed that when Sir Robert died in 1971 the club's loss was significant. Nothing was the same again.

His own parting from Celtic, in 1975, was far from satisfactory, but if he told me once, he told me 10 times, "I don't want a single word said against Celtic". The club that you and I recognise is the creation of Jock, Sean and Sir Robert. They transformed an amateurish football club into a legendary movement. He, more than anyone I ever met, never wanted a figurative goal scored against this legend.

Today we have lost one of the architects of all we hold dear, a man who achieved the Miracle of Lisbon. His insights reach back into the depths of our character. His decision to author an autobiography is a gift to you and me. I'll share many of his anecdotes between now and when it's published.

My sincere condolences to Myra, son Sean

and all the family. We have lost the man who was our greatest living legend but they have lost a great husband, father and grandfather. A remarkable life has come to an end.

ASonOfDan

R.I.P and God Bless Sean Fallon.

After helping Celtic win the Scottish Cup against Motherwell, Fallon said later: "As I walked off Hampden Park I felt I had got everything out of life I had ever wanted. I had become a member of the famous Celtic FC and holder of a Scottish Cup badge all in one year."

He lived the dream...

Tully57

Paul, A tear in my eye reading that tribute – well done.

I've had the pleasure of meeting Sean twice.

The first time was at an Allied Irish event and the last time was in the bar of his golf club – Pollok – about 5 years ago.

THE SINGING DETECTIVE DEMANDS THE RESIGNATION OF CAMPBELL

We had a great craic about Celtic at Pollok. My never-ending fascination with the 7-1 game meant I could actually talk to one of the legends from that game for the first time. He spoke about being delighted that Neilly Mochan was included in the team since there was some doubt beforehand and talked about the players' and fans euphoria after the game.

He spoke about the battles he had with Rangers defenders (ie in the games when he was played up front), including crazy off the ball stuff. He was a hard, hard wee man – and a total gentleman.

I was thrilled to be in his presence.

His original connection with Celtic involved one of our players whilst on a pre-season tour of Ireland, diving into a river in Sligo to save Sean's sister from drowning. The rest was history...Lisbon, 7-1, the lot...

As an aside.... and as a person with strong Donegal roots, and so proud of historical Donegal links with Celtic...including fan base and players...

I have to say that it is hard to beat what Sligo has given us...Brother Walfrid and Sean Fallon.

May you rest in peace forever, Sean – thank you.

Kilbowie Kelt

Today is not a day to be sorrowful. This is a day to celebrate the peaceful passing after a long life of the man who epitomises Celtic more than any other. Sean Fallon is the very soul of the club to which he gave his whole life. The coincidences that led him to Celtic Park & the unbelievable career that he enjoyed are the stuff of fairy tales, despite the fact that his playing days were, for the most part, times of struggle on the field. Surely the bravest & most enthusiastic Celt of all time, Sean's spirit & strength gave me some of the most precious memories I have, & will have as long as I live.

Thanks, Sean.

Brogan Rogan Trevino and Hogan supports Kano 1000

It was Fallon who persuaded Ronnie Simpson to come to Celtic, and who had to swiftly persuade a young David Hay and his dad to leave a hotel and come with him to sign for Celtic instead of waiting for the man they had intended to meet– another ex Celt called Tommy Docherty who was trying to get

young Hay to sign a contract that very day.. with Chelsea.

Any number of players will testify to Fallon's gentle and dignified way of persuading them to come to Celtic Park– not least Danny McGrain and Kenny Dalglish.

However perhaps the story that most emphasises the idea of "Lucky Sean" rubbing off on someone else is the one where he took a walk through Bellahouston Park.

It is said that he came upon a Sunday football game where jackets were being used for posts. A Bounce game between a group of young men, a bunch of friends if you will.

One young player is said to have caught his eye, and eventually the young man was called over by the genial Irishman and asked if he would be interested in trying out for HYPERLINK "http://www.celticfc.net/"Celtic? Within weeks, the young man had signed to play for Celtic, signing for manager McGrory on January 7th 1965.

His name was Jim Craig.

Thomthethim

RIP, Sean.

I had the honour of meeting him once at Celtic Park. It was the year of Jock's convalescence and Sean wore the " stripes". An engaging and friendly man.

My on-field memory is of an incident against Them. Sammy Baird, a talented but crude inside left, had just committed one of his trade mark tackles, leaving a Celtic player in a crumpled heap. Sean, from his left back position in from of the Jungle, made a diagonal beeline for Baird, who was around the centre circle. Sean never stopped until he put the offender up in the air.

The squeal of pain was clearly heard in the Jungle.

On field Tiger, off field Lamb.

Greengray1967

Beautiful tribute Paul. What Sean Fallon has done for our club will long be remembered and spoken of long after we are all gone. I will make sure my grandkids (when, if ever it happens) know of Sean, Jock and Bob. The first time I came across Sean was on the Original History of Celtic video in 1988. I remember thinking, as a young lad then that he was quite a scary and hard, got to meet him a few years later and that notion was totally dispelled. A pure gent. R.I.P. big man and thanks for everything.

Found this on Youtube earlier
http://youtu.be/ig5RAkgXaks

The Battered Bunnet

My enduring memory of Sean Fallon is of a severely grumpy looking man in a camel coat on the touchlines of Molls Myre of a miserable Saturday morning. The kind of miserable Saturday morning that was only possible in Glasgow in February in the 1970s. From Hampden in the Sun to Toryglen in the rain.

"D'you think wee Sean's Da's scouting

today?..."

Me, 10 years old, oblivious to all else except the possibility, the seeming inevitability, that wee Sean's Da would report back to Jock Stein that he'd found the next Kenny Dalglish.

"Did Mr Fallon say anything about me after the match Dad?"

"No Son, he was away sharp to get the team ready for the Morton game."

"Maybe he'll phone later..."

Odd socks.

Nylon tops.

Red blaes.

Mouldmaster days.

Garcia lorca

My enduring memory of Sean Fallon is of a severely grumpy looking man in a camel coat on the touchlines of Molls Myre of a miserable Saturday morning. The kind of miserable Saturday morning that was only possible in Glasgow in February in the 1970s. From Hampden in the Sun to Toryglen in the rain.

"D'you think wee Sean's Da's scouting today?..."

Me, 10 years old, oblivious to all else except the possibility, the seeming inevitability, that wee Sean's Da would report back to Jock Stein that he'd found the next Kenny Dalglish.

"Did Mr Fallon say anything about me after the match Dad?"

"No Son, he was away sharp to get the team ready for the Morton game."

"Maybe he'll phone later..."

Odd socks.

Nylon tops.

Red blasé.

Mould master days.

Thoughts with wee Sean and the family.

Junior

RIP Sean.

I knew Sean's father. He was an Alderman and Councillor. He was shot in WW 1 and the exit wound was devastating but never a word of complaint.

I knew Sean's brother Pauric an unbelievable character and like Sean so generous. He lived in Chicago most of his life and died in tragic circumstances.

connaire 12

How the memories flood back as we try to fend off the tears for a legend who will always have a place in the history of our club and was an example to us of what we should be as Celts.

My first memory of Sean goes back to the early 1950s when he came with the Cup to the St Laurence's Club in the Old Sailors' Res in Greenock to speak at an evening for the men of the Sacred Heart Guild. Even then as a very young boy, I knew I was in the presence of a Celtic Great.

My prayers and thoughts are with his wife and family. May Sean rest in the arms of the Almighty and find the other legends by his side.

Apricale

I'm lucky to be able to say that Sean Fallon was part of my youth – he was great friends with my grandfather, and they saw one another regularly (we only lived 250 yards apart in Kings Park), and I sat in on many conversations. These were great days, to quote Wordsworth, about another revolution, "Bliss was it in that dawn to be alive, but to be young was very heaven".

As so many others have said, he was a rock, in all the best senses. He also had to put up with a lot, but he never lost sight that he was lucky to be part of something bigger. Which I guess we all are.

Torontony

Very well said Paul, I know the Fallon family is aware of your wonderful words; I got a text from my brother (Martin) this morning who is with young Sean now, so well done sir.

I've told this one before on here, I only met Sean once. I was walking in the front door of Pollock golf club with my brother and young Sean. Sean snr was walking out and he stopped to chat and my brother introduced me saying "this is my brother Tony he's over from Canada" well He looked at me with a wry smile and said "I don't think much of the company you're keeping" we all burst out laughing. A true legend and a gentleman. A great Celt.

A big glass will be raised at lunchtime today.

Slainte

Tourtenay

Seeing him in the dugout many decades ago now with Big Jock, it was obvious that he was no passive observer. The club received and benefited from his huge contribution. The success that followed is evidence of his input and marks him as a Celtic legend. A light has gone out in the Celtic family. God bless and RIP. HH

Big G

Posted on the official club Youtube channel a couple of hours ago. Sean Fallon on This Man Craig

http://www.youtube.com/watch?v=mhqfXnRxCuQ

awsomeauldshilale

I usually lurk, but in the light of the sad news, felt compelled to say something, however inadequate. I was sent to do a repair at Celtic Park back in the early seventies, I found myself in the company of Mr Fallon as he was anxious for the work to be carried out as it was having an affect on his training schedule. Awaiting a part to be delivered, I told him it would be 20 minutes. I had the pleasure of his company for that time; I must confess I hadn't given Sean a great deal of thought up to that point. He quickly ascertained that I was a Celtic man and talked away about all things Celtic. It was all "we, "our", "us", not I, my, me. I was left with an impression of him being a real man of substance, while at the same time very self-effacing and modest. Celtic were taking a bit of stick in the press at the time, would you believe, and I asked him what he thought. He said "Ach we'll stand and see what happens!" I've never forgotten that phrase, or him. A class act. Above everything else the one thing that was most obvious to me, even as a lad at the time, he absolutely adored Celtic. God love him and his.

Ron Bacardi

Sean Fallon's part in Celtic's winning the Club Championship of Europe was not even thought of then. I remember being at the new Glasgow airport for an interview for a job in April / May 1967 and saw Jock and Sean coming through arrivals – having been to Italy to assess Inter Milan as it turns out. Shouted out 'Hell, Mr Stein', and he looked at me with a glower!

Praecepta

Paul - Nice piece on the sad passing of Sean Fallon – a true gentleman and an important part of the great tapestry that is Celtic F.C.

Had the pleasure of seeing him in action when I was a young Bhoy (including the 7-1 LC Final) and meeting him in later life.

My late father (a pass-keeper) was very fond of him and often chatted with him after Sunday Mass about the previous day's results. He often said the chats were; insightful, amusing and delivered by a man who had great love of the Club.

May he rest in peace!

Techter àr là

My father took me through to Edinburgh as a lad, to buy my first pair of football boots – well the first pair that you didn't need to nail the studs into - at Ronnie Simpson's shop in Rose Street.

Sean Fallon was also in the shop that day and whilst my dad was paying for the boots, Sean detected uneasiness from the young customer. Is there anything else then? No, I shook my head No that's it, shuffling my feet,

Thanks.

Right said Sean, How about I get Ronnie to autograph the box for you?

That would be brilliant, I replied...but only if you sign it too! The look on his face will stay with me always, as will the old shoebox – the one with the 2 signatures. God bless you Sean. YNWA.

Gordon

The numerous tributes and fond recollections are in themselves a testament as to how highly Sean Fallon was regarded by those who have Celtic at heart.

He certainly was an Iron Man on the park and he gave everything for Celtic each time he wore the jersey.

Off the field, as many others have posted, Sean was a gentle man. Decent, humble, respectful and always mindful of the club's reputation.

He was the manifestation of Celtic and epitomised the spirit of the club.

His contribution to our great success in the 60's and 70's is without question and he was of course the man responsible for recruiting some of our great players at that time.

He certainly was an Iron Man on the park and he gave everything for Celtic each time he wore the jersey.

Among his many other talents Sean could predict the future too!

The week before Lisbon, he wrote an article for the Sunday People headed "I Go For Celtic To Win 2-1."

The following week in a follow up article Sean wrote, "I told you we would beat Inter Milan 2-1 in Lisbon. We did exactly that...I am the proudest man you will meet this weekend.

Not only because I tipped the score correctly but because we proved beyond all doubt that we are the best team in Europe. In fact as far as I am concerned the best in the world."

And he was right; Celtic was the best team in the world in 1967 and all thanks to Jock and Sean.

They built the modern Celtic and elevated our club on to a global stage.

We have so much to thank them for.

As posted by garcia lorca earlier today, Sean was the honorary president of our supporters club, The Sarsfield from the Gorbals.

His connection with our club dates back to

when he first arrived at Celtic and he was good friend to us. I am pleased to say we renewed that friendship back in 2005 when we held an evening in his honour in the heart of the Gorbals.

I met Sean a number of times over the years (his handshake would crush a boulder) but two personal memories of him will linger.

Firstly, in January 1964, Celtic drew an all-conquering Morton side, then in the second division, at Cappielow in the Scottish Cup. It was an all-ticket match and some rascal impersonator had collected our ticket allocation from Celtic Park and left us ticket-less and in despair on the morning of the game. Sean heard about our predicament and worked a miracle (another one of his talents) and provided us with replacements. We won 3-1 and Yogi scored a screamer.

My other memory of Sean is from 1975 when Celtic played Valur of Reykjavik in Iceland and he was in charge of the team whilst Jock recovered from his car accident.

After the 2-0 victory the Celtic team retired to one of Reykjavik's many hot night spots (it was known as a disco in those days), as they were not due to fly back home until the next morning. I have to admit to being in that disco too and slowly the players

left and went back to the Loftleiðir Hotel. Apart that is from two who kept bumping and boogeying until the wee small hours. I must also admit to being there until the wee small hours and shared a taxi back to the hotel (I was staying there too courtesy of Holiday Enterprises).

When we arrived at the hotel we were horrified to see Sean sitting in the reception with a cup of tea and a look that would drop you at 20 paces.

Both players (they shall remain nameless), looking like mischievous schoolboys were summoned to appear before Sean and got the full blast of his Sligo brogue.

I slinked off to bed delighted for the only time in my life that I was not a Celtic player!

On behalf of our club I would like to express our deep condolences to the Fallon family.

Sean, son of Sligo and Lisbon Lion thank you for making Celtic great again.

CQN Magazine would like to thank all the contributors who we have quoted in this feature.

WHITECROOK TIM · AN DUN · JIMBO67 · CANAMALAR · THE EXILED TIM

SCOTTISH FOOTBALL ASSOCIATION
LAW T
THE CELTIC
RULE
EXPLAINED

To observe this rule in action you must attend a match involving Scottish Champions Celtic playing in domestic football. Please note that in European matches, as they have officials appointed by football associations other than the SFA, the rule will not apply.

Observe what happens when a Celtic player scores a goal. Instinctively, like

footballers across the world, the scorer may leave the field to celebrate with his team's supporters. This is especially the case is smaller, tight grounds where the fans are very close to the touchline.

Once the Celtic player indulges in some gratuitous celebrations with the paying customers the referee shall immediately produce a yellow card.

The SFA are very proud to champion this exciting new Celtic Rule and would like to encourage other associations across Europe to urge their referees to adopt this rule should they have the chance to ensure that Celtic progress towards London is hindered in every way possible.

WELVE

THE RULE: Any Celtic player who deliberately leaves the field of play without the referee's permission will receive a yellow card. Simple!

CELTIC PLAYER SCORES

CELTIC PLAYER CELEBRATES IN CROWD

CELTIC PLAYER GETS BOOKED

TEN MEN WON THE LEAGUE • THOMTHETHIM • MIGHTY TIM

MY OTHER L
FAR AWAY F
PLANET FIT

This article is the product of pure happenstance.

Actually, that is probably appropriate because what I will be relating here is largely the story of chance and timing. I really didn't mean to be here, I had no route map, but I'm here and I recently received an email that gave me reason to pause and think about that journey.

The commission from the CQN lads was quite simple, but quite attractive. They asked me to write about me when I wasn't charting Scottish football and the calamitous soap opera that has unfolded since the summer of 2012. Before I reported on the ignominious collapse to eventual liquidation, I did other things.

It made me stop and consider what I had been doing since the days when I wrote plays and articles about Ireland rather than blog posts and football books. Subsequently, I was happy to take up CQN's invitation to write about those 'other things'.

Once liquidation commenced in the summer of 2012, Planet Fitba entered a new dispensation. Subsequently, my own writing projects and other interests have slowly taken me away from the train wreck on Edmiston Drive. One recent email that gave me pause for reflection came from a community theatre group in Glasgow. They were writing to thank me for assisting them through social media to boost the profile of one of their productions and to sell tickets. Apparently it did the trick and I was

glad to help them.

I got chatting with their main guy and he told me that they were about to go into rehearsals for 'Juno and the Paycock' for the St Patrick's Festival next March. I'm a huge admirer of the work of O'Casey and it was when I was discussing the play with him that I had a light bulb moment; I realised that I was suddenly speaking about matters that had fully engaged me over five years ago, before I started on this journalistic journey into one of the biggest ever stories in professional football.

I told him that a play of mine, 'The Flight of the Earls', premiered in Donegal in 2005 and then toured the west of Ireland in 2007. 'Flight' was well received and after the tour I had another two plays 'in development', as the theatre lexicon would have it. So after talking to my guy in Glasgow I dusted down the PDF of 'Flight' and once more I was there again.

I could hear the voices of my characters and it re-energised me to the magic of the footlights rather than floodlights. I sent him the script and he read it at one sitting. He got back to me immediately to ask if they could stage the play and I agreed. Now Peadar O'Donnell and Daragh Gallagher will once again tell their story to a live audience, but this time in Glasgow. It will be the first time the play has been outside of Ireland and given the Donegal setting it is fitting that it will play in the city

FE ROM BA.
By Phil Mac Giolla Bháin

that is home to so many people with roots in Tír Chonaill.

The casting process has already begun. It is early days, but the signs are good and we already have one of the duo. The plan is for the play to have a two-night run in May or June. The opening night in the Balor Theatre in Ballybofey in 2005 was everything that experienced dramatists had told me about opening nights. Yes, I was nervous, but the cheering at the end for another encore from the two actors gave me a little insight into why people get hooked on acting.

After a period of script editing, funded by the Arts Council, the play then went down the west coast of Ireland in 2007 from Donegal all the way to my Father's County Mayo. When I was researching my first book, Preventable Death (about male suicide in Ireland), I had reason to interview the inspirational Father Aidan Troy at Holy Cross Church in North Belfast.

He knew I wasn't a person of faith and as we

settled into the interview I asked him: "How do you make God laugh?" Father Aidan gave a shrug indicating he had no idea and I think he was surprised to be asked this question by a professed atheist. I supplied the answer: "Tell him your plans." He laughed and the ice was broken into lots of little pieces.

I look back at my work in 2010-2011 with a degree of satisfaction. In the summer of 2012 it was frenetic and I was sleeping only a few hours a night, if at all. As I wrote in CQN last summer, the events of 2012 were epochal in Scottish football and all is changed.

This has been an unplanned journey I'm glad that I inadvertently stumbled onto this path five years ago. Once I was engaged with the story in all of its aspects then these other things that had filled up my life in the years before had to take a back seat simply because of time constraints.

The two other plays I had in development had to be shelved and on the shelf they have remained to this day. We have a saying in Ireland, 'on the long finger' - now that might sound rude to some, but it basically means that you'll get around to it sometime. Now that I'm writing this I can look at five years, half a decade, and allow myself a mild sense of satisfaction. I have no regrets in devoting this time to writing about matters fitba.

If everything in life comes back to The Godfather then the last year has definitely felt like The Godfather Part III. Just when I think I'm out they pull me back in! I'm not naïve to think that I can escape completely from this omnishambles. Even as I was writing this article I had to take some time out to demolish

a puff piece in the Daily Record about the London Stock Exchange giving the all clear. It was fantasy, and in all probability, the regurgitation of a press release verbatim under a house by-line.

The immediacy of social media means that people can get access to you directly to demand an update on the Carry On film. If I stopped providing this service entirely then there might even be social unrest, so I will continue, but not as much as I have been doing over the past few years.

Now another major project takes me away from Planet Fitba. A book deal is a deal and the one I am currently writing is out next year. The next book started as a movie script six years ago, discussions with one of Ireland's most respected young film directors was on going, but like many of these projects the raising of finances was just too difficult. I was prepared to cut corners in the production, but when it started to resemble a series of amputations I withdrew. The message wasn't the issue, but just the logistics around the medium.

Obviously, the printed page (and now increasingly the Kindle screen) doesn't have those restrictions. Just like 'Flight', that project is back off the shelf and characters that I created in a train journey from Dublin to Cork are about to have their coming out party. Moreover, it doesn't have anything to do with the fitba team on the Southside or its chaotic replacement. The new writing project is a blast. Well, it starts with a few explosions!

However, I have agreed with my publisher that this time next year I will return to Planet Fitba and make a fist of telling the next chapter.

JEEZ I THOUGHT BLINKER WAS PANTS • PRESTONPANS BHOYS

My view is that it is still too early to process the current tale into book form.

Aside from being a playwright, when I started writing about Scottish football in 2008 the previous five years of my life had been very different. Once upon a time I ran a tourism company specialising in hill-walking holidays and I was an operational member of the local Mountain Rescue Team. There were times when we could get quite busy and it was hugely rewarding in only the way a voluntary effort can be.

In one week in 2002, we rescued a Korean War veteran on vacation with his family - although he was past his 70th year he had been in the 82nd Airborne, so he was made of the right stuff. Then a few days later we got the call to rescue a Northern Ireland government minister who had gone wandering on Muckish Mountain with a mobile phone, but no common sense. Two days after that, I had to abseil down a 300 foot cliff in the dark to rescue a rather sheepish Beagle called 'Toby' who had gone down after his ball. Toby and I tied together had climbed back up the cliff in the pitch dark, but we never did find his ball.

I have promised the mother of my brood that I have to accept that with the passing of the years that I have attempted my last difficult Alpine route, but I still dream of the Matterhorn by the Hornli ridge once more. In the meantime, I have the Derryveaghs largely to myself most days. Well, not entirely by myself as my personal trainer and life coach Rusty keeps me on the right path. Nimble on her four paws and with a nose that picks up more data that the NSA she minds me along the way. Getting away from the craziness of the Fitba internet at times has been vital. In September/October 2010 I walked El Camino Santiago and it is something I must do again.

In the centenary year of the historic Dublin Lockout of 1913, my union, the NUJ, hosted the world congress of the International Federation of Journalists (IFJ). The theme of the gathering was to focus on the mounting toll of journalists

and other media workers who are killed in the line of duty. Here in Ireland we have lost Veronica Guerin (1996), and Marty O'Hagan (2001). The entire event was a reminder that democracy needs journalism and it does not matter the platform where the content appears.

Earlier this year, I was appointed the editor of the Irish Journalist (the NUJ's in-house magazine in Ireland) and the first edition under my stewardship was recently published. My union has been a great source of support to me over these years and I try to put a bit back in.

However, it is understandable that some in the Celtic support have a very low opinion of my trade. When writing the foreword for Downfall, Alex Thomson of Channel 4 News, himself named TV journalist of the year in 2013, had a far harsher take on the Fitba Fourth Estate that I did in my own writing about the Glasgow media. Looking back, I think I inadvertently provided a translation service to the spin that was permeating the Scottish media.

I think being able to physically and psychologically disconnect from this story has been a great benefit to me. When I close the laptop I close the door on Planet Fitba and I decide when I open it again. If I wish, I can seek out neighbours with no interest in association football or any interest in my work. Local gossip and the fortunes of the local GAA team are a great distraction from the craziness in Scottish fitba.

My affections for the Mayo football team augments the potential for the 'craic' to be had with me. Two years ago, Donegal demolished us in the All-Ireland Final and this year we were bested by Dublin by a single point. Given that I was blasting out "the Green and Red of Mayo" by the Saw Doctors on my car sound system around the parish in the run up to the final with Donegal then it seemed appropriate for me to go quiet for a while! However, it will soon be next year and the hope once more stirs that this next time will be Mayo's time.

James Horan, our Bainisteoir (coach), is staying

on and we edge closer to what we haven't had since my Father took the woman he wanted to marry into the Hogan Stand to watch Mayo lift 'Sam' for the second year on the bounce. That was in 1951. We haven't won it since and some of my kin believe it is because the last victorious Mayo team passed a funeral in Foxford and the widow put a curse on them.

The story goes that she declared that until all of that team passed away then the Sam Maguire would never again return to the County Mayo. And guess what? I've seen Celtic lift the European Cup, but Sam Maguire coming back to Mayo would allow me to die a happy man. No pressure then lads!

My Camino continues and I know I'm lucky to have had some excellent travelling companions, most of all my own clan, who know my back story; they are always there for me and chortle at the conspiracy theories that are invented around me by online crazies. I feel privileged that I was in the right place at the right time to report on this unfolding drama that changed the face of Scottish football. However, now it is time to look forward and get back to my future. However I will occasionally glance backwards with a sense of pride, and I know I'll never walk alone.

Phil Mac Giolla Bháin is an author, blogger, editor, journalist and writer based in County Donegal, Ireland.

He is an active member of the National Union of Journalists, sitting on the Irish Executive Council and the New Media Industrial Council.

He is also the editor of the "Irish Journalist" the NUJ's in house magazine for members in Ireland.

Phil was a columnist with An Phoblacht for many years and he has also contributed to

publications as diverse the Guardian, the Irish Independent, Magill magazine and the Irish Post

An established print journalist Phil has also built up a considerable online readership through his blog (www.philmacgiollabhain.ie).

His latest book 'Minority Reporter. Modern Scotland's bad attitude towards her own Irish' is available from all good book shops.

CQN
MAGAZINE

WWW.CELTICQUICKNEWS.CO.UK

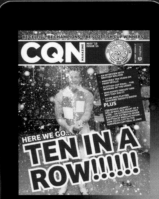

CLICK ON THE COVERS TO VIEW

MCDOWELL CELT • GARCIA LORCA • HOTSHOT • GOOGYBHOY

THE CASE FOR HAWK-EYE

Mike Maher reflects on Celtic's seemingly poor record of scoring from the spot, which thankfully didn't extent to Kris Commons missing against Spartak Moscow!

The game of football has changed much since the days when people kicked an inflated pigs bladder across an abandoned turnip field.

These days it is practically a science of its own. Balls are rounder, fortunes are spent on designing precision designed footwear, tops are made of magical alien material that "wicks sweat" whatever that means.

Sounds good if you have a speech impediment I suppose. Nutrition, medicine, exercise, tactics, you name it, the whole environment of football, both professional and amateur is now firmly geared towards precision.

Except for one thing. The chap in the middle of the field with his whistle,

and his assistants are still capable of making mistakes with alarming regularity. FIFA argue that one of the things that makes football the beautiful game is the unpredictability of it, the allowance for human error. Try telling any football fan of any club that it was beautiful when they leave a ground with the bitter taste of injustice in their mouths. That's not beautiful, its unfair, its robbery, and belongs in the history books.

There are of course different levels of mistakes, even "honest" ones, but at the moment there is a lot of discussion about goal line technology. Did the ball cross the line? Did it not? We have been hearing this for years, from the mistakes that they never stop going

about like Geoff Hurst in 1966 (never a goal) and Frank Lampard against Germany in 2010 (obviously a goal) to the ones that don't get

mentioned so much, like Johann Mjallby against Motherwell at Fir Park, the ball was so far over the line that a family of moles living in a cavern in the Falkland Islands who were fast asleep could clearly see it was a goal. The referee didn't.

Goals change games they say, and now with the game so global it is time to consider another game changer: technology. For years, the sport of rugby has used a video referee to step in at moments such as this. He is in the stands and views the T.V. replays of a contentious score from all the angles that the cameras have filmed, he can pause, rewind, view in slow motion and then has the final say over whether it was a proper score, he is able to have two-way

communication with the match referee via radio. It takes a lot of the uncertainty and doubt from critical moments. It does however have one major drawback: time.

Sometimes the video referee can take several minutes to view a definitive angle, rugby is a team game, therefore fluid and dynamic, and bodies are moving in several directions at the same time. Some scores can be obscured by the sheer number of people in the way.

This is another argument used by FIFA. Incorporate some form of goal line technology and it will break the flow of the game. Players could spend two or three minutes standing around waiting for a decision. That's all very well, but a bit ironic for FIFA to say that when they are yet to take action on teams and players feigning injury during games in order to do exactly that.

Some have suggested other forms of

scientific gadgetry, such as embedding a microchip in the centre of the ball and placing sensors on the line to detect when the ball is completely across the line, which does sound promising, but why not take advantage of something that already exists? Why not Hawk-Eye?

Tennis has incorporated the use of this to great effect in Grand Slam tournaments. Each player has two opportunities in a set to take advantage of Hawk-Eye when they feel the umpire has erred. Hawk-Eye uses a complex computer program, a minimum of four high-speed video cameras placed around the court, and uses triangulation

to track the ball movement, and then generates a computerised image of the trajectory of the ball to determine its final position. In both tennis and cricket the judgement of Hawk-Eye is final, and accepted.

Importantly, Hawk-Eye is also very quick so removes the FIFA argument of breaking up the flow of the game, it moves in almost real time, in fact in tennis Hawk-Eye has now added an extra level of audience participation where the spectators can view the image on the large screens and they can share in an "is it/isn't it?" moment.

There have been murmurings suggesting that Hawk-Eye could be allowed to be modified for football, and Jerome Valcke the FIFA Secretary General did reluctantly concede that Hawk-Eye would be "considered" if the developers could guarantee a 100% success rate...more than they ask of the humans. As of March 3, 2012, the IFAB (International Football Association Board) approved Hawk-Eye for a "second phase" of testing.

Nothing evolves by standing still. The game has to flow yes, but it has to flow fairly.

'THEY G US JAM MCGR

North East Glasgow has been represented by St Roch's ('The Candy Rock') of the Garngad in Scotland's non-league ('junior') football structure since our foundation in 1920 by Canon Edward Lawton of St Roch's Parish Church.

Canon Lawton's dream was for St Roch's to be a feeder Club for Celtic and our initial success in winning the Scottish Junior Cup in season 1921/22 was influenced by James Edward

('Jimmy') McGrory who almost immediately signed for Celtic and went on to become Britain's greatest ever first-class goalscorer with 550 in total, including an incredible 408 goals in 408 league games.

Subsequently, a number of other players stepped up to the senior level via St Roch's such as Frank Brogan, Jim Brogan and Dom Sullivan of Celtic, Denis McQuade of Partick Thistle, Johnny Rollo of Rangers, ex-Millwall

manager John Docherty and Gerry Collins of Hamilton Academical.

Denis helped Partick Thistle to a famous League Cup final victory in 1971 which many reading this would probably rather forget but we are very proud of his success in the senior game.

Jim Brogan of St Roch's was remembered by Celtic supporters more fondly (no offence Denis!) and arguably the hardest to ever

CLUB

'AVE ES RY'

wear a Celtic jersey so we are immensely satisfied to count a European Cup finalist from the team which unfortunately lost to Feyenoord in 1970 among our alumni.

In recent years, our fortunes have been mixed but we remain a member of the Scottish Junior Football Association and currently play in the Stagecoach West of Scotland League, Central District Second Division.

Our fixtures generally take place on Saturday afternoons with 2pm kick offs and therefore, clash with the senior fixtures of the day, most notably along the road at Celtic Park!

Nonetheless, we are here regardless in fairly close proximity to Parkhead and our continued existence is thanks to the assistance of the local community and

individuals who volunteer both their time and financial support to keep one of the special clubs in junior football alive.

A recent Annual General Meeting of the Club concluded with the election of a new Committee and Office Bearers, all of whom are united in their aim to grow awareness of and bring success to one of the very unique junior football clubs, whose formation was similar to that of Celtic's in some respects.

The above was recognised last year by the Celtic Graves Society, whom we are delighted to support in their efforts to recognise those instrumental in Celtic's formation and continued success thereafter.

Celtic Graves formally invited St Roch's to partake in their ceremony in October 2012 to commemorate the 30th anniversary of the passing of Jimmy McGrory and alongside members of the Lisbon Lions and Tony Hamilton of Celtic, our current President, Jim

Friel spoke at length on the Club's behalf, having personally contributed much of the research to John Cairney's biography of Mr McGrory, 'Heroes Are Forever'.

We extend an invitation to new fans and members to join us, particularly families who struggle to afford the inflated costs associated with modern professional football so all under-16s accompanied to our home games by an adult will gain free entry.

Standard entry prices are £4 adults, £2 for concessions and for the forthcoming 2013/14 season, an adult season ticket for 10 home league games will be only £30.

We are also pleased to be able to offer sponsorship packages to any interested individuals or businesses.

Car parking space is available for visitors and from Glasgow City Centre we can be reached at Provanmill Park, Royston Road, Glasgow by bus on the SPT number 329 service from West Regent Street to Stobhill Hospital as well as the First Bus number 19A service from Blairdardie to Robroyston.

The ground is located at the bottom of Broomfield Road within a short distance from the Red Road flats which are currently undergoing demolition works.

For further information, including upcoming fixtures, please follow us on Twitter @ strochsjuniors or email us at strochfc@gmail. com.

With thanks and kind regards,

The Committee for the time being of St Roch's Football Club

It was the smell of the grass that surprised me; that freshly cut smell in the middle of winter. The walk to the centre circle also seemed long, but perhaps I just wanted it to last forever. In truth, my son Tony dictated the pace for all four of us: his Mum Pauline, and his brother Martin and I. We were walking onto Celtic Park at half-time during the league game against Hearts on January 19, 2013.

In October 2011, Tony was diagnosed with a terminal illness that has at least three names, but only one wretched outcome. Amyotrophic Lateral Sclerosis (ALS) or

Motor Neurone Disease, is also known in the USA (where we all now live) as Lou Gehrigs Disease. The disease was identified in 1939 as¬ the reason for the debilitation and sudden loss of form by the New York Yankees baseball player.

Tony has been an active sportsman all his life: rugby, basketball, cricket, judo and gymnastics featured early in his life, but it was as a football goalkeeper and centre half that he truly found his métier. He played for Berkshire schools as goalkeeper, and in one England Schools FA game, prevented a young striker called Rio Ferdinand from

scoring. However, as with many keepers, Tony was convinced he was an even better outfield player. Unlike almost other goalies though, he was absolutely right: he was recruited to College in the USA as a centre back.

Tony has the same strain of ALS that claimed the lives of Celtic players Jimmy Johnstone & John Cushley. For Tony, it all began with a small but persistent muscle spasm in his upper right arm which defied initial medical diagnosis. A series of tests over 4 months confirmed our worst fears. He has now lost the use of his arms and hands,

CELTIC QUICK NEWS ROLL OF HONOUR 2013-14

HAT COLD AY IN ANUARY

"The first person who came up to us was eil Lennon himself, just after he finished his elevision interviews. He was funny, thoughtful, caring and very personable..."

while walking is only possible with great difficulty and he is largely confined to a specially adapted chair at home. He uses eye control to use his PC which is his only real mode of communication. Despite all of this, Tony continues to face life with fortitude and humour. When relatives from the UK recently visited him, he told them that his "weightlifting career was probably over now". One of his favourite moments since he was diagnosed was when he

arranged to meet James Johnstone, son of Jimmy, at Celtic Park in 2012. Never having previously met, the rendezvous point on matchday seemed a problem until James simply said "I'll see you at my Dad's statue."

The prospect of a trip to see Celtic play at Celtic Park has always brought a smile to his face, but the January 2013 trip was special. In view of his deteriorating condition, it would in all likelihood be his last visit to see his beloved Celtic play in Glasgow. I shamelessly contacted Paul Brennan and asked if he could suggest anything that might help make the trip even better. Paul contacted the club, simply

relaying Tony's story and the purpose of the trip. He warned me that the club get many such approaches and that it was entirely possible that nothing at all would happen.

On January 17, we left Charlotte, North Carolina, and travelling via Newark, New Jersey arrived in Glasgow at 7.30am on Friday January 18. Our Sunday morning return flight meant that we would spend two whole days in Glasgow! We indulged ourselves a wee bit though by paying for the complete hospitality package for the game. It would make for easier access for Tony and allow him & us to perhaps see or meet some of his heroes.

WEE BIG GEORGES FAN CLUB • CHARLES KICKHAM • HANKRAY

"Celtic jerseys are not second best...

After an expensive visit to the Celtic shop, and a fine meal in the Walfrid, we stood up to make our way to our seats for the kick off only to be confronted by a smiling man. Iain Jamieson (insert job title) introduced himself, and then astounded all of us by asking Tony if he would like to make the halftime Paradise Windfall draw on the pitch. Once Iain realized the extent of Tony's disability, he readily invited all of us to accompany him onto the field.

We sat down in the directors' box (seated next to men from Juventus who scribbled furiously throughout) and watched as Celtic scored two goals from Hooper & Samaras. Just before half time, we got the nod and made our way to the tunnel area, and stood like four dazzled school kids as the sweating players drifted past us to the changing room. We were waved on to the pitch, and, as we walked to the centre circle, the strains of Fields resonated round the stands. Somehow, we all managed to retain our composure as Martin helped Tony draw the winning ticket, and soon the lucky winner stumbled out of the North Stand to collect his winnings. He looked every bit as dazed as we felt.

We posed for official photographs and then took some of our own before resuming our seats. The Italians had left by now and Celtic completed their business scoring two second half goals. At full time, we had just returned to our table when Iain's staff invited us down

to tunnel/changing room area. Quite unable to believe what was happening, we took our 125th Anniversary strip with us in the hope that we could get some players to sign it. The reality exceeded our expectations.

The first person who came up to us was Neil Lennon himself, just after he finished his television interviews. He was funny, thoughtful, caring and very personable: telling Tony that he looked in good enough shape to train with the first team and that maybe Tony could shake things up a bit for him. He happily posed for photographs which we all treasure. Then, the changing room door swung open and the players drifted out, young & not so young, new and less so. Charlie Mulgrew, Victor Wanyama, Joe Ledley, Emilio Izzaguire, Scott Brown, Dylan McGeouch, Adam Matthews, and new signing, Tom Rogic. Kenny McKay also took the time to speak having also just joined Celtic TV, but two older men took our attention. Johann Mjalby signed the shirt and , for reasons that escape me, impressed Tony's Mum, while Lisbon Lion John Clark was a character. When I asked him to sign the shirt, he drily replied "I will if you really want me too." I told him that I had been at the 1965 Hampden Cup Final when we started the Stein era by beating Dunfermline 3-2. He looked unimpressed, but smiled a wee bit and then signed the strip anyway. We all smiled a lot that week-end, and still do when we reflect on how Celtic made Tony feel so very special on

that cold day in January.

Thank you Celtic, Iain Jamieson & Paul Brennan.

Tony has his own blogsite at www.dontshrink.com. The title has many roots: it refers to Jock Stein's comment that Celtic jerseys don't shrink to fit the player: to the nature of Tony's disease that deprives muscles of nerve stimulus until they gradually shrink to uselessness. It is too a reminder to all of us not to shrink from this disease or those who suffer from it. It could also quite easily be the shout from the team before every match. Don't Shrink!

STAN

When there are 60,000 inside Celtic Park the atmosphere is always electric. Yet the biggest crowd of the season was not here for a competitive first team match but to honour a Celtic legend and to raise a vast sum of money for charity. The Celtic way.

Celtic know how to put on a show. And at the Stiliyan Petrov's charity match, the world could see just how special a football club we have. For Stan there was a heart felt outpouring of love, support and admiration for him and his family.

The guests included Celtic supporter John Terry, former manager Martin O'Neill, Celtic legends Kenny Dalglish, Paul Lambert and Henrik Larsson plus from the game down south the likes of Jamie Redknapp, Gareth Barry, Gabriel Agbonlahor plus many more. Their presence was testimony to Petrov's popularity in the game and Celtic, Aston Villa and Bulgaria were all well represented at the match, which raised funds for Stan's new leukaemia charity as well as some local charities in Glasgow.

Gabriel Agbonlahor's no nonsense challenge on One Direction's Louis Tomlinson and the pop star's subsequent vomiting generated global headlines. Indeed more than a few supporters would have been surprised at the level of support for this young popstar – his band apparently are the biggest thing since the Beatles!

Celtic know how to put on a show. And at the Stiliyan Petrov's charity match, the world could see just how special a football club we have.

But the day was all about Stan. As the fans sang YNWA and his family joined him on the pitch, there were few dry eyes in the stadium. Stan left Celtic seven years earlier to join Martin O'Neill's Aston Villa in the Premier League in England. By the time he was forced to retire, another Celtic legend, Paul Lambert was his manager at Aston Villa. The Villa fans too deserve a special mention for their support given to Stan since the very beginning of this terrible illness.

CORKCELT · WEEFRATHETIM · GLENDALYSTONSILSCELTIC MAC

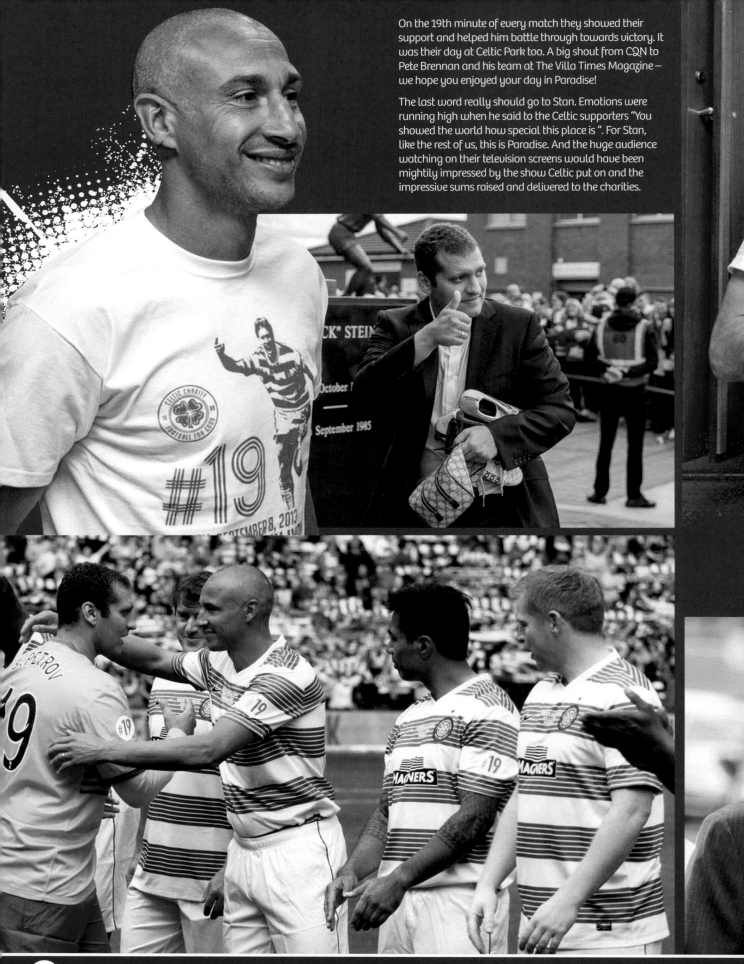

On the 19th minute of every match they showed their support and helped him battle through towards victory. It was their day at Celtic Park too. A big shout from CQN to Pete Brennan and his team at The Villa Times Magazine – we hope you enjoyed your day in Paradise!

The last word really should go to Stan. Emotions were running high when he said to the Celtic supporters "You showed the world how special this place is ". For Stan, like the rest of us, this is Paradise. And the huge audience watching on their television screens would have been mightily impressed by the show Celtic put on and the impressive sums raised and delivered to the charities.

A TRIP TO KAZAKHS

As one door shuts another one opens for Leftybhoy as he joins a select few Celtic supporters who, faithful through and through, followed the team to Kazakhstan...

The door with the opportunity to fly with the team shut late one night and the next morning another one opens. With a minute to spare before a 09.00 deadline a quiet unassuming Royal Mail postman delivers my Kazakhstani Visa application to the Embassy and the next door opens.

The door to book flights, hotels and arrange Worldwide travel cover opens up and the Champions League playoff first leg awaits. Surprisingly trips to Kazakhstan aren't covered by European travel insurance and I need to upgrade. So UEFA tell us Kazakhstan are in Europe and Insure & Go tell me otherwise? This must be the lateral movement that causes the Peter Lawwell to have sleepless nights. Now I understand!

A few days after Aberdeen are put to the sword we are on our way to Asia to see Celtic in Europe. A few stop offs on the way and before you know it we meet PaultheTim in Astana airport and we jump into a taxi at a ridiculous hour on Tuesday morning and head for a few hours' sleep.

TAN

A rendezvous at a nearby hotel and the elusive match tickets are acquired. A great opportunity to meet some old friends and make some new ones. Time to soak up the stunning views, some sunshine and enjoy a pre-match refreshment or two. Happy days! Or so I thought.

The centre of Astana very much had a western feel - vibrant, affluent with a splattering of large video screens on the buildings advertising top of the range cars to luxury apartments. With skyscraper office blocks and top end hotels with marble kerbstones this very much is one side of Asia.

Just outside the Astana Arena we saw the other side, a small shanty town with residents who clearly didn't share the wealth which was so apparent in the centre of town. Sights like this bring it home how poverty is still an issue which needs addressed.

The stadium itself looked fairly new, the shape of it reminded me of Tynecastle, thankfully we were made welcome here though

Throughout the day the locals were friendly and genuinely warm. Many requests for photos with us and heartfelt wishes "Thank you for visiting our country. Please enjoy your stay" was the response of the locals.

The stadium itself looked fairly new, the shape of it reminded me of Tynecastle, thankfully we were made welcome here though. Their fans like their Mexican waves, were excited every time their team made it over the half way line and generally made a lot of noise but not much singing if that makes sense?

Post-match was a hasty retreat into town. The bus journey back was an experience in itself. All of us crammed into a bus which was already bursting at the seams. Squeezed in and not a bit of air. Now I know what it's like to be a sardine! And despite all this the locals still manage to squeeze in another photo opportunity with us.

Analysis in the Chilli Peppers Bar was upbeat considering what we had just witnessed. The table next to us was occupied by the match officials and other members of the UEFA delegation who gave the impression that they would have rather been in our country.

On hearing news of our whereabouts Celtic director Brian Wilson took a detour around town and came and shook everyone's hand, personally thanked us for attending, then insisting on buying the entire company a drink. It was a genuine gesture from a genuine Celtic fan.

By the time the post-match analysis was complete it was the wrong side of 4.00am and some of us headed for some much needed beauty sleep. Others were starting their long journey home with the first flight

out for a few of the Bhoys scheduled for 06.30. Ouch!

The long journey home was mainly about a determination not to let 90 minutes spoil an otherwise pleasant trip and looking forward to Inverness game on Saturday. The feeling from the guys who were at the game in Kazakhstan was that we can overturn the result at a packed Celtic Park. With the will of the fans pushing the players on, Celtic can do it. By the time you read this you'll already know if we made it through.

Keep The Faith.

SEVILLE FROM C2N

COMING SOON

CATHEDRAL VIEW • OWEN • FANADPATRIOT • SPONSORED BY CHEETAH

HE BHOYS
HO CRIED
WOLF
R GET YOUR WITS
T FOR THE GHIRLS!

The reaction to the two blonde physiotherapists from Sweden set off an interesting debate among the Celtic support...

When these two sports professionals entered the field of play at Celtic Park they were certainly noticed! Wolf whistles and apparently some crude comments followed. Was this light hearted banter and just a bit of fun or was it offensive, sexist and unacceptable? An online debate raged the next few days after at Angela Haggerty, a prominent Scottish journalist, blogger and Celtic supporter noted her outrage in her own blog. You can read this blog posting here:

http://angelahaggerty.com/get-your-wits-out-for-the-ghirls/

We've noted some of the points that Angela makes below, and it is also worth reading the 80 or so comments on her blog. From my own point of view, we were sitting in the South Stand front and we had group of five boys aged between 11 and 18 plus myself. None of us heard any comments whatsoever along the lines outlined by Angela and the appearance of the girls and the reaction to them by the supporters seemed to be lighthearted, good natured although a little politically incorrect. The boys certainly enjoyed having their schoolboy banter about the girls – nothing obscene – and one of the boys had made an error in expressing a preference for the third "girl" who turned out to be the Elfsborg blonde haired pony-tailed substitute!

So what did Angela have to say on the behaviour of the supporters?

"It seems a juvenile minority of fans just can't stop themselves screaming sexually explicit statements at women in a football stadium" Angela observed.

She also noted that "before the Elfsborg physios took to the pitch, another woman from the Elfsborg staff warmed up not far from my seat along with two of the squad's players. She was subjected to the same nature of comments from the guys around me. She kept her head turned towards the pitch and never once looked in our fans' direction as she was goaded."

Later she noticed a tweet from a Celtic Underground writer who had witnessed the same behaviour. He was appalled by it too. It prompted her to put out a tweet of her own reporting what she had heard.

"The response was one of incredible fury that I had dared suggest women may deserve a little more respect"

Angela believes that Celtic supporters would not accept racist or sectarian abuse of any player, opposition player, member of staff, fan or visitor to Celtic Park "so why are women fair game among those who pride themselves on their progressive Celtic values?"

She continued "for those who are stamping their feet because people like me want to "take the fun out" of football", I'd suggest

therapy for you if indulging in occasional sexual harassment is necessary for you to enjoy yourself."

She concludes by saying that "Celtic Park is a women-friendly place, but a few men in Paradise need to learn manners."

When the dust had settled a little, we asked the supporters on the CQN Magazine Facebook page for their views and these are expressed below.

The general consensus seems to be that anything beyond wolf whistle is unacceptable. We even include a little cameo role from a Zombie who strayed onto the page and the put down at the end is excellent. Enjoy and Bhoys, mind your manners when there are ladies present!

THE VIEW FROM CQN MAGAZINE'S FACEBOOK PAGE

Simple answer to this. What would you shout if it was your daughter walking past ? These girls are someones daughter. Grow up. **(Blaise Pheln)**

FFS! Cut out the wolf-whistles lads. That's not allowed at Celtic Park! We'll be fecken blessing ourselves entering Celtic Park shortly. No farting either. What a thoroughly enjoyable experience it is at Celtic Park nowadays, Jeez! **(Stephen Reid)**

All I'm saying is its a good job McAvennie isn't playin with us anymore! **(Joss Duffy)**

He'd have feigned injury for a rub down! **(Criostoir de Piondargas)**

All these PC f*****s need to get a sense of humour. **(John McKenna)**

We are in danger of completely over sanitizing football. **(John Carlin)**

I think Elfsborg are a very lucky football team to have such fine professionals! What's the stats on groin injuries at that club??

More than any other club in world football I bet **(Craig Douglas)**

Gawd sake you are talking about a bunch of Gleswegian men who have probably had a couple of pints before the match. I know I struggle to make out half of what my bhoy says when he is like that! **(Judith Wooder)**

They were on Twitter saying they enjoyed all the attention. **(Paddy Whyte)**

Considering the highlighting of casual sexism on Twitter I have to say that as a woman reading some of the comments about these women I was left feeling a bit disappointed. Surely to goodness in this day and age a bit of respect? Next time you feel the need to make a remark about a woman based on how she looks as opposed to how she does her job think how your sister/ mother /niece/daughter would feel if they had studied or trained for years to achieve their employment and then are treated like window dressing. Peeved I tell you! **(Helen Traquair Loughran)**

People need to lighten up.The PC brigade really need to get a life! **(Gerry McGhee)**

Ah dont think there is too much wrong with wolf whistles but by all accounts the remarks were out of order. I think a good standard to work with would be to decide if you would like your wife, girlfriend or daughter treated the way they were. **(Kev Dickson)**

Shut down the section guilty of the wolf whistles. They can do it to other sections they disapprove of! **(Tam Mannion)**

Harmless banter, if they didn't mind then what's the fuss? As long as they were home in time to make their husbands supper I don't see a problem! **(Raymond Connor)**

As a wise man once remarked in a similar situation I witnessed," Man, you'd think fitba fans never get their h*** or something! **(Edward Anthony Coyle)**

Females entering a traditionally male dominated arena should be thick skinned enough to take the chants of the terraces.

In today's highly PC scrutinised world the utopia is everyone sitting down and being obedient; f*** that; banter, chants and wind ups add to the spice. So , ladies, grow a set. And may I add, the lemon curd on the right would look superb in her evening wear! **(Graeme Gillies)**

Blah blah blah. Welcome to Glasgow banter and humour. (Aldo Bove)

What I'd give for a wolf whistle! lol x
(Audrey Horan-Buchanan)

Hibs seemingly interested in signing both! *(Steven Rintoul)*

The reaction to it by certain "journalists" was an absolute disgrace! Would rather blog about it than challenge the offenders! There is no way hundreds of fans shouted/sang obscene comments all at the same time! All I heard was whistles and laughter! Complete over reaction. I had a twitter debate with the journalist in question she accused me of attacking her when I asked if she had challenged the offender, reported him to a steward or write to Celtic! There was nothing in 406 . *(Helen Dunese)*

They're barkin! I thought they were gonna be stunning the way everybody's been goin' on! *(Neil Young)*

Blah blah blah. Welcome to Glasgow banter and humour. *(Aldo Bove)*

Better than most Weegie 'burds', tbf. Not that most of us would even stand a chance with these two... *(Mark McCoy)*

I don't know what the crude comments were, but there is no need for them. However the wolf whistle etc is just a bit of fun. *(Peter McKenzie)*

Welcome to Scotland. *(Cary Griffin)*

Just attention-seeking, self-appointed spokespeople for the fans who got their knickers in a twist about it. It did raise a chuckle though when one was clamped over their previous tweets regarding Sammy. *(John Tolan)*

What about the Beatles, Osmonds And Boy Bands? Attacked by adoring fans clothes ripped assaulted etc if boys did that to the Spice Girls or other girl bands they would get jailed double standards most lassies love to get whistled at. *(James Gordon)*

Gillie 99% of the girls at football would agree with your sentiments, unfortunately the Internet gives the 1% a disproportionately large platform to air their views of how all male football fans are b*******.

Incidentally I have two sisters, two daughters a wife & a mother. If that's the worst thing they endure in their life I will die a happy man *(Colin Paterson)*

Since a group of women of various quality, heading to a hen weekend, wolf whistled at me on a flight to Majorca, one saying

she would like to rub sun tan lotion on me, I have been deeply traumatized and now wear 14 layers and a balaclava. Yours truly offended but slightly flattered really . *(Terry McCann)*

I'm taking back my wolf whistles , looking at these photos close up they look like a pair of spanners. *(John Manning)*

Wonder how many of the wolf whistlers would laugh it off if a half cut macho show off wolf whistled at their wife/girlfriend/sister/daughter.....ah what a laugh dear... that's just banter.
Or would they aggressively instruct the macho whistler to stop?
The irony of saying its OK but mocking a now dead club for its out of date attitudes. *(David Richardson)*

Stupid macho behaviour. *(Joachim Hacker)*

I say they are doing there job so feckin let them. Just like everybody else. It demonstrates a lack of respect/class... *(Harry Caulfield)*

Just asked my wife her view on it she said "it didn't really matter what they looked like they were woman and wolf whistles they would expect, but get your tits out for the lads went a bit far". They're you have it. Now I'll be wolf whistling at the beach all tomorrow. Sorry PC brigade. *(Tony Gibson)*

Are we serious here? Has a 1960's feel to this argument. If two big hunky men appeared unexpectedly at a well attended women's sporting event you'd get the same in reverse. No big deal. *(Lawrence mcNeill)*

Pathetic laddish behaviour that needs to be dropped. *(Criostoir de Piondargas)*

I am sure it was all light hearted but am sure the if they heard some of the rudeness then for them that's unacceptable so a tricky one.
(Fearghal Kane)

How many females have commented on the guy candy on the field.... maybe the odd hen night .. chippendales etc... Hope the pc brigade don't friend me - they might report my pics of Michelle Keegan in a bikini.
(Bernie Kilkie)

wit you exspect fi that mob o halfwits
(Zombie comment)

The word is expect ya halfwit! *(Kev Dickson)*

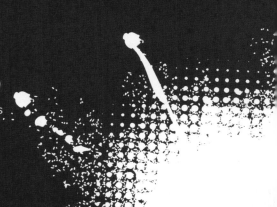

KEEPING THE LEGEND ALIVE

"As long as it's got green and white hoops any number between 1 and 11 will do me. I'd even settle for 12 or 13 sometimes. Numbers don't bother me, as long as I'm playing for Celtic." *Johnny Doyle, 1980*

A LONE WOLFS TONES · ATTICUSFINCH · WEEFRATHETIM · J67

Football fans, and especially Celtic supporters, are renowned for treasuring the memories and stories of the great players and matches, but a special place is always reserved for those footballers whose love for their club shines through. And none more so when they've supported that club from a young age.

Johnny Doyle was one such Celtic player. After his tragic death in October 1981 the headline in the Celtic View read 'And That Mighty Heart Lies Still'. More than 2000 people walked behind the hearse at his funeral in Kilmarnock. Only a year earlier Johnny had scored a fantastic header against Real Madrid in the European Cup and won a Scottish Cup winner's medal in the defeat against Rangers that led to the infamous Hampden Riot. His untimely death caused grief beyond his family to his team-mates, friends and thousands of Celtic supporters who'd seen his commitment shine through. To that support Johnny Doyle was simply one of them – a bhoy who, like his close friend Tommy Burns, lived the dream of wearing the green-and-white hoops.

One of the traditional ways in which the Celtic support have demonstrated their love for their heroes, living and past, has been through banners. A century ago, the fore-runner of modern supporters clubs were brake clubs and the centrepiece of the carriage those fans drove on their way to games was the banner – one of Tom Maley, from the club's first decade, still hangs in Baird's Bar. In 2006, as the 25th anniversary of Johnny Doyle's death approached, the Jungle Bhoys supporters group organised a fundraiser in MacConnell's bar in Glasgow city centre to raise monies for a banner in his honour. In attendance that night were Johnny's sister Anne-Marie and his daughter Joanna. With their help a memorial booklet of Johnny was produced which, along with the fundraising night and specially-made postcard, helped raise the necessary monies for the banner – which was proudly unfurled on the 21st October 2006 at Celtic Park before a game against Motherwell.

Five years later, the recently-formed Celtic Graves Society organised a ceremony at Johnny's graveside in Kilmarnock which was attended by his family, including his children Jason and Joanna, and former team-mates Danny McGrain, Peter Latchford, Dom Sullivan, George McCluskey and Lisbon Lion Bobby Lennox. Jim Scanlon of Charlie and the Bhoys played The Johnny Doyle Song at the graveside and, after that day's game at Rugby Park, the band played a gig in Johnny's honour back in Glasgow.

By that time the Jungle Bhoys had stopped

organising activities at Celtic Park and their last act was to use their remaining funds to set up a permanent, online memorial to Johnny in time with his 30th anniversary. The web address www.johnnydoyle.com was purchased, a site was designed and a Facebook page was also created – all in co-operation with Johnny's daughter Joanna.

Johnnydoyle.com launched on 19th October 2011 with a biography of this "running, tackling, up-and-down one man riot", galleries of pictures of Johnny in the Hoops, with his family, with Status Quo (!), quotes, downloads and an audio-visual page containing clips of Johnny's greatest moments in action. The Facebook page, originally designed in support of the website, has developed a character all of its' own

– with almost 1,500 friends it has helped unearth a mass of stories and pictures of Johnny from the support that many in Johnny's family hadn't heard or seen of before. Joanna Doyle's own interaction with the Facebook page has been one of the reasons behind its success.

Just back from following the Celts in Turin, Joanna recalled what it was like as a young girl before and after her father passed away: "I wasn't that aware of much in the early days as I was only 3 when he died. I do however remember him taking me to Parkhead and the team all shaking my hand! At that point however I had absolutely no idea of what my dad's profession was. As I got older, things became a lot clearer through the media and newspaper clippings etc. (which I still have) and I realised that my Dad had indeed been quite a well known footballer!"

As a Celtic fan, what does it mean to you to know how revered your Dad still is by the Celtic support? "It means everything. There are no words to describe the enormity of pride felt to know that your dad is still so widely idolised and missed this long down the line after his passing. That being the case, however, just sums up the Celtic supporters perfectly. That is what makes them special - and the best fans in the world. They never forget their own and keep in their hearts the pride and love for their club and all those past and present who have shown that same love and loyalty back to them. My dad always said that he loved playing for Celtic and that he would be content to sit on the bench for Celtic as long as it was them he was playing for. If those options were exhausted then he would be back in the stands with his Celtic scarf and the fans. He was a fan first and a player second, and that would never change.

Joanna confirmed that the impetus for keeping the memory of her Dad alive didn't just come from fans based in Scotland and Ireland: "We have many treasured friends from all over Italy known as The Italian Celts. They're a wonderful group of ghuys who are utterly devoted to the club even from hundreds of miles away. They visit Glasgow regularly and you only need to speak with them for a few seconds to know how utterly in love with Celtic they are. I came to meet them through the chairman of their club after a video was posted on You Tube of a group of them visiting my dad's grave. They arranged a mass over in Glasgow to mark the 30th year of my dad's passing and it is an absolute honour to know them."

The arrival and predominance of the internet was a key factor in fans abroad learning more about Johnny's life and heroics in the Hoops. Joanna recalled that she jumped at the chance to get something up and running online in her Dad's memory: "I had always wanted to make a website but did not have the first clue about where to start! There was no internet when my dad passed and so nothing to permanently keep his memory going which everyone had access to, so the website was the perfect way to do that – especially the stuff that we had in the family, some of which which had been used for the memorial booklet. On a website it was possible to put even more of our pictures and cuttings up though. I love the Facebook page because it's a great

way to interact and keep his memory going. Everyone has so much to share and I have met so many people through the page it's unbelievable. I love to hear as many stories and memories as I can from as many people as possible to add to all the wonderful memories of my own that I already have. I've been on Facebook myself for a few years but I think the wee man has more pals than me already!" (It's worth noting that Joanna's a fair bit taller than wee Johnny was!)

We asked Joanna if she had much footage of Johnny in action: "I have a videotape of a few of his games, which was recorded from home off the television so it makes it even more personal. It is a lot easier to access footage these days since the internet and you tube took off. It is through those sources that I have come to meet a multitude of fans from all over the world including the Italian Celts. I am still searching for a recording of him speaking

however, which unfortunately I have had no luck with. I would love to hear how he sounds as sadly that memory has disappeared through time."

Hopefully this is something that Celtic supporters reading the article or visiting Johnny's website can help to rectify as Joanna says: "The website is fantastic and hopefully through this article it will spread the word to let people know there is one out there. There is a part of it which I would like to see constantly being added to and that is the page for fans to submit stories, experiences or memories of my Dad. The family think it is amazing and it has taken off in such a big way in such a short space of time. To us that tells us just what an impact my dad had on the Celtic support. I am so utterly privileged to be his daughter. God Bless him."

www.johnnydoyle.com

www.facebook.com/johnny.doyle.735

johnnydoyle.com
the man who loved the green

"they arranged a mass over in Glasgow to mark the 30th year of my dad's passing and it is an absolute honour to know them"

NO, I'M NEIL LENNON "I'LL NEVER WALK ALONE" (FOURSTONECOPPI)

WHAT THE MANAGER SAID...

NEIL LENNON'S AFTER MATCH COMMENTS AFTER EACH OF THE OPENING THREE CHAMPIONS LEAGUE MATCHES...

MILAN STEAL THE POINTS

We dominated for long periods. I said to the players that when you're on top, you need to take your chances. I thought we were brilliant. Sometimes in football you don't get what you deserve. I couldn't see Milan scoring in the second half. It's funny you say that you have come away to San Siro and end up disappointed that you've been beaten. I'm very disappointed because we played well for a long time in the match and we were the better team. We didn't want to leave without three points. We were confident and had a lot of chances, so there is regret. We have done enough in terms of performance, of course, and our goalkeeper wasn't very busy during the second half.

I'm proud of my team. We were confident and had a good mindset. We have to face Barcelona, it will not be easy, but we want to compete with all these teams.

NEIL LENNON

BARCELONA INCHES FROM A REPEAT DEFEAT

I thought our shape was good and we limited Barcelona to very few chances until the sending-off and goal. We could have passed the ball better in the first half but in the second we were a lot better. For 25 minutes we were, I won't say equal, but comfortable.

My initial reaction [to Charlie Mulgrew's miss] was that it was in – but it flashed past the post. It was a great opportunity and you don't get many. Of course two minutes later Cesc Fàbregas scores the winner, so the game has hinged on those five minutes.

They'll be really disappointed that for all their efforts they didn't get something out of the game but they can take satisfaction and pride that they are competing, and competing well, against the toughest group in the Champions League.

LEFTHANDPILLAROLDJUNGLE • THE CLASS OF 67 • NEUSTADT-BRAW

I'm pleased with the result in Amsterdam [a 1-1 draw between AFC Ajax and AC Milan]. The double-header with Ajax, if we have any aspirations to qualify, is pivotal. NEIL LENNON

CELTIC WIPE THE FLOOR WITH AJAX

I said Ajax would give us as many problems as Barcelona and AC Milan and they did. That's a fantastic win for us. We are on our knees in terms of injuries in our squad, so it was a monumental effort from the lads. We grew into the game and, but for a few breakaways towards the end, could have won it more comfortably.

James keeps telling me he's never missed a penalty so with Kris out he kept his cool. It was a big moment and came at a good time. We were anxious at times in the first half, but as the second half went on we got better and thoroughly deserved to win. It leaves us in a very good position. We have to get a result at Ajax if we can. It'll be difficult, but on tonight's evidence not beyond us. It is a massive win in the context of the group.

We could have seen the game out more comfortably for my liking but it's our 19th game of the season, it was a heroic effort. We can compete with a lot of clubs at this level. We've been in every game and that's no mean feat with the calibre of teams against us. We've given ourselves a great chance now.

NEIL LENNON

FIELDOFDRAMS · PAPA JOHN · CELTICROLLERCOASTER · FRANTIC07

WHO BOOE[D] WEE FERG[IE]

C2N Magazine's Facebook page asked this question last month...

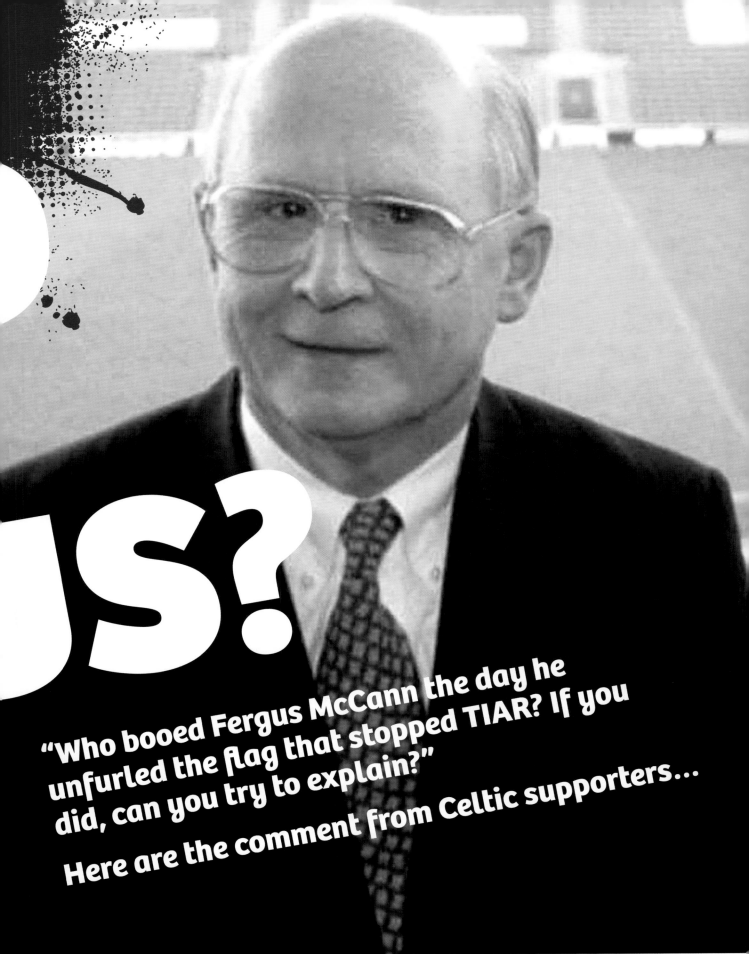

US?

"Who booed Fergus McCann the day he unfurled the flag that stopped TIAR? If you did, can you try to explain?"

Here are the comment from Celtic supporters...

HIGGS BOSUN · DIM SAM · AWE NAW NO ANNONI OAN ANAW NOO

Stephen Mullen - Easy, two word answer: Tommy Burns!

Chris Quinn - Never have, never will boo anyone while they are representing Celtic. Not a player, board member or any other member of staff.

Stephen Finch - I had this discussion with a mate of mine who hated him. He hated him for allegedly saying the fans were bigots rather than the issues with Tommy Burns.

I must admit I didn't know anything about those supposed comments.

The Bunnet doesn't get the recognition in our history he deserves IMO.

Joe Paterson - The treatment of Tommy Burns, and I'll tell you what, the memories still haven't faded with time and neither has my willingness to forgive or forget.

Bryan John Foley - I never booed personally but the ones who did probably subscribed to the media notion that Fergus was a tight wad who never followed Rangers(1872-2012) path to destruction.

Neil Young - Remember Jock Brown!

Kevin Brewer - Hail Hail The Bunnet. He sank RFC.

Jim Mulholland - I didn't boo, but I was in the main stand around ones that did. I remember seeing Tommy Boyd do the "gonny calm it" hand gesture to the crowd when they booed just as Fergus took the microphone. I think it was because they saw him as responsible for Wim Jansen leaving and not making any big signings. He liked keeping hold of his "One Thin Dimes," I seem to recall, but the booing was disrespectful in light of how he stepped up to save us when no-one else would,

Gerry Diamond - He was booed as he was trying to replace Celtic's Irish heritage with a more Scottish one. He had mentioned this publicly & had also tried to canvas support within the executive club.

The next time he addressed the fans he saw the error of his way & proclaimed 'the Irish flag will always fly above Celtic park'.

Fergus saved Celtic & I'd name the north stand after him!

Kevin McGoldrick - He was booed because of the way the Irish supporters were treated .

Damien MacAodha - I never booed. However people were angry at the treatment of Tommy Burns and the treatment of Wim Jansen. Celtic Football Club should not be solely about producing results (be it on the park or on the balance sheet). I like many other fans felt that Celtic owed these men much more than the treatment they received. The instability also robbed Celtic of the chance to build upon the progress and achievements the club made during the tenure of Burns and Jansen.

Garry Mccloskey - Like him or dislike him. He saved our club and he should be recognised. Name North Stand after him in my opinion. Without him stepping up we wouldn't have what we have today

Paul McMenemy - at that time I did boo. I was wrong .

Rab McCready - the man wi the bunnet dunnit, he did everythin' he said he'd do, & did that well, he was a business man, not an out & out football man, he made mistakes, e.g the Tommy Burns carry on, among others, but the club we know & love wouldn't be here in it's present state if it wiznae 4 him, hat aff tae the bunnet !!!!

James Campbell - Ashamed to say I did. Back then the media IMO intentionally tried and succeeded to divide the support, and because online sites like CQN were not yet around, the media was the only conduit for 'news'.

Barry Gallagher - Bhoys against bigotry, when we never had any bigotry.

Stevie Mac - Sometimes I question myself as a Celtic fan. Wondering why I don't go along with other fans point of view. Fergus made some very unpopular decisions but he made them for the club, not to p*** the fans off. At the end of the day he was/is a businessman and stuck to his business plan - to right the club and walk away again. He did that.

If you booed you are an absolute disgrace to the club

Stephen Lynch

He hired some people that some of us disagreed with, he cut players when they got demanding, he didn't bow to every supporters wishes and would retaliate. He was tough but that is business. Because of that, we are where we are. In the future, more unpopular decisions will happen at the club by others. We've already seen fans booing John Reid, booing Neil Lennon, booing players, booing Dermot and as always criticising the lack of spending. Yet in all of this, we have survived and gotten stronger in what is a very poor league. This was all instigated by Fergus. I never booed anyone at Celtic in my life. That won't change. If you do decide to boo, ask yourself why am I booing? Could there be another reason for this unpopular decision other than my own selfish point of view?

At that time I did boo. I was wrong.

Paul McMenemy

Sean McLaughlin - Some of these comments are ridiculous. Without him there wouldn't be a Celtic or Larsson or Lambert the list goes on. I can remember asking my Dad why are people booing and his words were because son some people are morons.

Colin Stephen - I wasn't happy with him for multiple reasons and especially for not signing big when trying to stop them getting 10iar, if we never stopped them doing that I honestly don't know if I would've forgiven him as he was getting plenty of money back at the time from the fans. But looking back to the day we stopped 10iar was probably the greatest day in my life and I agree he does deserve something named after him for saving our club and for choosing to pay the bills instead of doing what RFC have done, for that and building the stadium he deserves enormous credit.

Stephen Mcmaihin - I can honestly say yes I booed. Back then I thought he was penny pinching whilst the newco's oldco were spending like there was no tomorrow. It was only when they went bust last year that I understood why Fergus did what he had to do.

Brian Booth - I booed and my reasons were that, just like today, he allowed some of our support to be vilified. Remember the banner: "We're Irish, were catholic, we're Celtic fans, but were no bigots Mr McCann".......... I'd do it again and again!

Hugh McGarrigle - I didn't boo him and it was because he delivered what he said he would. He put plans in place for a new stadium, he put a team to be proud of on the park and left a legacy that lets us compete in the higher echelons of European competition.

Lawrence McNeill - Just the usual social sheepery. Boo-ing happens like a domino effect. Half of them probably didn't have anything against the man.

Gary Shek - I did boo wee Fergus that day. Because I was young and daft and read the Daily Record. Believed its lies and thus booed the number. However I did spend 1400 quid buying 500 shares from him which are now worth nowhere near. So I reckon we're even

Kevin McLaughlin - It was 15 years ago - the club has changed and moved on an awful lot since then. Of course Ferguson saved Celtic and no one can ever say otherwise - he took the risk but also left with a big fat cheque in his sky rocket !!! Celtic were as good for Fergus mcCann as he was for Celtic.

James Campbell - Looking back, Fergus saved the club and stopped 10 in a row. I was sad the day he sacked TB, but it WAS the right decision, would Tommy have stopped them doing 10? I don't know. Look at the man's legacy of his time at CP, he saved the club at the 11th hour (can you remember the feeling when the news broke? I shed a tear or two). He

built us a Stadium to be proud of. He took on the SFA and won (Farrygate) and he stopped the cloven hoofed ones from beating our record. Hail Fergus

Stephen Reid - Surely you never bought shares for profit, Gary ? It was an emotional investment. I wasn't happy with a few things around that time. But, I never booed him. I've never booed a player in the hoops either. I have slaughtered a few though, ha ! Hail wee Fergus. He did what he said he would do, he was true to his word. He also exposed the SFA for what they are (Cadette registration.) He stood up for Celtic. He never took any nonsense. How I wish he was here today. I wonder what his take would be on the Green Brigade situation?

James Campbell - When you look at the bigger picture being revealed now, With Murray, Masterton, Cummings etc controlling the finances of Scottish football through the BOS back then, it makes Fergus's achievements more impressive. He changed banks and kept the clubs finances from prying eyes.

Stephen Lynch - If you booed you are an absolute disgrace to the club .

Wayne Mcmullan - Fergus McCann we owe you so much always be grateful.

Kevin McLaughlin - It's always great to see how opinions differ - I agree with the comments against the booing but Fergus was no angel and wasn't immune from criticism. Wim Jansen was given far more resources than Tommy Burns to buy the players

Bhoys against bigotry, when we never had any bigotry. *Barry Gallagher*

that Burns had identified - Burley, Lambert, Reiper etc. Burns also was denied the opportunity to sign the likes of Colin Cameron, Neil McCann and an Italian playmaker who's name escapes me ... Allegedly after McCann had agreed the funds. He still saved us though, Fergus.

Mick Doran - He was booed from some due to his lack of spending in the transfer market .

Michael Johnston - have to say Fergus McCann was some business man - it did not mean you had to like him !

Ross Carroll - I think McCann was a business who was very cold, ruthless and focused. He sacked TB, he sacked Wim the Tim, he employed Jock Brown, he didn't invest in the team after we stopped 10 in a row. All of the above are reasons why Celtic fans were never universally won over by him. Also, the media did their best to portray him in a negative light causing further division amongst our support. We didn't have the likes of CQN back in 1998, more is the pity!

Kevin Cherry - Got to admit least you knew what you were getting with Fergus McCann. Never bullshitted said what he wanted to do with the club, team, stadium and the debt!!! He made mistakes, ie jock Brown,Tommy Burns and penny pinching on signings,

but at least he left his calling card on Jim Farry who if he had done his job fairly , we would have won the league in '96.

Cary Griffin - I didn't boo him, but I do believe that the people that did boo him believed the utter guff which was feed to them in the papers, which we all know now was being control by Sir Minty Moonbeans - pretty simple brainwashing really .

Macky Makatak - He did what he set out to do . Can't deny that.

Peter McKenzie - After his intervention and his transparent business plan I have always been a fan and grateful to wee Fergus. I have stated for years that he is such an important part of our great history that there should be some sort of statue at Celtic Park.

Robert Donnelly - Fergus was booed because of what he did to Tommy Burns, simple fact was Tommy would not leave quietly he left by the front door. I believe if the board had a little more insight and backed the manager a little more than they did, we would have stopped them a lot sooner. That's why I booed him and for that reason only. In hindsight he was the man that changed the direction of our club and I will be forever grateful to the man now

Daniel Birrell - The fans then in my

opinion were not as educated on club finances as they are now. I didn't boo that day I was young but my dad did and he told me it was because of 'the biscuit tin' etc. Also the sacking of Tommy Burns.

Edward Anthony Coyle - I can't honestly remember, it's all a bit fuzzy but I did have a few bones of contention with him. I seem to remember many articles regarding TB and Fergus, then later Wim. He made a few mistakes but I'm sure it wasn't easy for him. I'm sure he really wasn't fussed either way.

Thomas Cochrane - Get a statue up for him. I bought the shares, season book,all the stuff .....Those were the days I can tell you. Never to be forgotten! We are where we are to-day because of the guy. Ghod bless him,Tell you what we booed that big fat"Jock Brown every chance we got!

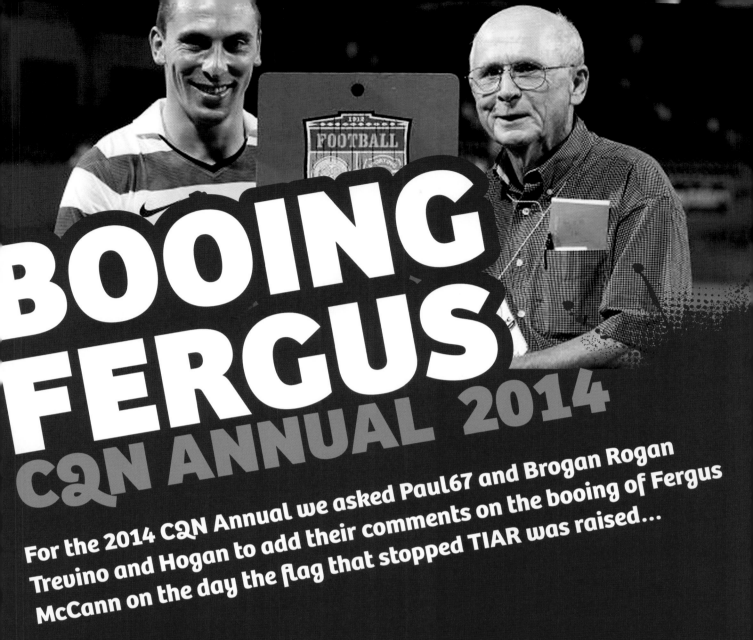

BOOING FERGUS

CQN ANNUAL 2014

For the 2014 CQN Annual we asked Paul67 and Brogan Rogan Trevino and Hogan to add their comments on the booing of Fergus McCann on the day the flag that stopped TIAR was raised...

BROGAN ROGAN TREVINO AND HOGAN

"I didn't agree with booing Fergus McCann then, and I agree with it even less now.

At the time I could not understand why fans couldn't see the difference between where the club had been and where it stood on that day when he unfurled the flag. There had been great progress made- but seemingly it wasn't enough for some in the ground.

Perhaps it was the "Three amigo's" antics, perhaps it was seen as his tight fistedness, or lack of ambition in challenging Rangers. When we look back now we have to be suspicious of the press reporting of the time and how they portrayed Fergus and his business acumen as it can be

seen now that the press' knowledge regarding football business has proven to be shocking. Further their football knowledge was pretty poor too—remember, Lubo was an embarrassment. Did the rubbish spouted by the press influence the cloud that day? Probably.

I would hope that the current fanbase would be smarter and more knowledgeable than they were back then."

PAUL67

It took until 13 years after he left until the full wisdom of Fergus McCann became evident. He left Celtic in March 1999, 10 months after unfurling the league flag at Celtic Park for the first time in a decade,

while being booed by a fraction of the support, frustrated that he hadn't authorised what some of us would regard as excessive spending. I was full of resentment at the time. For months newspapers told Celtic fans their team were being held back by a parsimonious management. What we actually had was a ruthlessly focused chief executive who delivered everything he promised before leaving us with an eminently manageable £2.5m debt. Fergus has been back on very few occasions but has always been given a rapturous reception. He avoided the limelight, declining a seat for Seville and the many cup finals, but he was here to address the Celtic Movement at the unveiling of the Br Walfrid statue and at a Celtic Charity dinner.

MHARK67 PRAYIN FOR OSCAR KNOX · SIXOCLOCKATTHECHAPEL

THE C
SHIR

Famous Celtic jerseys with very special memories for us all, collected and displayed on the fabulous Celtic Shirts website. Sit back and enjoy the memories....

ELTIC

The Celtic Shirt website was setup to showcase a number of match worn Celtic shirts from our heroes and legends that I'd been lucky enough to collect.

From a young bhoy going through the centenary season, the shirts the players wore had always fascinated me. Long sleeves!!! You couldn't buy long sleeved shirts.... Embroidered badges and not foam stick-on ones... the huge CR Smith logo... these where nothing like the Umbro replica kits you bought out of Roberts Stores!!

Player shirts where mesmerising!

1 - It took until 2008 for me to get my hands on my 1st match worn Celtic shirt and it was one of the Holy Goalies match worn shirts from the 3 in a row season. Not only a shirt worn by one of our greatest ever keepers, but a shirt worn during the season which culminated in us clinching the title at Tannadice in 2008

2 - My 2nd match worn shirt came along pretty quickly and it was David Hannah's from the memorable battle of Britain against Liverpool at Celtic Park in 1997. The atmosphere inside the ground was spine tingling as we went toe to toe with the English! I honestly believe that the spirit shown over these 2 legs set us up for the inspiring performances, which stopped 10 in a row.

Although, something still bugs me to this day... Why did no one take McManaman out?

3 - Talking of 10, who can forget the day we said cheerio to 10 in a row? With the sun shining and tears flowing, our captain, Tom Boyd lifted our first league championship since 1988 after wearing this shirt in the 2-0 win over St.Johnstone.

4 - The next big shirt that came my way was Paul McStay's 1990 League cup final shirt. The Holy Grail had been found.... Long sleeves!!!

BILLY BHOY • GORDYBHOY64 • BHOY67 • WICKLOWBHOY IN BAVARIA

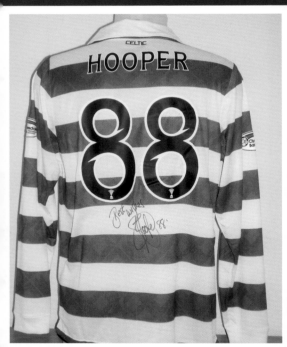

From a young bh
centenary season, th
had always fascina

The result behind the shirt is not one to dwell on, but a maestro match worn cup final shirt makes up for that. This style of shirt reminds me of growing up; watching Celtic and that is something no one can ever take away from me

5 - What could have been if John Hartson had been available to wear this shirt in the 2003 Uefa Cup Final?

A truly stunning shirt which I'm privileged to have in my collection and I'm sure it will stir many different emotions for us all from our time in Seville.

6 - Henrik Larsson's match worn shirt from the away leg v Boavista in the Uefa Cup Semi Final.

To me those words re-live Henrik's goal in slow motion. Henrik striking the ball, the keeper getting a touch, his touch not strong enough and the ball ends up nestling in back of the

net.

Queue Peter Martins radio commentary. Sheer joy... we where on our way to a European final

7 - In our 125th year of unbroken history, certain shirts in the collection make me proud as they are symbolic as to why Celtic Football Club was founded and how to this day, we still hold true to the principles Brother Walfrid laid down 125 years ago.

7.1 The National Famine Memorial Day shirts mark the tragedy of the Great Hunger (An Gorta Mor) in the 19th century when millions died or were forced to leave Ireland. Many coming to Scotland and directly related to the people in the East End of Glasgow who Brother Walfrid was committed to helping by the creation of Celtic Football Club.

7.2 The wearing of the Japanese Lettering shirts was a gesture of

ping through the
rts the players wore
me. Long sleeves!!!

support for the people of Japan and a tribute to all those who sadly lost their lives during the recent earthquake and tsunami which struck the country.

7.3 The Celtic Legends and Manchester United legends were watched by a capacity crowd at Celtic Park with a worldwide audience to raise funds for Oxfam's East Africa Appeal.

8 – Lee Naylor's match prepared shirt for the 2009 CIS League Cup Final.

In the past few Glasgow Derby Finals, we didn't have too much luck beating the club the former rangers football club, but on this day Celtic romped home with a 2-0 win.

Although Naylor wasn't in the match day squad, all members of the 1st team squad would've been issued a number of shirts for the cup final.

9 – The 2nd most popular question

people ask me is what shirt would you love to have in your collection?

To me it's between Billy McNeill's match worn shirt from the 1967 European Cup Final.

Such an iconic moment from our history that will forever live with us!

The most popular question is... How do I get all these shirts?

And the answer.... Well, That would be telling!

Hail Hail

TCS

http://www.thecelticshirt.co.uk

Twitter - @thecelticshirt

Facebook – http://www.facebook.com/thecelticshirt

ZIHUATANEJO • PAUL67 • FRED C. DOBBS • NALLY81 • SHADY • DOUGC

CELTIC
AND TH

3-14

HISTORY
THE WEB

NI · TINMHAN · HEBCELT · GREENGRAY1967 · TERRYMAC · TOMCOURTNEY

It's been so long since the Internet revolution began that really many seem to have forgotten what a change it has brought to all our lives. In Celtic circles, the profound change has been immeasurable with a fan-led presence that can surprise fans of every other club. True, most other major clubs have the forums, the article sites, the stats rooms and official club shops. However, one area definitely puts Celtic in a different sphere to the rest and that's the almost academic attention to the club's history.

I myself am one of the moderators on TheCelticWiki website, of which more later, but it is only part of an online presence of research on the club's history. The other major site is the wonderful Celtic Graves Society forum, and accompanying these sites are a myriad of dedicated sites to aspects related to our club's history that help to capture its magic (e.g. The Lisbon Lions, Belfast Celtic, Jimmy Johnstone).

The early days of online analysis

Back in the early days of the web, once a basic Celtic presence was formed on the net, the growth of forums is what I would say is what kick started the whole genre. Prior to the forums, the early sites were generally repetitive with back of the hand write ups on the club's history that delved only skin deep. In fairness there probably wasn't the bandwidth or capacity for

anything greater.

The forums were the ice breaker. Threads centring on nostalgia are a staple diet of Celtic forums, but one thing that became apparent quite soon was that these threads were more than just rehashes of old match reports. The informality of the forums allows supporters in as many or in as few a set of words to reminisce on any set of events. Take for example match days, the experience is not just the 90mins and fans are able to retell memories of the before and after the match, the good the bad, the humour the shocking and that which is long forgotten by all others.The threads captured a greater picture of the fans' experience than ever before, it was an information revolution.

Supplementing this were sites like imageshack which enabled ease of uploading and displaying of pictures. The great part of this was that old pictures in reports and photo albums could be shown for the interest of a wider set of people than ever before.

There is a catch. Forums are not a great long-term repository for information. Search functions can only work so well. Into that void is where the article sites step in which feature write-ups on players /events in a more formal format. Celtic Underground, The Lost Bhoys & E-Tims have plenty of these wonderful articles, although their

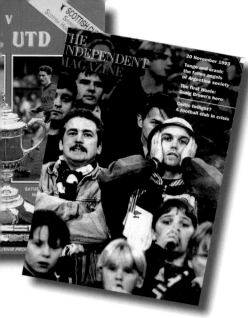

focus is current Celtic affairs and historical articles are really an extra. Strictly all the advances in Celtic research online were as a sideline from all else.

The Celtic research revolution begins

The big advance online was initiated on the kerrydalestreet forum. Moderator Fitzpas with the help of a group of people formed TheCelticWiki website (www.thecelticwiki. com). This site, for those unaware of it, is an ambitious undertaking of making a comprehensive online wikpedia on the Celtic universe, to capture as much about the club and document & list them for posterity. It's been a struggle, but personally I feel that the heavy work done on the site has paid off. It is a site that uses all sources available and transfers them to the web, taking information from books & the forums, pictures from papers and old scrapbook collections but also recording memories & anecdotes from the general support. There is also a huge amount of writing up on all aspects, be it player biogs, matches or events. Our main intention is to make them enjoyable as much as informing.

This site is a reference we feel that makes the history of the club more accessible to the general support, as it's free on the web (no adverts either) and the articles are generally in more digestible portions rather than directing people to have to go through an entire book. I'd like to hope the site helps to be a conduit that helps to get people interested to find out more and so will then seek out others sources, such as books, video or dedicated sites to discover even more.

In time, after the wiki, there came a bit of a boom in Celtic history analysis on the web (in small part due to the wiki but really a timely coincidence). This has included some excellent podcasts which have covered interviews with

ex-players or their relatives. The openness of podcasts has enabled players to open up and expand on topics & their careers in ways that are not possible in official publications, a good example of which is the George Connelly interview with The Lost Bhoys (a real coup). Even players who are not necessarily widely known have been interviewed and their input on the history of the club of their time has been invaluable, take for example the interview with Ian Young recently (again with The Lost Bhoys).

The only issue though with all the work done by everyone was there was little in the forefront and hands on for the general support. There are articles, pics and forum threads but as a support as we are, we want something more hands-on. Sites like TheCelticWiki and the rest are really in the reference and interest tools, but where was it to lead to? That was to all change with the formation "The Celtic Graves Society".

The Celtic Graves Society

Following a write up an article on the decrepit state of the gravesite of the legendary Willie Maley on TheCelticWiki site by the aptly named 'Maley's Spirit', word spread like wildfire across the forums and the response was incredible. Possibly the article generated for the first time across all the Celtic internet forums and sites a concerted focus on a single issue. In response, a set of supporters formed the Celtic Graves Society (CGS) with the wish to firstly map the gravesites of people linked to the club, and then to best service those sites to keep them in a good state.

The society have then organised regular remembrance services at the gravesites of

notable former players and staff. This provides a focus and helps to keep the name alive of the club's great players and key figures. It also means there is another practical way for people to be able to participate in to celebrate & promote the club's history. Their work has brought to life all that has been done by Celtic researchers.

Their forum (http://celticgraves.com) is a great starting place to get assistance on any help on Celtic history, although note that the different sites work alongside each other. There are people from TheCelticWiki working in the CGS, and people then also work on other sites too. We work with each other to help build up our Club's presence.

In addition, they have organised gravesite tours to help mark respect and tell the stories of our old greats, and have been involved on a number of different podcasts to help promote and educate on the history of the club. I'd very much recommend tracking these podcasts down; they have done a podcast now with all the main Celtic podcasts online.

The Celtic Graves Society, TheCelticWiki and general Celtic forums have even been a way for relatives to find out information on their old family links to Celtics. In turn they have provided the online Celtic community access to photos or information that has otherwise been locked up or unseen. We managed to get great info on many players whom we otherwise would never have been able to get info on.

The freedom of the web has even made it easy for supporters to be able to use our supporters links all over the globe. For example, a supporter in the US travelled for a few days by car to help track down the gravesite of

TTLE FOR THE CELTIC SOUL

Glasgow Celtic is a football club fighting itself as much as its ancient rival, Rangers. AMANDA MITCHISON reports. Photographs by JEREMY SUTTON-HIBBERT

a great old Celt. The CGS is also to hold a remembrance event in New York for the great Charlie Shaw, its first international event. Relatives of former players from as far as Australia & New Zealand have contacted the sites on help providing information on their forefathers. This has all been voluntary work by people and has been very humbling.

The Celtic supports love for its history

The question though is why the near obsession for the club's history? I don't think there is a need for me to repeat the already well-trodden road of our club's history and culture. In my opinion, I feel that it centres on the roots of the club centring on that the club was formed to serve a community but grew to be far much more than that. It's not about a business, a result, customers or a tournament. We view it as people with the supporters at its heart, something that is being lost at most other large clubs.

Reading through the history of the club, we are learn about the evolution of the communities we were brought up in, the multitude of stories weaving together to give us a portal to view the past. This is about our Scottish societies as much as it is about the success of an immigrant community. When you see how the lives and careers moved of our former players, you will get a greater understanding of the towns we live in, and the social events they lived through. Don't forget unlike today the players were no different to the rest of us, earning nominal wages and then moving into normal jobs (e.g. teachers, motor mechanics, ship yard workers etc). They also lived in the wee villages and towns we were brought up in, in the homes next to where we lived.

Some stories will even surprise but will broaden the minds of the support too. It's incredible to see the incredible number of Scottish Presbyterians who played a pivotal role in the early history of our club. It was not just a Catholic Irish success, something that in my opinion has been overlooked too often as Celtic historians can concentrate too heavily on the Irish roots of the club. The club has always been open minded and there are plenty of challenges they have faced and overcome, and for us to realise about and learn from.

Another reason for why there has been success for the internet Celtic historians, is because of controversy or perceived controversy. The web has allowed a dissection of issues that the club prefer to keep at arm's length due to various outsider's agendas who given an inch would stretch it to a mile. We've had contentious events in our history, we're not angels, and they are worth investigating. Official accounts of history are always diluted and can be saccharine sweet, so independent work can be far more thorough.

You could further add in that our club have had a poor relationship with the media and even the board at Celtic, hence this in itself created the drive for amateur historians to find out the truth rather than rely on the spin meisters in the media. It didn't help when the great Pat Wood's book (The Glory and the Dream) was banned from the Celtic stores on its first release (around 1986) due to a less than flattering overview of the forefathers of the then board members. Its honesty was refreshing but obviously not welcome by the old Biscuit Tin board. In an internet world, voices can't be stopped, and that means that there is freedom

to write as one sees it, no matter if others wish to either ignore it or see it different.

Don't get me wrong, the boom in historical analysis is not just a Celtic matter. In the new quarterly football journal 'The Blizzard', there was an article on the rising interest in investigating football in the old Victorian days. Maybe that is partly due to that modern football is leaving some people cold looking for a more sobre time, but maybe the greater ease of access to obscure sources is playing its part as well.

However, the scale of investigation from other supporters into their clubs has been quite minimal compared to that at Celtic. To our great surprise, few other clubs have wikis anywhere near similar to TheCelticWiki, even those who do (such as a Liverpool fan wiki) their sites are not as extensive in their coverage, and so far the Celtic Graves Society is itself wholly unique in football in what it does. Man City historians were surprised in the work done by the Celtic Graves Society on Tom Maley, and that was a huge compliment in itself. This reflects the genuine emotional attachment our fans have to the history of the club and our efforts to keep it alive, and illustrates that the support sees Celtic as more than a club.

The present and future?

We could go on, but this is not an ending history. The work to keep the history of the club alive continues, and all efforts no matter how big or small can bring out some valuable results. In future, who knows what the next big step will be in information dissemination. Tablets are a great area to make reading and research on Celtic even more convenient, but that's just a start. All I do know is that, whilst we have our club we will forever be in love with our history and will continue to pass it on to our next generations.

For anyone who wishes to get involved in any Celtic research (be it personally related or just out of personal interest), then feel free to register on any of the below sites and contact anyone off the site, and people will be very willing to assist:

The Celtic Wiki: www.thecelticwiki.com ; twitter: @thecelticwiki

The Celtic Graves Society Forum: http://celticgraves.com ; twitter: @celticgraves

KerrydaleStreet Forum (Wiki Section): http://kerrydalestreet.co.uk/forum/15926/

MAN IN THE MIDDLE

Shannon McGurin writes for CQN Magazine for the first time – in praise of her favourite Celtic player Joe Ledley

Joe Ledley added to Gary Hooper's first-half double at Hampden to help Celtic to a comfortable William Hill Scottish Cup final win over Hibernian, which completed the domestic double for the club.

It is fair to say, the Welsh midfielder is now one of the Scottish Premier League's best players and a key part of Neil Lennon's Celtic team.

After fourteen years at Cardiff City, Ledley signed for the Hoops in the summer of 2010 when his contract with the Bluebirds expired. In that same summer, Neil Lennon was appointed full time manager and fans were intrigued to see how his first signings would develop over the coming seasons.

In the 2010/2011 season, Ledley instantly had a strong and physical presence in the team and quickly formed a terrific partnership with Beram Kayal in Celtic's central midfield. It was obvious from the start, this was exactly the type of player the manager needed in his team as the club tried to put the previous season under Tony Mowbray to rest.

The Welshman demonstrates an ability on the ball that fits nicely into the possession hungry style of Neil Lennon, especially in the Scottish Premier League. Over the past few seasons he has became crucial to the team's tactical flexibility, he performs a shuttling role on the left side of central midfield, whether that be in a 2 or 3 man set-up. Neil Lennon can always trust Ledley to defend and attack as he is solid when it comes to putting in a tackle and a good passer. The only thing that Joe Ledley lacks is pace, however this rarely causes problems for the team when he plays alongside the likes of Victor Wanyama and Scott Brown who easily compensate for this.

The strong partnership formed this season with Victor Wanyama made our midfield almost unstoppable at times. Ledley played alongside the Kenyan for the most part this season, although the Welshman has had his fair share of injuries since signing for the Hoops in 2010. The central midfielder was out with a groin injury from the beginning of December until mid-January. Ledley is one of they players that's only really appreciated fully during his absence from the team because everybody is so used to depending on him to be there forming a strong midfield. The consistency and professionalism Joe gives can be somewhat lacking from his replacements.

Therefore, it is only really when he's out with injury that we see how much of a

crucial player he is in the team.

Ledley seems to excel in games were Celtic are seen as the underdogs and are up against it. An obvious example of this was on that memorable November night at Celtic Park against Barcelona in the Champions League group stages. Ledley worked as the midfield barrier alongside Kris Commons, Wanyama and Charlie Mulgrew that night with what can only be described as a display of sheer endeavour. Another example of the sort of game the midfielder relishes was the infamous 'Samaras Sunday' match back in January 2011 at Ibrox. Once again, Joe Ledley and Beram Kayal's partnership proved itself that day as they dominated the midfield. The Welshman finished off his fine display by setting up our opener with a superb long ball through to Samaras who gave us the lead. And, nobody can forget the 2011/2012 league winning campaign, after a dreadful start to the season Celtic began produce consistent performances again and the 15 point deficit in the SPL was overturned. In the last Glasgow derby of the year when a towering header from Ledley himself a towering header was enough to put Celtic ahead of Rangers in the league.

The William Hill Scottish Cup final win marked the end of the 2012/2013 season. All in all it seems a successful three years at Parkhead for the Welsh midfielder, with already two Scottish Premier League and two Scottish Cup medals already under his belt. In the past few weeks there has been rumours of a possible move back to his boyhood heroes Cardiff City but hopefully the prospect of more Champions League football next season and the chance to retain the SPL title is enough to keep him here. For his part Joe has been keen to stress that he enjoys playing for Celtic and is well settled in Glasgow. He seems happy to stay so Celtic have the opportunity of holding on to this very talented international midfielder.

A great deal has been said of Celtic's impressive transfer activity in the past few seasons under Neil lennon. Bearing in mind the club didn't pay a penny to Cardiff City for the midfielder, Joe Ledley can certainly be regarded as one of Neil Lennon's best signings as manager of the club.

I hope that Joe Ledley is a Celtic player for years to come.

OE LEDLEY 16

Over the past few seasons he has became crucial to the team's tactical flexibility...

LIVING IN
OF IMMIO

A couple of years ago, I was in the midst of a business meeting with three other guys when it was pointed out by one of our number that none of us would have been present were it not for the fact that all our respective grandfathers had taken the decision to emigrate to Scotland many years before. Further, by sheer coincidence, all three men concerned had arrived by boat and had come from a country beginning with the letter I--- Ireland, Italy and India.

All three men arrived in Scotland in the 1920's, and I suspect that they would have found Glasgow a somewhat frightening and inhospitable place to start with.

Many immigrants, especially from an Irish background, will have gravitated towards watching and indeed playing for Celtic due to the Irish roots that were imbedded within the club. Yet it may be surprising to some that Celtic

actually fielded an Indian player before they played an Italian. The barefooted ball juggler Mohammed Salim turned out for Celtic in 1936-37—several years before Rolando Ugolini deputised for the incomparable Willie Miller in 1946.

By playing Salim, Celtic became the first European club play an Indian so breaking all sorts of social barriers in so doing. Apparently he was a great entertainer—juggling and doing tricks with the ball—and all in bare feet!

Celtic FC have always been an inclusive club and yet for some reason there are those in Scotland who would seem to want to disparage the descendants of immigrants from the 20's, 30's and 40's— presumably for their sporting allegiance, possibly for their perceived religion and because they come from a background which is not traditionally--- well---- Scottish.

A CITY RANTS

Brogan Rogan Hogan and Trevino tells the story of one Celtic player, Matt Lynch, and those immigrants to Scotland who have shaped the club and Scottish society for the better...

Yet what is not often discussed is the fact that many immigrants from the three I countries were able to show a considerable work ethic, a desire for betterment and education, and a willingness to integrate with Scots and others that was not always shared by some who were born and bred along the banks of the Clyde and elsewhere in Scotland.

As the generations have moved on, so has the role of Celtic in this evolutionary process. Only a couple of weeks ago, a couple of Indian boys were training at Lennoxtoun,-- Mahhamed Salim had been asked to play his trial in front of 1,000 Celtic club members and three coaches--- and at the league match the following Saturday Celtic hosted some 300 members of the Asian community as guests. Think about that for a moment—300 members of the Asian community as guests of what is seen as a Celtic (with a hard C) Club?

Further, we fans are tempted to measure success at Celtic Park for a player (at least) in terms of the number of first team appearances—yet in true terms that surely cannot be the sole measure of success for the club itself or for someone coming to Celtic and hoping to make a success of life

through the club. In terms of appearances for instance, Jock Stein would probably not be held up as a Celtic great yet no one could deny that Stein was a true Celtic giant. When you think of people such as Neil Mochan, John Clarke, Sean Fallon and even Tommy Burns you don't just think of their first team appearances- you also think of what they put into, and what they got out of, the club over and above simply being a player

In social terms Celtic's community role has to be measured in a very different way. The club itself offered a social focus for anyone in the community—especially the immigrant from any nation, and of course the charitable roots and aspirations of the club are recognised by all.

Someone who came from an Immigrant background and who made his mark at Celtic Park was Matt Lynch. Like many families from Donegal the Lynch family came to Scotland in search of the better tomorrow. Matt was on the books of the club as a player for something like 14 years between 1935 and 1948. A right half or right winger, Matt was a hard tackling all action player who, it could be said, was not at Celtic Park in the best of periods—either for the club as an institution or for any

individual given the austerity of the time and the impact of war. The team had few stars in this era and unfortunately for Matt he was used more as a utility player- often deputising for the wizard like Delaney or for the impressive Chic Geatons.

It would be fair to say that Celtic was not well managed at the time and some players with potential were allowed to play bit parts in these years. Had certain players such as Matt Lynch been properly nurtured and coached, then their time at Celtic may well have been far more successful. As a result, Matt probably made fewer appearances than his ability merited yet he remained faithful and loyal to the club and its ethos throughout.

However, it is away from the field of play that I want to discuss Matt Lynch. He went on to gain a degree from Glasgow University- something unusual for a footballer especially at the time-- and for many years was a respected Maths teacher. Clearly immigration was a success for Matt and his family and he grabbed the opportunity to better himself and his lot with both hands.

However, after the playing days were over, Matt continued to serve the club for many

EDWARD URSUS · HUTCHYBHOY · JOHNNNYQUEST · THISISTHEONE

years as the Honorary President of the Celtic Supporters Association, and I recently came across a photo of him presenting the player of the year award to Bobby Murdoch in 1974.

For Matt, it was not just about playing for Celtic—it was about representing Celtic, being part of Celtic, and supporting Celtic and all that Celtic represented. I got to know him slightly in his later years and had a few drinks with him in his local-- Harvie's Bar in Paisley—and he would happily talk about all things Celtic including his playing days alongside one of my own relatives Charlie McGinley.

The makeup of the Celtic support has greatly changed since the days when Matt Lynch or Mohammed Salim pulled on the green and white shirt. With the advent of air travel, European competition, and television the pull of Celtic Football Club has ceased to be solely local and the club is a very different beast to the institution that existed before the middle of the last century.

A far greater proportion of the support are now University educated yet it is clear that education and the opportunity it brings is not something that is taken for granted. Anyone who follows the pages of CQN will know that posters regularly report with pride that a son or daughter, grandson or granddaughter has attained a degree in some discipline or other and is set to go on to a chosen career.

The very pursuit of a university degree and a following career has given rise to what might be described as the further adventures of the immigrant families who came to Glasgow— with many young people pursuing degrees and jobs far away from the banks of the Clyde whether that be in England or much further afield such as The USA, Australia or elsewhere.

The result of this is that the Celtic support is now to be found throughout the world with new immigrants arriving in far off lands and cities—and again it seems that the support of the Celtic Football Club becomes a social focus for those who have left "home" to find prospects and the better tomorrow elsewhere. There are Celtic Supporters Clubs and bars in some of the most unlikely of places.

Further the "local" home support now includes many ethnicities and this increases each time Celtic signs a new player who comes from Japan, Honduras, Poland or wherever. When I go to Celtic Park these days I see people from not only all walks of life—but whose families originated from many corners of the world--- and all with a green and white scarf around their neck. That is something that the club should be rightly proud of—and never ashamed to highlight or promote.

Over the course of the weekend, I received a message or two via twitter from a young man I know. I haven't seen him in a couple of years as he has been away studying at the University of Chicago. He will graduate this year with a degree in Law and of recent he has been editing the Sports section of the University Newspaper.

His dad's family was one of those who made their way to Glasgow from India—again in search of the better tomorrow—and his father went on to be a University graduate and is now a community doctor in the West

LYNCH

of Scotland. His mother graduated as a lawyer, but eventually chose to move away from mainstream law—in fact away from law altogether-- into a career whereby she gives advice and support in the community through one of the Government agencies which are vital in an urban society.

Both parents are Celtic fans, and mum in particular is to be found at most Celtic home games. Perhaps that is not surprising as Matt Lynch was her uncle and her father Jim—Matt's brother—was every bit as much a Celtic man as Matt—he just didn't play at the same level.

The Young man in Chicago gained entry to the University partly on the basis of a soccer scholarship, and in support of his application he stressed that he had played for Celtic FC at youth level.

Whilst the young man concerned and his family undoubtedly take great personal credit for what he has achieved thus far, there is no doubt that Celtic Football Club can take some pride in a young fella who played in their youth ranks and who has and will go on to make his mark away from the football field—Much like Matt Lynch did with his teaching career after he hung up his playing boots.

The makeup of the Celtic support has greatly changed since the days when Matt Lynch or Mohammed Salim pulled on the green and white shirt.

Celtic Football Club, those who play for the club, work for the club and those who support the club, have come a long way from the austerity of the 1930's in all sorts of ways. There is far greater integration in Scottish Society and perhaps more importantly there is a far greater instance of the Celtic Fan making their way in all walks of life in many different countries.

The Club itself has a far greater function—including an ever growing educational function—than merely putting a football team of highly paid stars out on to the pitch on a Saturday.

Unfortunately, Mohammed Salim became homesick after a few months and eventually made the decision to go back to Calcutta although the story goes that his family retain an uncashed bank draft from Celtic for the sum of £100 (the sum was sent by the club to help Salim through some hard times) and a Green and White hooped shirt in memory of a young man's time at Celtic Park in the '40's.

Celtic success cannot merely be measured by the number of first team appearances made by any one individual or even by the number of trophies won--- that is a very narrow definition of success.

For those of us whose Grandfathers and Grandmothers made the brave decision to take a boat to Scotland in search of a better tomorrow, and who have grown up listening to stories about Celtic, watching Celtic and

As the generations have moved on, so has the role of Celtic...

doing things in the Celtic way there is a never ending sense of pride in hearing stories about young people who have achieved something in their own chosen fields—yet who still retain an undying affection for a football club—no matter where they are.

Ciaran Kohli Lynch told me that when he comes home in the summer he may look to play football at Junior level while he continues his journey through life. No matter what he level he plays at—like his Grand Uncle Matt—he will have walked through Parkhead's gates and learned to play football—and the game of life--- The Glasgow Celtic way.

Last week an Italian by the name of Andrea

Pirlo said that Celtic were a true European force in football—not just because of the calibre of player they field or the size of the stadium they play in but because of who and what the club represents.

I believe he was talking about all those people who took a boat to Glasgow from another country – some starting with the letter called I and elsewhere long ago in times of hardship--- and the generations that followed who , today, still look for a better tomorrow on the back of that boat trip and who follow a football club that welcomed all then and still does to this day.

ANGELGABRIEL · CONNAIRE12 · CLINK\0/ · FIN75 · FISHERMHAN

A H
TH
OF

YMN FOR DAWN THE FREE!

Mike Maher takes us on a journey down memory lane to the early sixties and recalls that his father was wrong in thinking that the new Jock Stein era at Celtic would be another false dawn and remembers how the mainstream media of the day managed to blame "The Old Firm" after Rangers fans rioted at Hampden Park…

Apparently Jock Stein had only one photograph in his office. Not the Lisbon Lions but the 1965 Scottish Cup winning team. It was said that things might have turned out as well for Celtic if they had not won that game. However I feel that Big Jock's second trophy was also important in setting Celtic on their new path. It was the League Cup and the opponents were — Rangers.

I had been following Celtic for 5 years before Jock Stein arrived. In the 10 Old Firm League encounters during that period Celtic had managed one victory.

5 League Cup games with the Ibrox men had yielded one win and 4 defeats. A draw was the best Scottish Cup result with 2 defeats in that competition. Celtic had managed a couple of wins in the Glasgow Cup but even allowing for the fact that the latter trophy still had some importance in those days the conclusion was all too easy to come to-Celtic could just not beat Rangers.

Big Jock's first Old Firm league game ended in a 2-1 defeat. "Still can't beat the Rangers" were my father's sad words as I returned from Ibrox that September

day. Another false dawn? Surely not. With Jock Stein in charge things just had to change. We would soon get another chance as the 2 teams were to meet in the League Cup final in just over a month. The previous season Celtic had won the first Old Firm League encounter only to go down 2-1 in the League Cup Final. Maybe that would be an omen in reverse as it were.

So it was some confidence I met up with a school friend, John Fagan, to join him, his dad, uncle and cousin on the Kirkwood CSC for the journey to Hampden. It was a bright autumn afternoon as we walked down Aitkenhead Road and into the stadium. We climbed up the steep steps to the top of the Celtic End and then went down the dilapidated terracing to a vantage point near the front where we had a great view of the action. And action there was. In those days Rangers were to me epitomised by players like Bobby Shearer, Harold Davis and Sammy Baird. Hard, crude men who used physical intimidation as part of their game. However on this occasion the Celtic players showed that for a change they were not going to be intimidated. Tackles were fierce with no prisoners taken. However there was skill too. Mostly from the Bhoys in green and white. In particular John Hughes. "Big Yogi" had one of "those days". He seemed to be unstoppable. In one incident out on the left touchline in front of the North Enclosure he stood, hands on hips, with the ball at his feet inviting Rangers full back Kaj Johansen to tackle him. The Dane went for the ball and Yogi almost contemptuously knocked it past him and left him sprawling. And it was Yogi who scored Celtic's goals, both from the penalty spot. The first in 18 minutes after Ronnie McKinnon inexplicably handled in the box and 10 minutes later after Ranger's left back Davie Provan brought down Jimmy Johnstone inside the penalty area.

The Celtic End was a happy though not over confident place during the half time interval. John's dad remarked that a referee who gave Celtic 2 penalties in one game might find himself in bother. (as it was the referee, Hugh Phillips,

retired at the end of that season). Someone else reminded us that it was the same half time score as the 7-1 game.

However this was never going to be a high scoring game. The second half was also an uncompromising affair. Celtic showing a new steely determination and although Rangers scrambled a late goal we held on for a deserved victory.

Big Billy was presented with the League Cup and the Celtic team then came out onto the park and brought the trophy to the Kings Park end to show to the Celtic fans. As we were cheering I noticed that at the other end of the ground some Rangers fans had come onto the track. That was not always unusual in those days. If a fight started on a packed terracing people would come over the boundary wall to get away. However this was more sinister. The Rangers fans were now on the field and were making their way towards the Celtic players. Thankfully the players realised in time and raced for the pavilion. Some fans did get close to them though and I recall

Neilly Mochan and Tommy Gemmell having to manhandle some of them to get to safety. More Rangers fans now came onto the park and were involved in fighting with the police. At the Celtic end we stood and watched. The pitch invasion actually subdued the Celtic support to an extent but the celebratory feeling soon returned as we made our way back to the double decker bus parked in the Toryglen football pitches. As we pulled out of the bus park the bus convenor- John Daisley's dad- started the singing with "Kelly the Boy from Killane"

" What's the news, what's the news oh my bold Shelmalier with your long barrelled gun of the sea Say what wind from the south blows his messenger here with a hymn for the dawn of the free Goodly news, goodly news do I bring youth of Forth, goodly news shall you hear Bargy man"

I don't know if he thought the words were relevant or he just liked the song but I could not help but feel that it was somehow appropriate.

When we got back to Coatbridge I waited outside the Big Tree Bar in Whifflet to get the evening papers the "Green Citizen" and the "Pink Times" to get the first reports on the game. Then home to share the joy with my father and brothers. Later that evening we watched the highlights on "Scotsport" and I at last saw the goals my nerves had prevented me seeing at the actual game. I had turned my back as each penalty was taken. For once I went to bed on the night of an Old Firm game contented. Not only had Celtic won but the Rangers fans had rioted. The Sunday papers would surely make great reading.

A couple of years earlier I had been at Ibrox for Celtic's Scottish Cup semi-final with St Mirren. With

I had been following Celtic for 5 years before Jock Stein arrived. In the 10 Old Firm League encounters during that period Celtic had managed one victory.

their team down 3-0 many of the Celtic fans invaded the pitch with the intention of getting the game abandoned. Quite rightly they were heavily criticised by the media and I recall the sense of shame not just for the Celtic support but also for the wider Irish Catholic community with whom Celtic were more closely identified in those days.

However when I read the papers that October Sunday morning I discovered the Press had a different attitude to the previous day's riot. It was apparently an Old Firm problem. We were told that both clubs did not do enough to rid themselves of their bad element. Some of the blame was even aimed at the Celtic players for coming out on the pitch with the trophy. Virtually none of the media ventured to suggest that Ranger's non –Catholic signing policy might attract some of that "bad element" to them. If that subject was mentioned at that time it was always countered by the fact that Celtic flew the Irish flag. Amazingly even some Celtic supporters felt there was logic in that. That particular war would take a bit longer to win but at least on the pitch Celtic had won a major battle. They had stood up to Rangers and had at last beaten them in a major game. With that monkey off our back and Jock Stein in charge who knows what we could go on to achieve? Goodly news, goodly news indeed!

OYS BRASIL

It all began on 14th June 1982. The legendary yellow shirts of Brazil took to the field in Seville to play their opening game of the world cup against a strong Soviet Union side...

As a young boy sitting in front of the television in Glasgow this was not only my first taste of world cup football, but the first time I would see the famous Brazilian national team in action.

Spectacular late goals from Socrates and Eder eventually overcame the stubborn Soviet defence. Scotland, New Zealand and Argentina were also put to the sword before the dream ended in a classic world cup encounter with Italy

I was hooked on this exciting and exotic brand of football, seduced by the thought of watching one of the best teams ever to play the game.

This childhood nostalgia lead to some excitement when the 2014 World Cup was awarded to Brazil. This could be the one when Scotland actually qualify! Surely it must be fate that Brazil and Scotland would meet again?

Two home draws soon kicked that idea into touch. However I had another trick up my sleeve. My forthcoming marriage to the lovely Andrea was being arranged for Easter 2013 and I wondered whether the honeymoon location might be somewhere vibrant and exotic, somewhere to relax on

the beach but also with a sense of adventure. The name Rio de Janeiro sprung to mind.

We have all seen the iconic pictures of Christ the Redeemer, Sugar Loaf mountain and Copacabana beach and the thought of combining that with a little bit of Brazilian futebol meant that I had my heart set on Rio. To my delight Andrea was in agreement, even with the football part!

With the honeymoon booked the next step, as for all good Celtic fans, was to consider how I would get to see the matches when we were away. The first Saturday would be the 6th of April against Hibs at Celtic park. A quick search online threw up the Rio Fergus McCann CSC also known as the Bhoys from Brasil. After exchanging a few emails with the guys in Rio we set up a rendezvous at their current watering hole, the Blue Agave pub in Ipanema. (surely it should be the Green Agave?)

Browsing through their website www.rioceltic.com I also began to appreciate the work that the CSC did for charity and in particular to help support a boys football team. The

Further adventure was to follow including a ride up the cable car to sugar loaf mountain...

team from Santa Margarida on the west side of Rio is located in a poor neighbourhood and run by a local coach and ex Flamengo player Gerson. (not THAT Gerson by the way!) He never quite scaled the heights of Brazilian football like his namesake from the 1970 dream team, but at least can claim a Brazilian championship success with Flamengo in 1987, as an understudy to the legendary Zico no less. Gerson's role now is far more important than his time as a player. He now works tirelessly for the kids as coach, role model, mentor and advisor. Helping children with a less fortunate start in life both on and off the pitch. With this in mind I took the opportunity to contact the PR department at Celtic and ask about the possibility of helping out with some Celtic related gifts that I could take over to RIo. I received a prompt response offering to provide me with some kids Celtic tops that I could pick up from Celtic Park. With 12 Celtic tops safely packed away in our luggage we made the long trip to Rio on Wednesday 3rd April. After arriving late at night in our Ipanema hotel we awoke on a beautiful Thursday morning to see a spectacular and bustling city. A long walk down Ipanema then Copacabana beach allowed us to get our bearings and see some of the sights. First up was a trip up to Cristo Redempto (Christ the Redeemer) the world famous statue of Christ that overlooks the

city. Despite being a humid 25 degrees at the bottom, the mist then the wind and rain eventually enveloped us on top of the mountain. More like Ben Lomond than Rio! However, we braved the elements to take some nice pictures. Saturday morning brought the long awaited trip to meet the Fergus McCann Rio CSC. Drew, Jim, Stan and Raymond welcomed Andrea and I to Rio for the 11am kick off. Some technical problems meant we missed Kris Commons first goal but with the beers flowing no one seemed to mind. With Celtic cruising into a three goal lead, thoughts soon turned to Fir Park where Motherwell were losing to St Mirren. I had thought it would be written in the stars that we would see Celtic winning the league in Rio. If scores had stayed the same, a title party was in the offing. Unfortunately a late James McFadden equaliser deflated us just a little, but the post match party continued anyway through the afternoon. A ceremonial handing over of the kids Celtic tops took place with Drew and he duly promised to hand them over to Gerson at the earliest opportunity. Jim then taught me how to fold the 'fleg' and with that it was boa noite as we walked back to the hotel. Further adventure was to follow including a ride up the cable car to sugar loaf mountain and a trip down the Costa Verde to the small colonial town of Paraty. A fabulous honeymoon and a fantastic experience made

all the more special by meeting a great group of bhoys who have spread the Celtic gospel on the other side of the world. For those thinking about whether to go to the World Cup next year, just do it. A fabulous country with beautiful people awaits you. And I'm sure the Bhoys from Brasil will make you feel most welcome. We can't wait to go back! With thanks to Jim, Drew, Stan and Raymond for the Rio CSC t-shirt, the flowers for Andrea, tourist tips for Rio and Paraty and all the beer on the day! Many thanks also to Karen and Eileen at the Celtic PR dept for organising the strips.

THE RAVEN · JANE FIELD STREET · ANDY CORR · BONZODOG

THE ELEPH IN THE ROOM

Tony McCann considers th price of match tickets…

It is rather a curious turn of phrase; the elephant in the room. This idiom creates an image, in my head anyway, of a rather quaint room with a few people, almost stood about like a it was a party or gathering, talking nervously, but never about the pachyderm stood nervously in the corner, too nervous in its manner to be furniture and too pronounced a threat to be glared at directly so the edgy banter in the room never broaches the subject of its presence.

I wonder how long it will take for someone with a voice louder and infinitely more respected than mines to point out that there is a large land mammal skulking in the corner, upsetting the Feng Shui. Don't hold your breath for the assorted punditry and bevy of Sky Sports beauties to concern themselves with this. Or even journos that meander back to source to become an official mouthpiece, having previously adopted this role voluntarily.

And do not labour under the illusion that vitriol is preserved only for those outside the Celtic boat micturating in. Everybody in football is ignoring this elephant and it is to their peril I believe. Have I stretched this analogy further than Alberto Undiano Mallenco stretched the interpretation of the rules when we hosted Juventus? Possibly, but this is a big elephant we are talking about.

Let me commence my explanation by saying that the average price of a ticket to see Borussia Dortmund is €15. That's £12.99. Dortmund are at an equivalent level within the Champions League as Celtic, challenging languidly behind Bayern for the title. And speaking of Bayern, a team packed with stars, it is a paltry €17 to see them take on Werder Bremen in their next home match.

So why is it that we are asked to pay £23 (less booking & postage) to watch Dundee? Celtic are not the worst offenders, but are on the radar, even for a difference of £8.30 with Bayern. We all know about the well-documented and recent furore over Arsenals tickets. Have a look at this:

The elephant isn't ticket prices, that's maybe just the trunk and possibly a tusk. The great hulking beast is what is behind this ticket price issue, which also extends to our fellow SPL clubs and seems to pervade every level of English football; League One, the old second division, which was the old Third Division, anyway, the prices in the 3rd tier of English football are the equivalent to the top tier of Scottish football which is more expensive than Germany and, yes, Spain. On average.

The elephant is perhaps an attitude, pervaded when demand has sufficiently increased with supply remaining unchanged, the inevitable shortage occurs, leading to a higher equilibrium price. Ticket prices are rising, the cost of TV subscription is rising and so too are salaries all round. Robbie Savages hair ain't gonna style itself and Alan Hansen is unlikely to get £40k per appearance in any other line of work. Mostly as the only other line of work suitable would be as a bookend or doorstop. And lest we forget the talent on the park, able

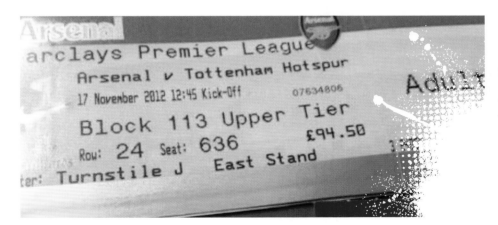

to rightfully bemoan their lot in life whilst staying in at New Year and not partying. As an enlightened Scouser pointed out to said talent via Twitter, there is a lot one can tolerate for £80k per week. I'm paraphrasing but not prevaricating.

The Rio Ferdinand tweet I am referring too sums up the general dissatisfaction of the fan. The Arsenal ticket rifles home precisely the nature of the previously unspoken of animal; the fan is being squeezed; the mug punter mentality is laid bare.

We started out as a charity and have gone on to be more than I doubt our founders could envisage. But we are betraying this heritage if we don't carry that noble sentiment forward. The price of a day out to see Celtic could reasonably be paid for out of the cost of two Arsenal vs a title contender home tickets, but nonetheless we could do more than just be cheaper than some. Some teams have free child places, some German teams tickets can be used on public transport on match day, not to mention standing, responsible drinking at football and I could go on.

But I shall say that until we ask the question: what are we paying all this money for and no longer get a reply along the lines of 'who do you think pays for camouflaged Bentleys?' The way in which fans are treated has not yet had a deleterious affect upon footballs popularity but how long before being pumped ever so increasingly violently for money in a declining economy, one which demands innovation not exploitation, can the average fans head remain unturned?

The next time you are listening to Alan Hansen pontificate on TV, ogle the delectable Sky Sports News ladies, watch a small African countries' GDP in salaries run after a ball, or indeed cough up more than you think is acceptable for a ticket, think about the riddle of value and ask yourself whether it is time to talk about that elephant.

OUT OF AFRICA

Celtic's historical ties and charitable endeavours are noteworthy. So too is the club's increasing interest in this continent as fertile territory for signing high quality first team players. Chris Collins investigates for CQN Magazine…

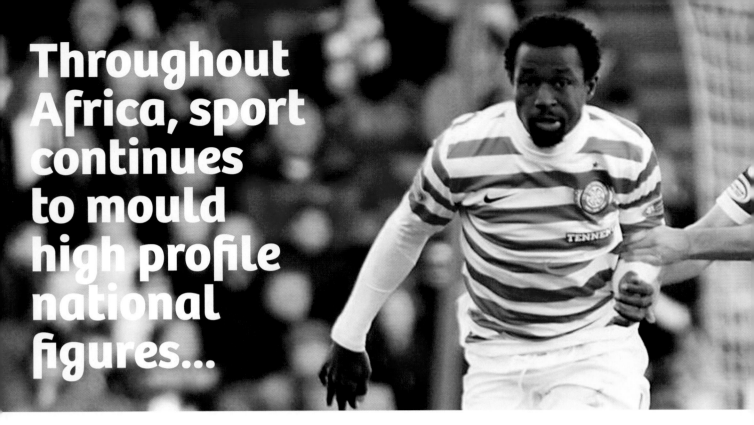

Throughout Africa, sport continues to mould high profile national figures...

To the outsider, the continent of Africa is a complex dichotomy, a region where the joyful expressions of tradition and culture take place amid the reality of dire poverty and chronic malnutrition, forming contradictory images in the minds of non-African observers. Home to over one billion people and thus resistant to easy generalisations, Africa is often referred to as the birthplace of humanity, but often viewed as neglected suburb of the modern world. The African contribution to global progress has historically been restricted by exploitation, and more recently, hampered by the corrosive effects of political corruption and civil war. Despite endemic structural problems, fifty four independent African nation states strive to make their mark on the world, with all the opportunities, obstacles and barriers presented by the unstoppable force of globalisation.

Celtic's historical ties and charitable endeavours on the continent are worthy of consideration.

Throughout Africa, sport continues to mould high profile national figures, who their compatriots aspire to emulate and it is in this arena where modern Africans have earned worldwide distinction. The African footprint is strongest in distance running where Ethiopians and Kenyans continue to dominate, but over the last twenty years the footballing world has been alerted to the outstanding qualities of an increasing

number of players from this emerging football territory, many of whom have made it to the very pinnacle of the game. Indirectly, Celtic have acquired the service of a small but growing number of African players in the last few decades, currently evidence by the presence of Ambrose and Wanyama in particular, while the club continues to increase charitable work in the region, a point we will return to later.

The nascent European obsession with African footballers can be partially explained through the cultural influences and physiological attributes they bring to the game. In his excellent book Feet of the Chameleon; A History of African football, Ian Hawkey notes the prevailing stereotype is for the muscular defensive midfielder but argues there is a high degree of skill and ability forged on arid, dusty pitches. Consider the outrageous ability of Jay Jay Okacha and the power of Michael Essien for examples of both. Hawkey, who believes laughter to be an "instinct" for Africans, sees "something unique in the way they interpret the game." It might also be suggested they have a unique insight on how to interpret life, given their natural propensity for self expression, noticeable traits in the current African contingent at Celtic. Think of Ambrose' exuberant celebrations after scoring in Paisley or Rabui Ibrahims propensity for pitch side dancing, draped in the Nigerian flag. And for those who follow Victor Wanyama on twitter, you may be familiar with some of his uplifting

communications, including this gem:

"Morning people, arise and shine, we thank God for the gift of life."

However, Hawkey also hints at a strong desire to succeed and achieve, highlighting the fact that there are over 2000 professional African footballers now employed in Europe. Unfortunately this desire is so great that it has led to a lucrative market in human trafficking as dodgy football academies charge families costs they can barely afford with the promise of a European career. Hawkey notes that the brutal reality can be busloads of young men being taken to live in squalid conditions in neighbouring African countries, playing no football at all.

Thankfully, success is more common. The lower tiers of the European game have seen a huge increase in exports over the last twenty years while a swift glance at any Champions League team sheet will provide numerous examples of African talent.

Two days prior to Celtic's 2-1 victory over Barcelona, the African football conference announced the short listed candidates for the African Player of the Year award 2012, which included John Obi Mikel, Demba Ba, Didier Drogba, Yaya Toure and Alex Song among others. The list will be narrowed to three and the winner announced at a prestigious gala event in the Ghanaian capital of Accra, on December 20th. The grandeur of the ceremony will symbolise

the growing importance of African footballs contribution to the worldwide game, a contribution which has enriched and improved domestic leagues across Europe, delivered a dash of colour to World Cups and greatly enhanced the Champions League as a spectacle. The player awarded the accolade, voted for by managers of all African football nations, will follow in the footsteps of greats such as Milla, Weah, Kanu, Eto'o and Kanoute.

At the same ceremony, Victor Wanyama will find out if he has earned the titles of African Young Footballer of the Year for which he has been short-listed. In January, Ambrose and Lassad will have the opportunity to enhance their reputations during the African Cup of Nations, for Nigeria and Tunisia respectively. It's not unreasonable to suggest that there will be a residual effect from Celtics employment of African talent as the club's exposure in the continent continues to grow. Neither is it inconceivable to suppose that in the years to come, a Celtic player will make the shortlist for African player of the year. The most likely candidate, assuming he hangs around long enough, is of course Wanyama, who has made a seamless transition from Kenya to Kerrydale Street, greatly enhancing his profile and reputation in the process.

These players have joined a small tribe of African players who have worn the hoops, most of whom hailed from the West African strongholds of Senegal, Ivory Coast, Nigeria and Cameroon. Several were brought in on loan, including Badr El

Kaddouri, Diomansy Kamara, Henri Camara and Landry N'Guemo; others permanently; Oliver Tebilly, Mo Camara, Mo Bangura, Momo Sylla, Jean Joel Perrier Doumbe and of course, Bobo Balde, who until the emergence of Wanyama, had arguably made the greatest impact at Celtic of any African player.

Islam Feruz, to our great misfortune, is the one that got away.

Now a UK citizen and Scotland youth international, but born and raised in war torn Somalia on the east coast of Africa before he settled with his family in Glasgow aged six, Islam was the precociously talented striker who Celtic coached, nurtured and educated as kid. Tommy Burns spoke on behalf of Islam and his family at a deportation hearing in Glasgow and helped secure their status as legal immigrants, citing the contribution he would go on to make to this country. Unfortunately, Feruz moved to London to sign professional forms with Chelsea as a sixteen year old thereby denying Celtic fans the chance to witness him fulfil his potential in green and white. Those inside the game are unanimous when discussing the outlook for this striking prodigy: Islam Feruz will be a superstar. Far from harbouring any bitterness, Celtic as a club should be proud of their role, not only in his sporting development, but in his life as a whole.

While Celtic's employment of African footballers - the vast majority of whom were already plying their trade for European clubs before arriving in Glasgow - may or may not be part of a wider strategy to market the club in the region, there is another interesting component in this emerging Celtic – Africa story, as alluded to earlier.

Jane Maguire, manager of the Celtic Charity Fund, estimates that the club have donated in the region of £600,000 to various causes in Africa, not including a huge number of in-kind donations (thousands of shirts, footballs, signed merchandise) in aid of work all over the continent. She provided details of the official partnership the club has formed with Kibera Celtic, a club founded on the principles of openness, social inclusion and assistance for the poor in one of the largest and worst slums in Kenya. The Kibera Celtic Foundation run male and female football teams and deliver programmes linking sport with community projects designed to improve health and education. 27 volunteers from the Celtic Charity Fund will travel to Kibera this year to work in local schools and orphanages.

The Legends match between Celtic and Manchester United last year, attended by 55,000 fans in aid of Oxfam's East Africa Food Crisis Appeal, was memorable for

many things, most notably a remarkable gesture by youth coach and ex Celtic player John Kennedy. His decision to donate his share of the gate receipts and pass on hundreds of thousands of pounds from a match that was originally scheduled to be his testimonial, summed up the spirit of the event which raised a huge sum for those affected by famine in Kenya, Ethiopia and Somalia. The staff and volunteers at the Celtic Charity fund continue to work in the background on these and many other worthwhile causes across the world. Even if the two are mutually exclusive and this article is a futile search for a non existent link between Celtics African footballers and charitable work in the region, there is no reason why one should not augment the other, as in the case of Wanyama's messages of support for the work of Kibera Celtic.

As football at the top level becomes ever more corporate, a disconnect can develop between Celtic fans and those charged with running the club. The 'supporter or customer' debate is re-ignited every so often but by definition, we are both. In the boardroom and the stands, representatives of Celtic, a modern club with a global fanbase, appear to understand that their social responsibilities extend far beyond the parameters of Scottish society, and staff and fans work diligently in the background to ensure those responsibilities are met.

The 125th anniversary celebrations focused minds on the true roots of a club that was formed to assist the poor, reminding us that the glory of Celtic is not measured exclusively on trophies won, but also in adherence to the original ideals of its founders. The clubs involvement in Africa, particularly in Wanyama's homeland of Kenya, is a noble venture in keeping with that ethos.

In a globalised world of instant information and imagery, the needs and attributes of ordinary African citizens will not be ignored; neither will their enthusiasm for the beautiful game. If Celtic can continue to attract established African internationals while expanding social justice projects in areas of need, the Celtic-Africa story will continue to be mutually beneficial. Sport is often a great leveller in societies beset by inequalities and like distance running decades earlier, football has proven to be a unifying force for the betterment of many, in a continent of extremes. For most of the clubs history there has been a strong fan base in Ireland, North America and Australia so perhaps in 125 years time there will be Celtic Supporters Associations the length and breadth of Africa, from Nairobi to Dakar and everywhere in between, as Celtic become the pre-eminent club in a more stable, confident region of the world.

PERCEPTI
LENS

Why should a subjective perceptive lens reduce the market value Celtic should expect for our playing assets? Tony McCann explains for CQN Magazine...

"He is just unlucky that Joe Hart is in front of him", said Jamie Redknapp with an austere seriousness, after heaping massive amounts of praise on Fraser Forster, a major component in our fantastic victory of FC Barcelona. I agree with Jamie Redknapp that big Fraser is unlucky to have Joe Hart in front of him.

At the time of writing this, with the joyful exuberance of watching Tony Watt double our advantage of Barca only beginning to subside, Fraser Forster has completed 450 minutes of Champions League football, conceding 7 goals in 5 games, being in the losing side only twice thus far. Contrast this with Joe Hart who has conceded 10 goals in the same number of games. Perhaps it has been the dazzle of such sparkling gems in front of him that has put him off?

But the reason I have concentrated on the Champions League as opposed to domestic league performance is that both players are competing in the same competition against an agreed similar level of opponent; indeed both Celtic & Manchester City have the two widely recognised best club teams in the world, Barcelona & Real Madrid, in their respective groups. This settles the trifling question of opponent calibre delightfully.

Leading me nicely on to my next supporting argument, Man City spends roughly £3.3m in wages per week vs Celtic's estimated £600,000. Celtic have managed to lead Barcelona for 95 minutes over 180 minutes of football; Manchester City failed to hold such an advantage over Real Madrid who, along with Celtic are the only team to inflict defeat upon the Catalans this season. Also the one important fact that whatever happens against Spartak Celtic are guaranteed European football next season. The billionaires of Manchester cannot say the same.

In the inexorable march towards the January transfer window the same rumours pop up and this time it is of Gary Hooper's exit to the EPL with QPR, a team with relegation eagerly beckoning to them. Yet nobody questions the absurdity of this; even though Gary is playing and scoring in Europe's premier competition against top class opponents he is only good enough to be considered for a team with the relegation vultures circling.

And this perceptive lens is damaging, particularly to us. Although we are not primarily a selling club we cannot ignore that our excellent scouting system is bearing fruit. Indeed in six months if one was to draw a graph of Victor Wanyama's value it would yield a very steep slope, one, which we daren't even guess it's summit for fear of jinxing our fast rising star. But given the pejorative tones of our football we are its ambassadors and we're not exactly doing bad job. Indeed our exertions this season have introduced additional player fatigue and new requirements to rotate players that we are still becoming accustomed to which has shown that in the absence of Rangers there are other clubs willing to fight to secure second and even challenge us for dominance.

The SPL has vibrancy to it this season and although I have no doubt we shall win it, it won't be because it is the Mickey Mouse set up our cousins down south would have you believe and our hapless administrators are perennially inclined to make out we are, no it shall be because we were the best team in a league threatening a very promising revival. Granted this revival shall be driven by those keen to get some much needed European income and the prestige that follows. And I for one would love to see another Scottish team in Europe, even just to revel in the momentary absurdity of seeing Hibs, Aberdeen or Motherwell come out to the Champions League theme.

But before I drifted off into a tangent I was going on about the damage this poor perception of us has. That damage is inflicted on potential revenue streams. Viewing our players as lesser than the grotesquely overpaid benchwarmers of the Premiership promised land results in lower fees for our players. This in turn has ramifications for the rate of return on our investment in a both the youth and scouting policies. It is foolishness to not consider that we should be trying to maximise our investments and it is ignorant to assume that this is only a minor issue. Why should this perceptive lens reduce the market value we should expect for our assets?

Listening to talking heads like Jamie Redknapp et al wheel out this tired and boring rhetoric programmed into most of them with a ruthless and careless efficiency is more than just banter. The simple matter is that things have value and this can be measured. Perhaps opposition to measuring value and seeking parity on value would surely shake the tree so hard that Alan Hansen (£40k for ever appearance on Match of the Day just to give you a flavour) and his fellow pundits would come flying out with nothing but their P45s, only for the rest of the whole horrifically over priced farce to come collapsing down about everybody's ears. Perhaps not, but to listen to pundits drive home this worn out and grubby message repeatedly has to be challenged.

The only way to challenge this is with reason and results. I sincerely hope that other clubs in Scotland can rise to the challenge too. For too long we have been derided whilst a Murrayesque feat of financial doping allows the English, our principle football trading partners coincidentally, to view us through a tainted lens. We may never achieve parity or perhaps deserve to, but potential revenue streams or indeed key players international aspirations do not deserve to be tainted by this perceptive lens, tainted as it is.

MUNGOLIAN BHOY · TONYDONNELLYG7 · DUBAIBHOY

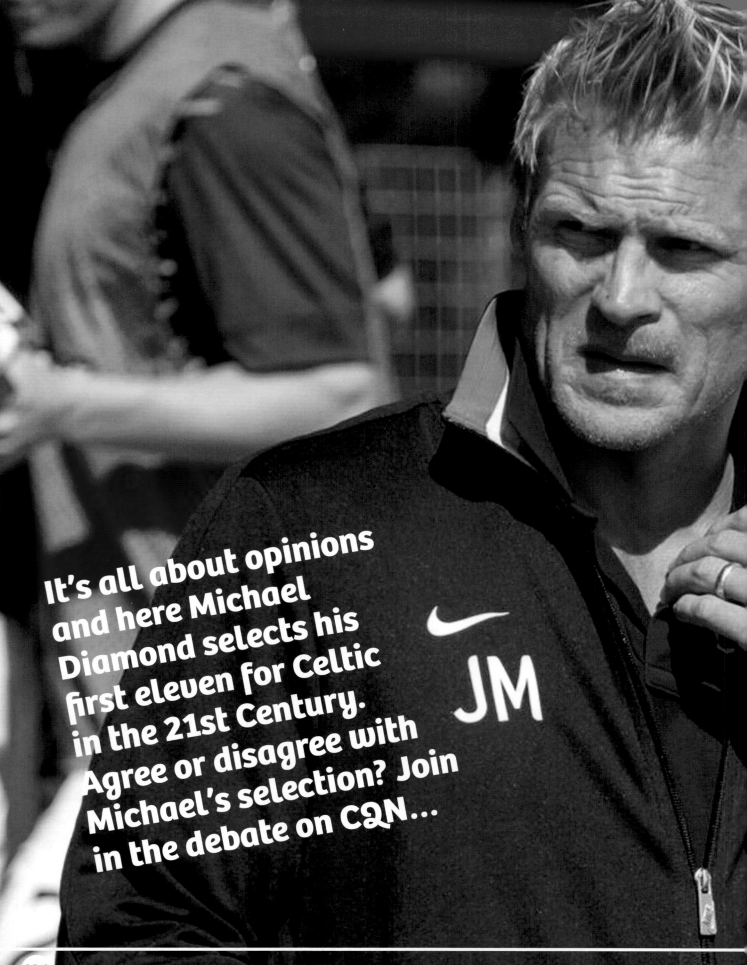

It's all about opinions and here Michael Diamond selects his first eleven for Celtic in the 21st Century. Agree or disagree with Michael's selection? Join in the debate on CQN…

MY CELTIC TEAM OF THE CENTURY

Celtic welcomed the new millennium in a precarious position. Managerial uncertainty, an under achieving team and losing the league by a staggering 21 points were among The Hoops' biggest concerns. In the summer of 2000, Celtic appointed Martin O'Neill as the new manager and hoped that he had the key to success, given his overwhelming achievements at Leicester City. When O'Neill addressed the Celtic support on a sunny day at Celtic Park, little did we know what was ahead. O'Neill's Celtic was the foundation for a strong decade for Celtic with many players becoming legends in the green and white. From O'Neill to Lennon, through the European dreams realised by Strachan, we have witnessed some great moments, and even greater players. The question begs to be asked: who is the team of this century so far?

Goalkeeper: Fraser Forster

Englishman, Fraser Forster joined Celtic on a season-long loan in August 2010 from Newcastle United. Forster had a mixed first season at Celtic; making some crucial saves but also being at fault for a handful of goals, which saw him, criticised by sections of the Celtic support and the mainstream media. Neill Lennon clearly saw enough quality in the Hexham born stopper and signed him for a fee of £2.2m in August 2012. This has proved to be a bargain (so far) after a collection of heroic goalkeeping displays. Gallant performances in the Champions' League have seen him branded 'La Gran Muralla' (The Great Wall) in Spanish newspapers. A great start to his career, as well as an international call-up, will have Celtic fans very excited to see what is still to come from this young, promising goalie.

Right back: Jackie McNamara

McNamara joined The Hoops from Dunfermline Athletic for a fee of £650,000 in 1995. In addition to being a crucial player in the late 90s, McNamara continued his excellent form well into the new millennium. Scoring the opening goal in the 2001 Scottish Cup Final, scooping the Football Writers' Player of the Year in 2004 and being named Celtic captain in the 04/05 season will be among McNamara's greatest achievements in his career. His loyalty to the club saw the full back awarded with a testimonial game in May 2005 with a game against the Republic of Ireland to mark his 10th season at the club.

Centre back: Johan Mjallby

Signed by Dr. Jozef Venglos from AIK for a fee of around £1.2m, Mjallby made an immediate impact after a rousing debut performance in a 5-1 Glasgow Derby win. Mjallby played a key role in Martin O'Neill's team and was crucial in The Hoops' journey to Seville in the summer of 2003. During his time at Celtic, the Swedish defender won 3 SPL titles, 2 Scottish Cups and 2 Scottish League Cups in what many Celtic fans will remember fondly as being a very successful period for the club. Many Celtic fans would say that the foundation for this success was a solid defensive line, in which Mjallby played a vital role.

Centre back: Dianbobo Baldé

Joining Celtic in 2001, Bobo went on to make 232 appearances for The Hoops. Renowned for his size and no-nonsense playing style, Baldé played a pivotal role in Celtic's UEFA cup bid and was a regular in O'Neill's side. Bobo was always a fans' favourite at the club and the fans' sentiments were mirrored by the Guinean. Looking back on his career at Celtic Park, Baldé said: "Celtic was a great adventure for me in my career. We reached the UEFA Cup Final, were league champions five times and won several Scottish and League Cups. There were a lot of great matches in the Champions League and I'm very happy with the experience I had at such a fantastic club and stadium."

Left back: Emilio Izaguirre

The Honduran signed for Celtic from Motagua in August 2010 and immediately caught the attention of Celtic fans. Izaguirre hit the ground running, and a marvelous display on his debut against Motherwell saw him draw plaudits from managers, fans and pundits alike. This is something Emilio would become accustomed to. After an outstanding season in 2010/11, Emilio won all of the individual awards available to him including the Clydesdale Bank SPL Player of the Year award. Injury plagued Emilio's 2011/12 season after suffering an ankle break at Pittodrie. This season has seen Emilio return to form and many will be looking forward to seeing Izaguirre rediscover the form of his iconic 2012/11 season.

Right midfield: Aiden McGeady

Childhood Celtic fan, Aiden McGeady, came through the club's internationally acclaimed youth system and ascended to stardom in the green and white. Scoring just 17 minutes into his Celtic debut against Hearts, many could see that the fresh-faced McGeady would go onto great things. A large section of the Celtic support will have particular memories of moments of sheer brilliance, but McGeady was more than just a showman. He was a very important player and was often seen as the playmaker in the team who, on occasion, could chip in with a goal or two. McGeady's form saw him awarded the 2008 SPFA Player of the Year and Young Player of the Year awards. Aiden's excellence caught the attention of many foreign clubs, and the Irishman left for Spartak Moscow for a staggering fee of £9.5m in 2010.

Centre midfield: Victor Wanyama:

For just under £900,000, Celtic may have found themselves a real gem in Victor Wanyama. In July 2011, Wanyama became the first Kenyan to sign for The Hoops and immediately endeared himself to the Celtic family by selecting the number 67 in honour of the Lisbon Lions. Wanyama continued to impress on the field by stringing together a series of robust, classy performances. Wanyama's splendid, mature displays have seen him become one of the first names on Neil Lennon's team-sheet. While Wanyama is a defensive midfielder, he has helped himself to some very important goals for Celtic, most notably a late winner in a must-win game against Hearts and the iconic header against Catalan giants, Barcelona. Having been so impressive at the tender age of 21, Celtic fans will be very excited to see what is still to come from the Kenyan.

Centre midfield: Stiliyan Petrov

Joining John Barnes' Celtic side for a fee of £2m, Stan rapidly developed from a young player into a modern day great. After playing in some interesting positions under Barnes, Petrov looked at great ease in the centre of midfield.

Petrov was the definition of a box-to-box midfielder who was always eminent at both ends of the field. Playing alongside two experienced midfielders in Lennon and

Lambert, Petrov did not look out of place as a young player in a very successful and decorated Celtic side. Petrov's efforts were recognised by winning the 04/05 Celtic Player of the Year award. Petrov's glowing performances sparked interest from teams all over Europe, but the Bulgarian would join former manager, Martin O'Neill, at Aston Villa for a fee of £8m in 2006.

Left midfield: Alan Thompson

Martin O'Neill signed Thompson for a fee of £2.75m in 2000 from English side, Aston Villa. The left sided Englishman slotted perfectly into the left midfield position in O'Neill's 3-5-2 formation and was key to Celtic's successes at the time. Like McGeady, he was a creator but also contributed a collection of crucial goals for The Hoops.

He will be fondly remembered for his trademark left-footed strikes against Liverpool on the road to Seville and in the dying seconds of a Glasgow Derby at Celtic Park. On the pitch, Thompson contributed more than just ability. He often seemed to be one of several 'captains' in Celtic's fabled 'Seville team.' Such leadership skills and rapport with fans and staff saw Thompson appointed as Celtic first team coach in June 2010.

Striker: Henrik Larsson

It is impossible to condense the heroism and majesty of Henrik Larsson into mere words. Hailed as being Celtic's greatest ever signing, Larsson joined Wim Jansen's Celtic side for an insignificant £650,000 from Feyenoord in July of 1997. After a deficient debut at Easter Road, Henrik went on to inspire a generation in his time at Celtic and write his name in the club's folklore as one of the greatest of all time. Scoring 242 goals in 320 appearances in a Celtic jersey, Larsson's goals were often not only crucial but things of great beauty. A certain chipped finish will remain in the memories of those in attendance on the 28th of August 2000 for a lifetime. 'King Henrik' also scored a brace in the UEFA Cup final against FC Porto in 2003, which The Hoops tragically lost in extra time. Among Larsson's personal honours are a European Golden Boot, 5 SPL Top Scorer Awards, inclusion in the UEFA Euro Team of the Tournament for his performances with Sweden and induction into the Scottish Football Hall of Fame. There are many who will consider Larsson to be the greatest ever Celt; that is a point for contention. A matter of fact is that he was one of the all-time greats in green.

Striker: Chris Sutton

In the summer of 2000, Martin O'Neill spent a sum of £6m to bring the English target man from Chelsea to Celtic Park. Sutton came with a wealth of experience at the highest level having also played for a Premiership winning Blackburn Rovers side before playing joining Chelsea in 1999. Sutton immediately endeared himself to the Celtic support after scoring on his debut at Tannadice and bagging 2 goals in the Glasgow Derby just weeks later. The Sutton and Larsson strike partnership was a catalyst for success under Martin O'Neill and the pair were renowned throughout the continent for their prolific scoring record. Sutton was awarded the SPFA Player's Player of the Year Award in 2004 for his contributions in the green and white.

With so many great names not being included in this team, and many of the current team showing an abundance of potential, the mind begins to wander into places that would have seemed inconceivable in the mid 90s. With Celtic currently being the only Scottish force capable of competing on the European stage, the future looks bright for The Hoops if finances allow the current players to stay put and develop their game at Celtic Park. This season's return to Europe's top table has been a testament to the return of Celtic as a force to be reckoned with. One can only hope that the current team can reach, or even exceed, the achievements of the great ex-Celts mentioned in this team.

12 MILLI
WELLS

Tony McCann considers value for money in football and what you get for a transfer budget....

ION PENT

Understanding value is a tough. In any given marketplace, take for example the pub, £3.50 a pint would seem to be more or less the UK average; in my experience anyway. I think that it is an acceptable price for a pint but perhaps a pensioner operating on a budget lower than Kerry Katona's sense of self worth might argue.

At the time of writing this Champions League, double FA Cup, Premiership and Community Shield winner Daniel Sturridge has just completed his £12m move to Liverpool. Aged 23 with an impressive looking CV only further bolstered by caps for both England and Great Britain it gives his agent plenty to draw attention away from his 39 goals in 141 outings. That's one goal every 3.61 games.

Another striker Chelsea sold for £12m was Tore Andre Flo. Now granted this was in season 2000/01 and omitting such vagaries as inflation, 2007's minor economic blip and the resulting aftershocks, Rangers paid £12m for a striker who had scored one goal every 3.26 games (based on his Chelsea stats alone to keep things fair with Daniel Sturridge who has yet to ply his trade beyond his home country). Of

course Flo was considered in the prime of his career having played 163 games for Chelsea alone prior to his Rangers move. This is more than Sturridge's total number of games played thus far.

But how does one discern value for money, or rather whom can you tell your £12m has been well spent?

Well one way to measure impact of expensive assets is Champions league performance. For most this competition provides the greatest pecuniary reward per goal scored after all. In Flo's first season at Rangers he scored 3 times in the Champions League qualifiers. Not enough for Rangers to reach the group stages and therefore all three goals not marking a solid return on investment thus far.

It is worth pointing out though that Rangers had the opportunity to progress in the Champions League thus dramatically increase their earnings whilst Liverpool do not. As per the Lottery advert sentiment; you need to be in it to win it. Liverpool are indeed struggling, having been a traditional and ostensibly perennial member of the top-four quartet now placidly perched at 8th as I type this. Based on the

Football pundits can influence the market values of players, particularly on high profile programmes like MOTD.

prize money awarded in the English Premier League season 2011-12, each league spot was worth £755,062 (which is what Wolves got with Man City coining in £15,101,240 for winning the competition). TV rights to Premiership alone yields £32,552,737 per club in revenue, so assuming that Sturridge's goals (this season alone) boost Liverpool's league position by a generous 3 places he would have generated £2,265,186 additional revenue for the club. A jump from 8th to 5th would also secure UEFA cup football for another season and yield up to another £10m in income typically. So assuming all goes well Sturridge's contributions could allow Liverpool to claw some of the transfer fee back on additional revenues, less wages naturally. But 3 league places based upon the work of one man drafted in at the season's halfway point to a team not necessarily firing on all cylinders and, well, its safe to say 3 league places boost might be quite generous.

From the above example Rangers were in no position to sit back and wait for the annual washing in of the EPL cash tide, so this accelerated need (disregarding a certain owner's galactic ego) to bring in an expensive fix. As it happened Flo's Scottish goal scoring rate cashes out at 1 goal roughly every 2 games, which is not at all bad. However he did not repeat the same

feat in Europe making him a high priced flop.

When examining the value of the Sturridge deal some points should be noted before we continue: Liverpool are in a cash rich league and as such are far more able to afford £12m than most other European clubs therefore the risk £12m represents is smaller than to a club such as Celtic or even our perished foes circa 2000/1. Liverpool can also take a bigger chance on securing a young, promising talent. But why should they?

Given that Liverpool's owner is a self-proclaimed admirer of Billy Beane's "Moneyball" ethos it seems strange then that the man signing the cheques as it were would not look at someone like Marouane Chamakh. He has scored 90 goals in 368 appearances or a goal every 4.08 games. Compare this with Daniel Sturridge at a goal every 3.61 games and it seems odd, based on this statistic alone, that Liverpool would pay £12m for a 0.47 delta vs the nominal loan fee. Granted Chamakh has completed far more games and is older, but this can alternatively be read as more experienced and factoring in the transfer fee he is far less of a risk. This wildly simplistic view is going somewhere though...

Last issue I wrote about "The Perceptive Lens" and the damage it could do by reducing probable transfer fees for our

stars. Mull over Gary Hooper's stats for a moment. He is 24 and with 367 appearances and 160 goals has a rate of a goal every 2.29 games. His CV doesn't include a Champion's League winner's medal, but unlike Sturridge Hooper has been a vital part of Celtic's current success in Europe. Sturridge cannot claim to have been quite so pivotal in Chelsea achieving parity with Celtic on European Cup wins.

Only those at Celtic can answer this correctly, but if we were offered £12m for Gary Hooper I am certain we'd accept and also as I have written about previously (Taking a Punt on The Market, Issue 6, Pg 38) we should be looking to relinquish our assets prior to them depreciating or going on a free. Not that I am suggesting we should be trying to sell Hooper, not quite yet. What I am saying is that when filtering out all the media white noise, the facts tell a story very different to the pundits and other assorted mouthpieces.

If we believe what the assembled "experts"1 have to say then a whole host of other

CELTIC QUICK NEWS ROLL OF HONOUR 2013-14

factors come into a player valuation and I wholeheartedly agree. Just not with the other factors coveted so much by the former pro's warming TV studio sofas, hogging tabloid column inches or just generally stealing oxygen. A vast amount of emphasis is placed on Premier League experience and being able to, as Pat Nevin puts it, "stand up to the intense rigours of the top flight English game". There may be some truth to this, but without any empirical evidence this is just opinion and Swansea's signing of Michu (13 goals) at £2m or Southampton's capture of Rickie Lambert (8 goals) for circa £1m, just to cite two examples, show that opinion to be less than watertight.

The question remains though, what is value? If Marouane Chamakh had went to Liverpool and scored half the number of goals in between now and the summer that Daniel Sturridge does will he be deemed a success or a failure? I think I would see the value there, but I cannot say the Liverpool fans may agree. An Arsenal reject to save the day? Perhaps not, but it is worth thinking about what value actually is in football and more importantly, just how much of YOUR money is being channelled into footballing ventures. Personally I would rather my cash was spent bettering the youth scheme and giving local boys a better chance rather than lining a multitude of agents jacket pockets.

I can only suspect that had Liverpool spent £12m on Gary Hooper that they would have bought a more rounded and effective player than Daniel Sturridge, albeit from the lowly SPL. But I would hasten to point out that Liverpool's most prolific striker Ian Rush was signed from a lowly club (Chester City). One has to wonder how much all his previous top-flight experience figured in his ascent into club folklore & legend.

I suppose what it comes down to ultimately is what are you buying for £12m or whatever the sum maybe. The Moneyball principle works simply by filtering out the superfluous data and focussing squarely on the attributes a team needs. To that extent games per goal tells you only about how prolific a player has been. Averages are but a pixel in the entire data display. But low-resolution information can at least be of some use. Gary Hooper has managed to maintain a scoring average greater than a goal every 2 games since 2008 when on loan at Hereford. By looking at goals per game alone since going on loan to Hereford Gary Hooper has been remarkably consistent at various in clubs in a variety of different competitions and leagues This feasibly points to the player being adaptable and ambitious. And at 24 with a great deal of experience under his belt, a favourable scoring rate including in The Champion's League one has to question what £12m should get you. Perhaps not Gary Hooper when put like that.

How goals are scored, where from on the pitch, number of assists, type of assists, percentage of tackles won and where, fitness, time to complete a 100m sprint, the list is endless and doubtlessly the headaches as interminable whilst trying to calculate a formula to tie all this data together coherently, fairly therefore factoring in adjustments for age, condition and so forth. The Adidas miCoach is a positive step towards a system that allows prospective clubs a more efficient means to ascertain player value based on accurate data it. Rolled out in the MLS and worn by every player it works using GPS to track player movement and health, which can be analysed in real-time by coaches using an iPad. Tools like this open up possibilities to know so much more about a players. Mining this data has a lot of promise to minimise risk on transfer fees. By opening up data, which can be referenced to video footage of games scouts, would be able to build up a more detailed analysis of a potential target.

Any system that could be used to discern value based on unbiased and dispassionate analysis is likely to be met with scorn

The question remains though, what is value?

by those it threatens. The entire football cabal currently has stratospherically high volumes of cash to pumping through it. Any attempt to reduce that flow away from the current recipients will be alleged to be nothing short of a knife to the very heart of football. So for Celtic as things stand that means we need to be clever.

The cleverest thing we can do is to continue to develop our scouting system. An extensive scouting system is an investment, one that if done well should be profitable therefore it makes perfect sense to arm scouts with any new tools, ones that allow proper in-depth analysis rather than going solely on gut instinct, which thus far has hardly shown to be infallible. Andy Carroll for £35m anyone?

As Celtic fans we enjoy a unique perspective. We are expected to sit and hold our own at Europe's top table on a comparatively shoestring budget and we have been known to do it on occasion. We can safely say that, whatever the result against Juventus we deserve to be there solely on merit, both playing and scouting. Unless Of course you feel your scouting doesn't have to go beyond listening to an agent's sales pitch, after all what do figures, statistics or the agent's generous fees matter when the stakes are low, £12m is a great deal for a Champion's League winning striker, right? And should this transfer not work out then hey at least it is progress; 12 is significantly less than 35, surely that's value? Right?

THE PET DOWDS STORY

THE GREAT EVER ALL ROUND CE[LTIC]

ER

eter Dowds of Irish parentage and the son f an iron miner was born and died in the ame house at 27 Graham Street, Johnstone in the space of 25 years. It is what he packed into those years that will be of interest to Celtic fans.

He was a hometown football player with Johnstone Harp before arriving at Celtic via Broxburn Shamrock at the tender age of 17. He played in the same Johnstone Harp team as future Celtic and Scotland international Goalkeeper Willie Dunning, who he would join at Celtic and again on his football travels south of the border.

Making his debut in March 1889 v Clydesdale Harriers Peter established himself as a player of worth and partnered future Manager Willie Maley on the left in his next game v Abercorn. He scored in Celtic's first ever silverware haul - a 6-1 victory over Cowlairs in the final of the North Eastern Cup at Barrowfield (Clyde's ground) in May 1889.

Before the start of the first ever league in Scottish football in 1891-92 season, Celtic were much in demand playing games on tour and at home to the well established English teams. Peter featured in many of these earning himself a reputation against the likes of Newcastle, Bolton, Burnley, Preston N.E., Sunderland, Blackburn and Everton. In August 1889 Peter bagged both goals in a 2-0 win over Rangers.

Emphasising Peter's versatility, Celtic's first two Glasgow Cup wins saw him emerging as the victor playing in two different positions. He also played at centre in Celtic's first Scottish Cup win at Ibrox v Queens Park.

As the Scottish league commenced in 1891-92 season Peter featured in our first official match in a 5-0 win v Hearts at Tynecastle. He was off being treated for a severe eye gash for ten minutes and returned to the field, head bandaged with fifteen minutes remaining. The match report continues, "Dowds who was now playing outside left, easily walked round Adams, and with a fine screw kick put the ball out of McKay's reach for the fifth time...."

The following game a hat trick came his way and soon after he had a golden spell scoring 9 goals in 5 games, 4 in one match, 2 in another including "a backward shot with his heel" against Clyde in the Glasgow Cup at Celtic Park! In our first league season he became the first Celt to be an ever present, appearing in every league game and was Celtic's top scorer as well!

KLBHOY · HOOLAHOOPS · DICK BYRNE · WILLIE WALLACE · CELTICLOVER

With professionalism established in English football from 1885, payment of players in Scotland, although common was viewed

as a stain on the amateur game. Marie Rowan's excellent book on Paisley born Dan Doyle points to the sign that all was not well for Scottish players.

Willie Daly, a friend of Dowds met him in Paisley after his victorious scoring appearance in a Glasgow cup final. Daly asked what he got for winning - perhaps with a cash bonus in mind. Dowds brought out the medal from his pocket and said, "That!!" He dropped the medal and kicked it as it fell, into some grass nearby before walking on. Medals alone were no use to a man with little money who now had a wife in tow by the name of Mary Smith.

With Scottish football lagging behind England in a professional sense, Dowds was now a highly treasured commodity with clubs south of the border aware of his precocious talent willing to pay enormous sums of money to a young man who clearly needed money!

Tom Maley ex Celtic teammate of Dowds and brother of Manager Willie Maley wrote this during the First World War in 1916 while manager of Bradford Park Avenue.

"To tamper or try to wheedle a Celtic player from Parkhead was about as fatal a task as to trifle with the fuse of a big shell."

"Dick Molyneux Secretary of Everton tried to nobble Dowds, one of the best all rounders I can remember. Through the kindness of a friend the movements of Molyneux and Dowds were disclosed.

They were driving from Glasgow to Johnstone. We drove after them, overtook them on the High Road, and bored them so to speak into a hedgerow. Then having compelled them to stop with gloved hands disposed of in pistol shaped fashion, sternly ordered Peter to get off and up — off the Everton machine and on to the Celtic. This removal effected we gave Dick and his pal the order to git!"

"The next day a telegram reached Dowds from Fred Dewhurst on behalf of Preston N.E., desiring Peter to meet him at a certain hotel in Glasgow. That wire I replied to. "Peter can't come. I will." and signed it in full. Fred didn't wait to meet me."

Reminiscing on the start of the 1892 season Willie Maley wrote in a Weekly News article in 1936, "At half we had reckoned on keeping Dowds as he first of all went to Aston Villa in July, changed his mind and returned to us in August and actually played two games. Suddenly he shifted his mind and never returned."

Peter played one season with Aston Villa, Joining up with fellow Harp and Celtic team-mate Willie Dunning, and the next with Stoke City.

Again Willie Maley recounted a Dowds tale in his series of articles. "When he was a Villain (Villa player), Peter once made a bet on the occasion of a West Brom match that his opposing wing would not get the ball during the game. Peter's bet was promptly covered but he was the winner."

Celtic Manager Willie Maley, also highlighting the quality of player Dowds was continued, "Peter Dowds was a wonderful footballer, his versatility was unique. Talk about class all rounders. There never has been and never will be finer. It did not matter in which position Peter played. He distinguished himself. I admired him most as a halfback. He was the perfect middle man, playing the ball all the time and every time. Peter did not have to throw himself about to get contact. Contact came to him by his own intuition. He did not find the ball. Nothing so common. It found him."

Peter Dowds was to die tragically young within a short timescale on his return to Scotland.

Willie Maley in 1931 remembered remarks made to him by a footballing friend in 1895 at the graveside. He paraphrased, "To the present generation Dowds is not even a name, but to old timers he was the greatest ever, at home in any and every position. The equal of a Doyle or Kelly in defence, of Madden on the right, Campbell on the left and Cassidy at centre."

Peter returned to Celtic after an absence of two seasons in 1894 with Scotland embracing professionalism the season previous. He played at the new Celtic Park and also played in the inaugural game at St.Mirren Park, Love St. in September in a 0-3 victory.

In the match report in the Paisley & Renfrewshire Gazette it quotes, "Dowds lagged somewhat during the game and the stalwart Maley had to do his own work and assist Peter also."

This was the first indication that he was not physically at his best.

Unbeknown to Celtic they had re-signed a 24 year-old man who should have been at his peak but was in fact suffering from an illness that would be terminal. Peter Dowds would be dead in a year. He had Consumption (Tuberculosis), a bacterial disease that was a horrific ailment with no cure available.

His last game as a Celtic player was away against Manchester City at Ardwick Road in December 1894.

It's ironic that his death certificate states as his occupation "Professional Footballer," as he had to leave his country to become one. Peter played only three league games as a professional in Scotland for Celtic.

It is especially poignant that he returned to the club he loved and played so few games in what would have been a great future if illness hadn't intervened.

Peter died in September 1895 and lies buried in an unmarked grave in Abbey Cemetery, Elderslie.

Written by Iain Reynolds for CQN Magazine.

"To tamper or try to wheedle a Celtic player from Parkhead was about as fatal a task as to trifle with the fuse of a big shell."

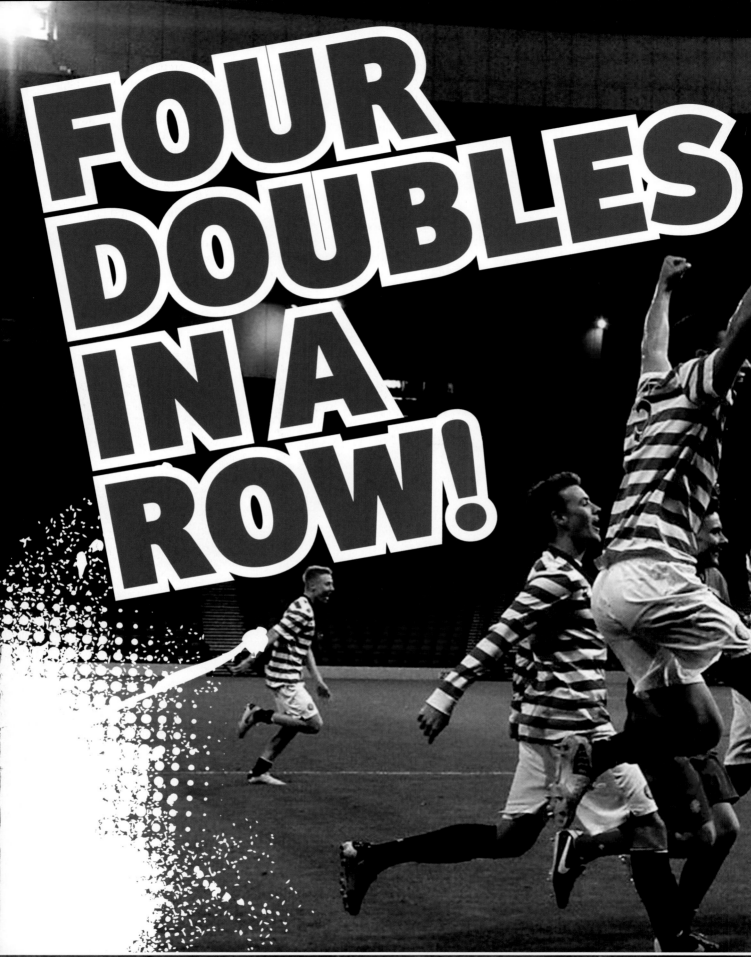

FOUR DOUBLES IN A ROW!

A quadruple double. What an achievement for any team, at any level. This is exactly what the under 20 Celtic squad managed to do on 1st May 2013. They made history by becoming the only under 20 team to do so. The youth team have played magnificently throughout the whole season, and have won the league by a significant margin. The 'win every game' mentality of Celtic seems to be cementing a place in each of the youth players, something that has gone somewhat astray within the first team.

Callum McGregor said before the Cup Final: "At Celtic there's an expectation to win every game and to play well and with a certain style. It's no different for us, you need to have being a winner as part of your make-up. There's a lot of excitement in the squad as we are going for four doubles in a row. We're chasing history." When I read these comments, I was very impressed with the attitude of McGregor, it's great to see how important they see the results,

John Kennedy was full of praise for the youth team, he said: "It's great for our Academy to go and win the league and cup four years in a row. It's credit to the work that goes on from grassroots up. We're here to develop players, but nights like this are about developing their mentality too." I think it's great to see that this winning mentality goes from the bottom, all the way to the top. It's crucial to have this mindset and mentality as a Celtic player. The fans expect nothing but to win every game. (Joseph Ruddy)

M • FNG • TIMBHOY2 • LENNYBHOY • OLIVIA K • MAYANMAN

THE SPI
RELATI

CELTIC QUICK NEWS ROLL OF HONOUR 2013-14

CIAL
ONSHIP
BY GREG MARTIN

GALLOWGATE MAD SQUAD · FLEAGLE1888 · EKBHOY · DJBEE

"No, not the Boston Celtics."

For a Celtic supporter living in Canada, this phrase is hardwired into the brain; your chances of meeting a random Tim on the street are about as good as your odds of not getting frostbite on the walk from your car to your house. Supporting Celtic can be something of an ordeal here: the 6 a.m. wakeups; the arctic conditions in the only bar with Setanta for 100 miles; the distinct lack of beer. But, as any Celtic fan and indeed any football fan will tell you, it's all worth it.

Growing up as I did, as a Celtic fan in northwest England, is also a strange experience. No one English believes you don't support either Manchester United or Liverpool, and no one Scottish believes you support Celtic, what with that silly English accent. But when I used to go up for matches with my dad, I generally wasn't allowed to wear my Celtic shirt around the city, on grounds of it being perhaps a

temptation of fate. I could hardly believe, in my youth, that wearing my green-and-white hoops should be even remotely dangerous, but with extra years the starkness of the tension between the two colours of the city became more and more evident to me.

I am sure that the possible dangers of flaunting my allegiance were greatly exaggerated by a protective father, but the fact that these precautions were even hypothetically necessary is symptomatic of an incredible zealousness in the hearts of all football supporters, a fervor that goes unmatched in North America. In very few, if any, places on this vast continent is it possible to find such a large group of people so devoted to a sport, and to a team. Undoubtedly, there are devotees of American football and NASCAR who would argue until they were blue in the face that their dedication far outstrips anything

we could muster on our tiny little island, but I stand by my belief that supporting a football team goes deeper than merely showing up on match day with your foam finger and your watered-down Budweiser.

Nowhere else is this more true than in Glasgow, where supporting Celtic is something that is ingrained from birth and forms an integral part of your youth. It is an almost ideological divide that runs down the middle of the city, something that sadly runs over into a cultural and even religious conflict. Explaining the history and meaning of Celtic to the uninitiated is often quite trying: yes, since the 1800s; yes, as a charitable cause; yes, we've always played in Glasgow; yes, I'm serious no, absolutely no vuvuzelas.

This gulf in enthusiasm became glaringly evident this past autumn, when the National Hockey League franchise owners

locked out its teams on salary disputes, effectively bringing the entire hockey industry to a grinding, shuddering halt. While these kind of pedantic goings-on are now fairly commonplace in North America – in the last twenty years, I count nine work stoppages in the professional sports leagues – the idea of even one matchday being cancelled due to labour disputes is inconceivable. Football fans wouldn't stand for it. The season finally begins January 19th, and while the players who signed with Russian teams in the interim were on the first flight home, the number of fans I have informally polled over the last two weeks who say that they will not be returning to the bleachers, or who are even selling their season tickets, is staggering.

Perhaps it's the franchise system, whereby any team deemed to be performing undesirably can be unceremoniously uprooted at any moment and moved to a

city with deeper pockets, but there does not seem to be the same camaraderie between hockey fans, the same unity of purpose or strength of devotion that you see in football.

The atmosphere at the games for my local team, the Ottawa Senators, is nearly non-existent, even on a sellout night. The closest thing I ever get to the goosebumps of hearing "You'll Never Walk Alone" is being confronted with the prospect of an eleven-dollar slice of pizza. Whenever I hear about someone's plans to visit Scotland, I implore them to visit Paradise, just to experience the walk to Celtic Park, the songs, the love, the hatred, the mason in the black, and the feeling of 62,000 people's collective will being exerted on a tiny leather ball.

Obviously I accept that I am by no means an unbiased auditor of the situation.

But even on my trips to Anfield and Old Trafford, even on my trips to see Northwich Victoria take on a field of part-time decorators and electricians in front of a crowd of 32, there's still something intangibly more special about cheering your team on from the stands and hurling vicious insults at the paltry away support. And even if you can't be there, even if you're stuck in a freezing cold pub at 7 a.m., clutching a coffee and staring stubbornly at the flickering Setanta feed, you know that you share an unspoken bond with every bleary-eyed, unshaven Tim in the pub, and indeed all over the world; in some ways, it's just like being there in the flesh.

When Fraser Forster joined Celtic on loan from Newcastle United, he was very much unheard of to the Celtic fans. He came recommended by Paul Lambert after a good season in League 1 for Norwich but despite coming from England, he was, just like most of the signings under Neil Lennon, a name we only first heard when the rumours started to fly around in the days before the transfer. Forster would go on to become an integral part of the Celtic team and its European success. However, the move did not seem quite so ideal in the beginning.

His first season was to most Celtic fans, myself included, less than convincing. Despite, with the help of Lukasz Zaluska, breaking the record for clean sheets in an SPL season, and showing glimpses of what he could become in the future, most Celtic fans were not keen on making the move a permanent one due to his supposed lack of aerial command despite his size. With hindsight it can be argued that his unconvincing performances were down to Celtic's less than brilliant central defensive options including Majstorovic and Hooiveld.

Newcastle were undecided on what future Forster had at their own club and so were reluctant to let him leave permanently. Celtic were keen to bring him back to the club and so after Newcastle boss Alan Pardew said that there was no chance Forster would return due to the low standard of the SPL, the clubs came to an

agreement for Forster to join Celtic on loan for another season. He would go on to win round the Celtic support.

At the end of 2011 Forster began to win over the masses. In particular rescuing the three points with a last minute penalty save against Hearts before putting in an outstanding performance away to Udinese were the turning points for Forster. His form continued in that vein throughout the season as he broke the record for SPL clean sheets in a season for the second year in a row and Celtic brought the title back to Paradise for the first time in four years.

For the second season in a row Celtic wanted to bring back Forster on a

GRAN URALLA

permanent basis and this time the Celtic support was very much behind the move. Again Newcastle were undecided on Forster's future. They had a number of goalkeepers and wanted to see them all in action before making a decision. After some pre-season action Forster was told he could leave and Celtic wasted no time in making their move, signing the giant for a reported £2 million. This would go on be a sale the English Premier League side would regret.

Forster's season this time was even better. Winning a league and cup double as well as being instrumental in the club's European success, as well as the honour of receiving his first call up to the England squad in October. He even earned the nickname "La Gran Muralla" or "The Great Wall" amongst the Spanish press after a top class double header against Barcelona in the Champions League group stage and has earned a reputation as a top class penalty saver having stopped a number of spot kicks across the season. To cap it off, Forster was described as one of Europe's top young goalkeepers by legendary Juventus stopper Gianluigi Buffon who said he had the potential to rank amongst the likes of Manuel Neuer and Joe Hart sometime in the future.

Despite such an impressive season Forster has made sounds about potentially leaving Celtic to move back south of the border in recent weeks. Forster's England ambitions have been stunted by playing in the SPL and with the World Cup in a year's time he seems desperate to make the squad. This is the same arrogant attitude that comes from England that meant Alan Thompson and Chris Sutton couldn't get into the squad regularly during their time at Celtic and the same attitude that means it is likely Gary Hooper leave Celtic in the summer.

No matter the outcome Celtic cannot lose. Either we will be able to hold onto a top class goalkeeper and maintain, and hopefully build on, the success of the current team, or we will make a large profit on him and we will be able to attract more top young players with the lure of putting themselves in a shop window for a move to the lucrative English Premier League and a range of other top European league. In addition he will have been a major part in bringing back the title to paradise and an even bigger part in one of the most memorable nights in recent years and perhaps the clubs history.

GREEN NINJA — THE PAINTINGS OF DANNY MCGRAIN

NOT ALWA
EASY BUT
WORTHW

'S ALWAYS ILE!

Joe Ruddy rounds up what people in the game have said about Celtic and the Celtic supporters...

GREEN NINJA • THE PAINTINGS OF DANNY MCGRAIN

"We know Celtic have a special group of fans…" "The Celtic fans deserve to be in Europe. They have been amazing in both games we have played against them recently. We knew what they were going to be like in Glasgow but the way they were in Barcelona after they had just lost in the way they did was amazing. I have never seen anything like that before." - **Lionel Messi**

"The Celtic fans are incredible. It is always great to play there." - **Cristiano Ronaldo**

"Celtic, like Barcelona, are more than a football club. Our clubs are a symbol of a culture and community that has not always been made welcome in their respective countries."

"The atmosphere generated by the fans in Celtic's stadium for our visit was the most impressive I've ever witnessed. The grounds of Liverpool and Manchester United are good and the hostile feeling of playing against Real Madrid in the Bernabeu is also excellent, but the atmosphere against Celtic was the best." - **Xavi**

"The Celtic fans are very special and the club and players can be very proud of them. They are the best I have ever heard" "I have played many games for Spain/Barca but I've never heard fans like Celtic, they were amazing, not quiet for a single second!" - **Andres Iniesta**

"I have never played in such an atmosphere…" - **Michael Owen**

"Celtic fans are some of the greatest supporters I know." - **Clarence Seedorf**

"It is absolutely spectacular to see the fans like that." - **Alberto Gilardino**

"The atmosphere here tonight was unbelievable and it's an honour to play in such an arena." - **Oliver Khan**

"The incredible thing was the people, for an opposition player it is quite incredible, i have not seen a better atmosphere from the grounds I have visited." - **Steven Gerard**

"When we played at Celtic Park for Bayern in the Champions League it was unbelievable and I think all our players said the same thing afterwards. The atmosphere was just totally unique. I've played in lots of big games and stadiums but I've never witnessed fans making that much noise in 90 minutes." - **Owen Hargreaves**

"Celtic are popular for testimonials because everyone knows they will fill the stadium – and I've always had great admiration of them. Their fans have a reputation as one of the best and that's on merit because of the great atmosphere they create." - **Eidur GudJohnsen**

"The match against Celtic in Glasgow was amazing. The atmosphere there was the best I've ever seen or heard. I couldn't shout to my team mates two yards from me. It was amazing, I loved it. Celtic Park was ten times noisier than it was in the Maksimir for Serbia versus Croatia." - **Nikola Djurdjic**

"Celtic enjoys a greater community spirit than any other club in the world." - **Archie MacPherson**

"Football will survive because of teams like Celtic and its fans." - **Age Hareide**

"This is what we need in Italy, this type of environment. This was the essence of sport. To hear the Celtic fans singing and chanting after the game was incredible." - **Carlo Ancelotti**

"It will stick in my mind for ever that after the game the Celtic players were extremely good sportsmen and, together with their supporters, they gave us a standing ovation when we were receiving the cup." - **Eddy Pieters Graafland**

"Celtic have all the cool people supporting them. Rangers have me and Wet Wet Wet!!!" - **Alan McGee**

"Anyone going to Celtic Park now is saying, 'You've got to beat that atmosphere, the energy they spend in their games'. We would love to have an atmosphere like that, but…" - **Alex Ferguson**

"I fell a bit in love with Celtic, because the atmosphere was amazing and the crowd was magnificent, the way they behaved with the Porto fans."

"When I was at Porto my team also played in the UEFA Cup final against a Scottish side – but it was Celtic. I've never seen such emotional people. It was unbelievable!" - **Jose Mourinho**

"Celtic appear to have magical powers of obtaining new players and in a few months instilling them with the Celtic Spirit." - **James Gordon**

"This is the most fantastic support in the world." - Franz Beckenbaur

"Celtic fans, you are great, you are marvellous!" - **Sepp Blatter**

"The atmosphere inside Celtic Park is one of the best in Europe it's absolutely incredible." - **Sven Goran Eriksson**

"I have never experienced anything

like it. This is a lesson for all football clubs about how to be proper football supporters, This is the best club in the world. Every club wants to play Celtic. They love Celtic. They want to go to Celtic Park because of the type of club they are." - *Michael Platini*

"I speak for everyone when I describe the behaviour of the Celtic supporters as immaculate, with all the bother concerning racial insults and hooligan behaviour, these fans were a breath of fresh air." - *Barcelona Police*

"In my experience, which embraces big matches at Old Trafford, Anfield, Ibrox, the San Siro & the Nou Camp, there's nowhere else remotely like Celtic Park in full flow." - *Brian Viner*

"It will be a real pleasure to visit Celtic Park and feel the atmosphere of a great UEFA Champions League night at such a great venue. The Celtic supporters are fantastic, in fact the best travelling supporters in the world as we have seen many times. I know that Celtic supporters are extremely passionate about their club, a club which I believe, like FC Barcelona, is different. We know that supporters will travel in huge numbers to follow their team, but we also know the great reputation of good behaviour which Celtic fans enjoy and clearly we are looking forward to hosting the Celtic fans in the city once again. We hope all Celtic supporters enjoy their visit to Barcelona." - *Laporta*

"Celtic doesn't need to be defined, they are a historic team in the world of football. They have such great passion for the sport." - *Andoni Zubizarreta*

"Nothing could put me off Celtic. Even poking my eyes out wouldn't stop me from going If that happened, I'd still turn up for the atmosphere. Celtic is more than just a football club it's a cultural icon. It's an emblem of the Irish diaspora which is very important to me. My father took me to my first game against Dunfermline in 1962. We won but I don't know the score. I just remember the sea of green and white. There were 70 to 80,000 Celtic fans really crammed in it was the biggest crowd I'd ever seen. The Irish flag flew then, as it does now over Parkhead, and I thought I was at home." - *George Galloway*

"I can't think of fans creating a better atmosphere, anywhere, than those at Celtic Park." - *Alan Green*

"I have got a friendly, good perception of Glasgow Celtic, now they are my second team. I have got a sympathetic relation with the club, with the history of that club. I will be very happy if Glasgow Celtic goes to the second round." - *Carles Vilarrubí*

"There isn't a better atmosphere in world football than Celtic Park." - *Ray Wilkins*

"Celtic fans a couple of years ago went to Seville in the Uefa Cup Final and took over 3 times the amount of fans there. There was not one bit of trouble as all the fans that had no tickets stayed in the square and had a big party. Every team should follow Celtic's fan behaviour and that mentality." - *William Gaillard*

"You may have it good here at Anfield but the Celtic fans do it best." - *Eurosport*

"The best fans on the continent." - *El Mundo Deportivo, Barcelona*

"More than a club, a people." - F*rench Newspaper L'equipe*

TOP 5 QUOTES

1. "This place makes the hairs on the back of your neck stand up, there is nowhere like it in football, and I can see how the people love to play here and speak so highly of it." - *Samuel Eto'o*

2. "Every professional footballer should seek to play at least one game at Celtic Park. I have never felt anything like it." - *Paolo Maldini*

3. "That horizontally striped white and green jersey is the uniform of a club worthy of the applause of the world. The fantastic Celtic fans gave a real lesson in civility in sport. The chants and insults which blight too many games in Serie A are light years away from the spectacle of education and sportsmanship that the people in the Celtic away end offered." - *Calcio Mercato*

4. "The atmosphere the fans at Celtic Park generate is something that is unique in football and it is a factor that, for me, makes it impossible to predict the outcome of the game. The noise is unbelievable and it's constant, from the moment the opposition players walk on the pitch they will not get a moment's peace until the final whistle. If you haven't experienced Celtic Park in full cry, it is very difficult to play your normal game. Players are used to playing in hostile grounds all over the world, but I can tell you that there is nothing to compare with Celtic Park." - *Lou Macari*

5. "Being a Celtic supporter is not always easy, but it is always worthwhile." - *Fergus McCann*

A SUCCESS SCOUTING STRATEGY

FUL

Kieran Caw looks at Celtic's scouting policy and the influence of John Park since his arrival from Hibernian…

Over the past few years many young and talented individuals have worn Celtic's famous shirt; individuals whom most of the world would not have heard of before. The scouting team, led by John Park, had come to terms with the fact that the days of attracting the calibre of player such as Di Canio, Henrik Larsson, Chris Sutton, John Hartson and Paul Lambert were gone. No longer can Celtic afford to tie players down on £35,000 per week deals. In the same way, marquee signings like Tommy Gravesen, Roy and Robbie Keane, Craig Bellamy, Diomansy Kamara and Freddie Ljungberg were also unaffordable and not beneficial to the club's long-term goal.

John Park is key to Celtic's recent success in the transfer market – this after creating a new strategy due to Tony Mowbray's failings in his short spell as manager. Some say he's more important than any other member of the back room staff and even many of the footballers. After all, countless English Premier League sides wouldn't be chasing his signature for nothing.

In 2007, Celtic recruited Park from Hibernian where he was responsible for producing one of their best ever squads which included the likes of Steven Fletcher, Scott Brown, Kevin Thomson, Gary Caldwell and Steven Whittaker – many of which subsequently joined either Celtic or Rangers after their success in Edinburgh. Since John Park accepted the job offer – one he couldn't refuse – he has continued his outstanding record in finding and helping produce some of Britain and Europe's best young talents.

On joining Celtic, Park stated "If the Celtic job hadn't been here I would have gone to West Brom. But you could go to West Brom and still be hankering for the Champions League, while I can miss all that out, and go direct to the Champions League without passing other stations to get there. No-one in their right mind would pass up on that." This has been West Brom's loss and Celtic's gain ever since as Celtic will continue to prosper in Europe with a very young squad, many of whom are on considerably low wages and are eager to showcase their skills on a worldwide stage.

Celtic supporters have now adjusted to and accepted the current financial climate they are working in. When the club announced the signings of Fraser Forster, Emilio Izaguirre, Beram Kayal and Gary Hooper in the summer of 2010 (at the expense of Aiden McGeady who was sold for £9,000,000) many fans were concerned at the risky prospect of buying relatively unknown footballers with no real experience in European competition. A few weeks prior to those signings Neil Lennon was close to signing David James, Sol Campbell, George Boateng and Jimmy Bullard – all journeymen who wanted their last big pay cheque – which shows the extent Celtic would be worse off by without John Park's intervention (although the buck ultimately stops with Neil Lennon!)

These signings were, or course, proven to be gambles worth taking as Izaguirre picked up all awards in his debut season, Gary Hooper scored 22 goals, Beram Kayal received deserved praise and Fraser Forster broke a new clean sheet record, also in his debut season.

The important aspects of the majority of Neil Lennon's signings are both the age of player and transfer fee. Celtic signed those four players for a combined total of £4,200,000. Now, Lennon could easily ask for double that figure for half of his squad. A staggering amount considering more than half of the squad including Joe Ledley, Charlie Mulgrew, Adam Matthews, Kelvin Wilson and Mikael Lustig were signed on free transfers.

Ki Sung-Yueng is the most recent success story from Park's 'new' plan. Swansea bought the South Korean last summer for a reported fee of £6,000,000 possibly rising to £8,000,000. Considering Ki could not regularly hold down a starting spot in the fiercely contested midfield, Celtic had struck gold once again.

Celtic's long-term plan is of a similar model to that of clubs like Benfica and Ajax who buy and sell on for profit, although on a much higher scale. This is the only way for big teams in small leagues to compete with Europe's elite – and it seems to be working for Celtic. With an average squad age of around 23 and a highest paid transfer fee of £2,400,000, Celtic did not look out-of-place amongst the likes of Barcelona, Benfica and Spartak Moscow in this seasons Champions League competition.

As Ajax, Benfica and Porto have also shown, the youth set-up is equally important to

on-field success. Emerging talents such as James Forrest, Dylan McGeough, Lewis Kidd and Marcus Fraser are currently attracting interest from Europe's elite with Tottenham and Ajax hot on the heels of Forrest and Kidd after their standout performances in the Champions League and the NextGen Series. John Park also played a pivotal role in taking Tony Watt to Celtic for a fee of £80,000 from Airdrie – a player who conquered the might of Barcelona at Celtic Park in November.

Many of Celtic's young stars have caught the eye of top European Clubs after their excellent performances against the world's best. Victor Wanyama, for example, is attracting attention from Manchester United, Fraser Forster is apparently top of Chelsea's goalkeeper wish list and Juventus are said to be keen on tying up a deal for Gary Hooper. All credit must go to the scouting system who are one of the best in the whole of Europe at the moment.

Losing players is always going to be a blow for Celtic, which is arguably the negative side to this strategy, but that blow could be softened by the hefty transfer fees such teams will pay to gain their services. The then Kenyan teenager, Victor Wanyama, who cost little under £1,000,000, is being heavily touted to leave for at least ten times that amount which is all part of Celtic's sustainability plan, headed by John Park, who will aim to achieve further progress in Europe's premier competition to ensure Celtic will become contenders to reach the knockout stages each year.

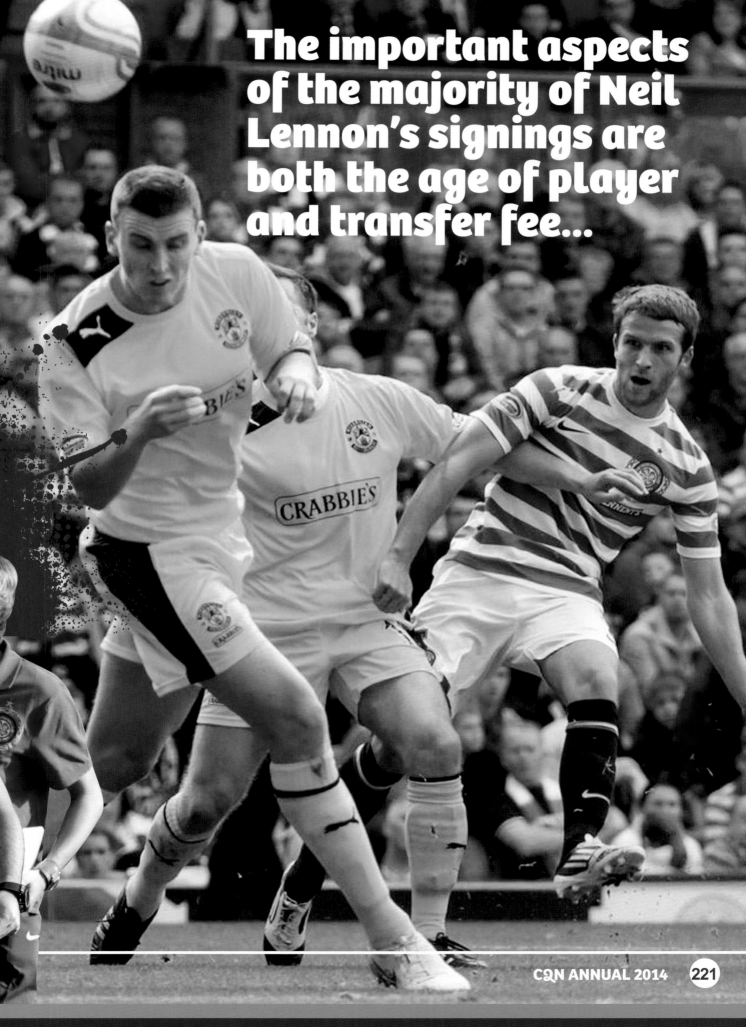

The important aspects of the majority of Neil Lennon's signings are both the age of player and transfer fee...

READ THE AWARD WINNING CQN MAGAZINE ON CQN

COME ON YOU GHIRLS IN GREEN

Graham Ward updates CQN Magazine on Celtic's women's senior team as Celtic aim to beome the leading side in womens football in Scotland...

CELTIC FIRST CELTIC LAST AND CELTIC OVER ALL

Celtic's clash with Rangers on June 9th is a crucial must-win clash for the women's senior team. The young squad had the most difficult possible start to the season with matches against last year's runners-up Hibs and two back-to-back games against seven-times Scottish champions, Glasgow City.

All three matches were lost and that left Celtic out of the League Cup and trailing nine points (with a game in hand) behind leaders Glasgow City who have maintained their 100% records after 8 matches. The team have fought back well and put together a run of four victories in a row and now lie a point behind Rangers in fourth place.

The Celtic women's development academy was founded in 2007 and Celtic have been in in the top three of the SWPL every year since, except for a fourth place finish in 2011. Silverware to date has been limited to a League Cup final victory over Spartans. in 2010.

Following a management shake-up at the end of last season, Celtic are now managed by Peter Caulfield, who remains the most successful manager in Scottish women's football history after leading Glasgow City to five Premier league titles and numerous other domestic honours. To add to the turnover, at the same time there was a loss of a number of experienced players to other clubs. In particular, Celtic lost players to Rangers who now have ex-Celts Karen Penglase, Rebecca Storrie, Megan Sneddon, Michele Barr, Hayley Cunningham and Natalie Ross in their team this season. This left Celtic missing experienced players and internationalists for the start of this season and has meant a rapid promotion to the first team for a number of the younger players from the academy. This season Celtic have only four players above the

age of nineteen. It has also meant that Rangers have become more of a threat this year since they brought in an experienced group of ex-Celts who were trained, tried and proven as a team unit at Lennoxtown and are now likely to significantly improve on their ninth place last season.

The strength of Celtic's academy system has allowed the team to remain competitive by promoting players from the reserve team who play in the SWPL 1st Division. The youngest player in the team is midfielder Abigail Harrison who, at only 15, has already impressed with her technical skills and goalscoring abilities. Her style is fluid and seems to have roving position playing off the main strikers and is most adept at using her speed and ball control to run on to through passes from deep and create scoring opportunities for herself and main striker Heather Richards. With her potential, a great career beckons for Abilgail once she adds a little more aggression and a striker's confidence to command space and demand the ball.

Last season's defence has had to be largely replaced but is still marshalled by Rhonda Jones who has 115 caps for the Scottish national team. In such a young defence, Jones' experience is essential as, in recent weeks, her positional sense and competitive drive have pulled Celtic out of a number of exposed positions and allowed the team to stay ahead at crucial points in various matches. The loss of Barr and Ross from the left of defence this year has meant that a huge responsibility has fallen onto 19 year old Emma Brownlie and 18 year old Kelly Clark who were recruited this year from Hibs and Forfar. Brownlie's speed on the overlap brings an extra attacking option to Celtic.

The strength of the team is their individual skill, pressing game when not in possession and movement off the ball. A number of SWPL teams have distinct channels through which they develop attacks but Celtic have the ability to attack more fluidity from midfield with great distribution from Mairead Fulton and surging runs from Emily Thompson. Celtic are capable of attacking from all angles.

Celtic are now managed by Peter Caulfield, who remains the most successful manager in Scottish women's football history...

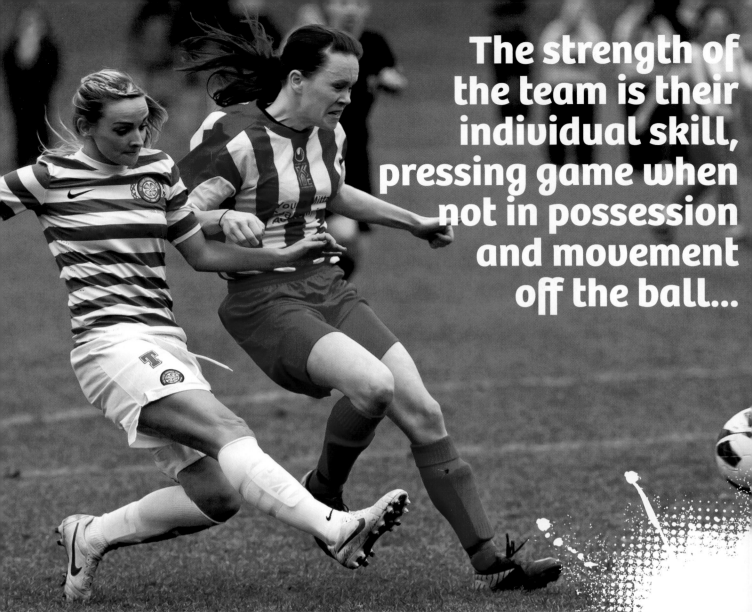

The strength of the team is their individual skill, pressing game when not in possession and movement off the ball...

Realistically, Celtic's goals this year must be to rebuild the team and focus on the Scottish Cup as a chance for silverware. The experience of matches against Glasgow City was that a team like City, which has played in the UEFA Champions league for the last few years, are able to control the midfield and stifle Celtic's creativity. In the second of the two games Celtic did not have a shot on target as City pressed the Celtic youngsters out of the match. Celtic's passing needs to be improved as too often passes don't reach a player in the hoops and too often players are dispossessed after being caught in possession. These are clearly things to be worked on in the training ground and the new coaching staff will no doubt be focussed on blending the new team even more than now.

 226 VISIT **WWW.CELTICQUICKNEWS.CO.UK**